P.F.WELBURN.

ANS COBOL
SECOND EDITION

£6.75

ANS COBOL
SECOND EDITION

RUTH ASHLEY
Co-President
DuoTech

in consultation with
NANCY B. STERN, Ph.D.
Hofstra University

John Wiley & Sons, Inc., Publishers
New York • Chichester • Brisbane • Toronto

Editors: Judy Wilson and Martha Jewett
Production Manager: Ken Burke
Artists: Carl Brown, Winn Kalmon

Copyright © 1979, by John Wiley & Sons, Inc.

All rights reserved. Published simultaneously in Canada.

Reproduction or translation of any part of this work beyond that permitted by Sections 107 or 108 of the 1976 United States Copyright Act without the permission of the copyright owner is unlawful. Requests for permission or further information should be addressed to the Permissions Department, John Wiley & Sons, Inc.

Library of Congress Cataloging in Publication Data

Ashley, Ruth.
   ANS COBOL.

  (Wiley Self-teaching guides)
  Includes index.
   1. COBOL (Computer program language)--programmed instruction. I. Stern, Nancy B. II. Title.
QA76.73.C25A83   1979   001.6'424   78-27717
ISBN 0-471-05136-5

Printed in the United States of America

79 80 10 9 8 7 6 5 4

How to Use This Book

Each chapter in this book consists of many small segments called frames. Each frame includes a question to answer or a problem to solve and is followed by the correct answer or solution. When you work through this Self-Teaching Guide, use a piece of paper or a large index card to cover the answers, sliding the card or paper down to the dotted line while you read the frame and write down your answer. Most of the time you will be right. When you do find that you have made an error, find out why before you go on. Look back over the preceding frames and make sure you understand the correct answer.

Each chapter will take from one to three hours to complete. Whenever possible, try to complete a chapter in one or two study sessions. Stop only at the end of a chapter or a section within the chapter. The material will be more difficult for you to learn if your work is frequently interrupted.

Each chapter ends with a review, often a program for you to write. After you have completed the chapter, check your answers. If you make a mistake, review the appropriate section of the chapter. If you make many errors, you may find it helpful to repeat the chapter.

Contents

INTRODUCTION 1

Chapter 1   COBOL PROGRAMMING   3

         COBOL Coding, 4
         Identification Division Entries, 8
         Environment Division Entries, 11
         Data Division Entries, 13
         Procedure Division Entries, 18
         DISPLAY Statement, 21
         ACCEPT Statement, 22
         Review, 25

Chapter 2   DATA MANIPULATION   28

         Optional Identification Division Entries, 28
         Data Division Entries: Group Data Items, 31
         MOVE Statement, 35
         Review, 40

Chapter 3   ARITHMETIC CODING   45

         Picture Characters, 45
         Usage Clause, 51
         Numeric Literals, 52
         Arithmetic Operations, 54
         COMPUTE Statement, 61
         GO TO Statement, 66
         IF Statement, 68
         Review, 73

Chapter 4   CARD FILES   78

         Data Description Entries, 79
         Environment Division Entries, 84
         File Description Entries, 87
         Procedure Division Entries, 92

READ Statement, 95
WRITE Statement, 99
Review, 102

Chapter 5   PRINT FILES   105

Environment Division Entries, 106
Data Division Entries, 107
Record Length in Files, 109
Editing Data for Printed Reports, 111
Heading Records, 118
Procedure Division Entries, 122
Qualified Names in Data Descriptions, 123
Review, 126

Chapter 6   TAPE FILES, CONDITION TYPES   132

Environment Division Entries, 133
Data Division Entries, 133
Card-To-Tape Procedure, 138
Relational Conditions, 141
Condition-Name Conditions, 146
Review, 149

Chapter 7   PRINTED REPORTS   154

Editing Alphanumeric and Numeric Data, 154
Editing of Signed Values, 157
Floating Insertion and Zero Suppression Characters, 160
Vertical Spacing Options, 165
Review, 170

Chapter 8   FLOW OF PROGRAM CONTROL   174

PERFORM Statement, 174
TIMES Option of PERFORM, 180
UNTIL Option of PERFORM, 182
VARYING Option of PERFORM, 185
DEPENDING ON Option of the GO TO Statement, 192
Review, 195

Chapter 9   TABLES   197

Table Description Entry: Single OCCURS, 197
Double-Level OCCURS, 215

Chapter 10	MASS STORAGE DEVICES (DISK FILES)	221

                Standard Sequential Files on Mass Storage Devices, 222
                I-O Option of OPEN Statement, 223
                Direct Files, 230
                Procedure Division Entries, 234
                Indexed Sequential Files, 238
                Comprehensive Program, 243
                Summary, 253

Appendix A	ANS COBOL RESERVED WORDS	254
Appendix B	COLLATING SEQUENCE OF COBOL CHARACTERS	258
Appendix C	SUMMARY OF FORMATS	259
Appendix D	SUMMARY OF FD CLAUSES	262
Appendix E	SUMMARY OF EDITING CHARACTERS	263
INDEX		264

Introduction

COBOL is a computer programming language that was designed to solve the data processing problems of business. A number of years ago, a national committee, under the auspices of the U.S. government but with representatives of most computer manufacturers, studied the many versions of COBOL; almost every large installation had its own version at that time. The standardized COBOL that was adopted by the committee became American National Standard, or ANS, COBOL. Today, again, many compilers have variations, but they are extensions or modifications to the basic ANS COBOL. Reference manuals clearly indicate where the variations differ from the standard.

The ANS COBOL you will learn here will not be "structured COBOL"; however, the statements and techniques you will learn will apply to structured coding as well. "Structure" refers to an approach to programming that emphasizes ease of coding and readability of programs for future maintenance. While many installations today are leaning toward structure and clarity, sometimes at the expense of computer storage space, a basic knowledge of ANS COBOL is critical to both traditional coding and structured coding. Another Self-Teaching Guide in this series, Structured COBOL, also teaches ANS COBOL; the statements and rules are the same—only the focus is different. In this guide, we shall stick as closely as possible to ANS COBOL. The guide is self-contained, including all the materials necessary for you to study ANS COBOL; you do not need access to a computer to learn how to write a program in COBOL. Of course, you will need access to a computer to develop what you learn here into actual programming.

When you complete this Self-Teaching Guide, you will be able to write COBOL programs that will require no alterations to run on most systems, and only a few changes for others. The Environment Division in the COBOL program, because it describes the machines and equipment used, contains most of the material that varies among systems. When you begin actual running, therefore, you will have to find out what the standard Environment Division entries are for the system you will be using. The majority of the ANS COBOL program, however, is machine independent and will run equally well on almost any computer system.

You will not learn to run your programs in this guide, since we don't know what system your installation has, and we can't tell you just how to go about it. You will probably need guidance from an instructor, a fellow student, or a congenial programmer. And before you run any programs, you will also find it useful to review the COBOL reference manual for your installation. You will find that this guide doesn't teach you all there is to know about COBOL. There are many more options than those presented here, some more statement types, and various aids to testing your programs can be used. If you are using this guide as part of a course, your instructor will have more information for you.

The ANS COBOL program you write is called a <u>source program</u>. This source program is then fed into a <u>source computer</u>, where it is <u>compiled</u> or translated into a machine-language program, the <u>object program</u>. One ANS COBOL statement may be translated into as many as fifty consecutive object statements, since extremely detailed instructions must be given to the computer in terms it understands. At the compilation stage, many of the errors (or bugs) in a program become apparent. Errors in spelling of the special ANS COBOL words, omission of required spacing or punctuation, and use of incorrect formats are just some of the factors which hinder the compilation of your source program into the machine-language object program. Learning to program in machine language does not circumvent these problems; machine-language format, syntax, and sequencing require even more attention to the details of both the language and the system. When you program in a higher level language, such as ANS COBOL, the compiler provides error messages from the source computer, which will help you correct your program. The <u>object computer</u> is used then to execute your mechanically correct program.

PREREQUISITES

Before studying this guide you should have a basic background in data processing, know generally what programming is, and be able to read a simple flowchart. Another Self-Teaching Guide, <u>Introduction to Data Processing</u> by Martin Harris, would provide these prerequisites, as would many other introductory books or a course in elementary data processing. Access to a computer and previous programming experience are not required.

CHAPTER ONE
COBOL Programming

American National Standard COBOL (ANS COBOL) is a high-level computer programming language. You write a program using words and syntax similar to English, then the computer translates this source program into machine language, producing the object program. This translation process is called <u>compilation</u>. The computer expects to find certain elements of the language to react to. The compiler cannot function if words are misspelled, for example, or if required punctuation is not included. Certain elements of the program must be placed in specific columns. The COBOL language requires you to be meticulous in your programming. It can repay you by providing the precise output you need.

Spelling, punctuation, and format are mentioned here because they are crucial elements for correct compilation. When you check your responses, be sure to check the details too. Even the placement of periods makes a difference. Attention to such fine points will enable you to spend less time debugging your programs.

In this chapter, you will write a simple program to use input, perform an operation, and product output; you will write all the required entries for a COBOL program. You will identify the program to the computer, describe the machine on which the program will be compiled and run, describe the data used in your program, and, finally, write the statements that will be executed by the computer.

COBOL is an acronym for <u>CO</u>mmon <u>B</u>usiness-<u>O</u>riented <u>L</u>anguage. COBOL was specifically created for handling the masses of data that are necessary in business data processing. Ordinarily, data is stored in <u>files</u> which allow for efficient processing of similar sets of information, such as customer records. In these first few chapters, however, we are going to avoid files. Their use involves much "housekeeping" coding, which can sometimes distract the novice programmer from more critical aspects of programming. We will still use input and output, but with statements for small amounts of data. In this way you will be able to do actual coding of short programs without doing the mechanics of COBOL programming which involve a great deal of writing.

Specific COBOL features you will learn to use in this chapter are:

- Identification Division entries
    IDENTIFICATION DIVISION header
    PROGRAM-ID paragraph

- Environment Division entries
    ENVIRONMENT DIVISION header
    CONFIGURATION SECTION header
    SOURCE-COMPUTER paragraph
    OBJECT-COMPUTER paragraph

- Data Division entries
    DATA DIVISION header
    WORKING-STORAGE SECTION header
    Level number 77
    PICTURE clause
    Picture character X

- Procedure Division entries
    PROCEDURE DIVISION header
    DISPLAY statement
    ACCEPT statement
    Literal entry
    STOP RUN statement

COBOL CODING

It is not really essential to write COBOL statements on special forms, called coding sheets. The programs, once written, are either keypunched or entered into a terminal. However, the special coding sheets make it much easier to keep statements in the required format. For this reason, we have included segments of COBOL coding sheets wherever you are asked to write a program entry. Feel free to use separate coding sheets, however, if you wish.

1. Every COBOL program has four parts:

    The Identification Division identifies the program—it includes the program name, the programmer, the data, etc.

    The Environment Division gives the hardware environment—it specifies the input-output devices to be used.

    The Data Division describes the data to be used in the program—records in files and work areas.

    The Procedure Division includes the instructions that the system will follow in solving the problem—it includes the procedure coded by the programmer.

Which division might each of the following be in?

(a) The name of the computer the program will be compiled on. _____

(b) The number of card readers involved. _____

(c) The instructions to calculate gross pay. _____

(d) The variables you will need in the program. _____

(e) The name of the program. _____

- - - - - - - - - - - - - - - - - - - -

(a) Environment Division; (b) Environment Division; (c) Procedure Division; (d) Data Division; (e) Identification Division

2. COBOL programs include many words dictated by the language itself. The division titles, called "division headers," for example, are used to begin each division. All words specific to the COBOL language are called reserved words; you cannot use them in program names you make up. You can't tell a program PROCEDURE, for example, because the word PROCEDURE is reserved for COBOL.

   Appendix A includes a list of COBOL reserved words. You will notice that many common words are reserved. Refer to the appendix and check off the words below that are COBOL reserved words.

   _____ (a) VALID
   _____ (b) INVALID
   _____ (c) PRINT
   _____ (d) PRINTER
   _____ (e) DIVISION
   _____ (f) DIVIDEND

- - - - - - - - - - - - - - - - -

b, e

3. In COBOL, many entries in a program fit into a hierarchy. The highest level entries are the division headers: Identification, Environment, Data, and Procedure divisions. Each of the division headers occurs in the above order in each program. As you will see, a division may contain several sections. A division or section may be made up of several paragraphs. And paragraphs may be made up of simple statements and sentences. Which of the following is true? (Choose one and write the letter in the space provided.)

(a) A paragraph may include several sections.
(b) A section may include several divisions.
(c) A paragraph may include several statements.

_____

- - - - - - - - - - - - - - - - - -

c (In the hierarchy, the division comes highest, then sections and/or paragraphs, and then statements.)

4. Some of the rules for coding COBOL programs help us to keep track of the hierarchy of entries. All division, section, and paragraph names must begin in columns 8 through 11. Look at the coding sheet (reduced size) on page 7. What are the columns in which division headers must begin called?

(a) Sequence
(b) A
(c) B

_____

- - - - - - - - - - - - - - - - - -

b (A, called the "A margin," includes columns 8, 9, 10, and 11.)

5. Statements, and all other entries that are not division headers, section-names, or paragraph-names, must begin in the B margin. Look again at the coding sheet. The B margin includes columns _____ through _____.

- - - - - - - - - - - - - - - - - -

12 through 72

6. The very first line of every COBOL program is a division header. This could begin in:

(a) the B margin   (c) column 8
(b) column 12   (d) column 10

_____

- - - - - - - - - - - - - - - - - -

c, d   (In examples in this book, A entries will begin in column 8. B entries will usually begin in column 12.)

7. As we mentioned, every COBOL program has four divisions, always in the same order: the Identification, Environment, Data, and Procedure

COBOL Coding Form

SYSTEM		PUNCHING INSTRUCTIONS			PAGE OF
PROGRAM		GRAPHIC		CARD FORM # *	IDENTIFICATION
PROGRAMMER	DATE	PUNCH			73] [80

SEQUENCE (PAGE) 1 3	(SERIAL) 4 6	CONT. 7	A 8	B 12	COBOL STATEMENT 16 20 24 28 32 36 40 44 48 52 56 60 64 68 72

A margin: Division headers
Section names
Paragraph-names
Level 01 and 77

B margin: Statements
All other levels

1 3 4 6 7 8 12 16 20 24 28 32 36 40 44 48 52 56 60 64 68 72

8 ANS COBOL

Divisions. A division header—the division name followed by a space, followed by the word DIVISION, and then by a period—goes in the A margin. Which of the following division headers is written correctly?

(a) IDENTIFICATION.
(b) ENVIRONMENT DIVISION
(c) DATADIVISION
(d) PROCEDURE DIVISION.

---

d (Most programmers use all capital letters on program sheets to facilitate keypunching; you may use small letters if you wish.)

IDENTIFICATION DIVISION ENTRIES

8. The very first entry in any COBOL program is the header for the Identification Division. Write this header below.

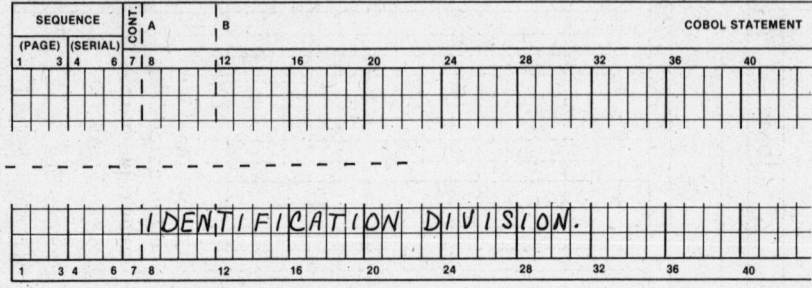

Don't forget the period.

9. The Identification Division is used to identify the program to the computer. It contains, in addition to the division header, a special paragraph named PROGRAM-ID, followed by a program-name which identifies the program. We will use a format like this throughout the book to show you how to make entries in COBOL:

> PROGRAM-ID. program-name.

The capitalized words are the exact words you must include in the entry. The lower case words indicate the general kind of entry you would make; you, as programmer, must supply the exact words.

Here, when you enter the exact words for "program-name." onto a coding sheet, you would write whatever name you have decided to give your program (and remember, you can't use reserved words).

At least one space must follow the period after the paragraph-name, PROGRAM-ID. In fact, one or more spaces must follow a period wherever it is used. The paragraph-name need not occupy a separate line. Which of the entries below are correct?

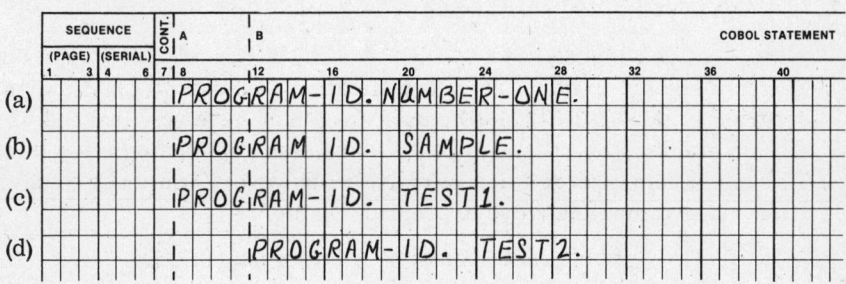

----

c (In a, no space follows a period. In b, no hyphen is included in PROGRAM ID. In d, the paragraph-name does not begin in the A margin. Notice in c that TEST1 begins in the B margin, but not in column 12.)

10. Write a PROGRAM-ID paragraph to name a program PRAXIS.

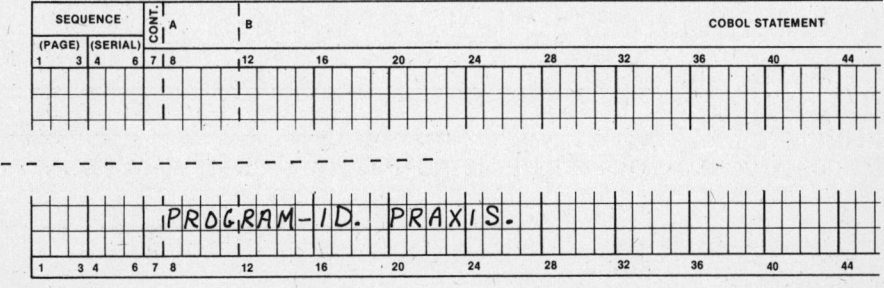

----

11. Write a division header and PROGRAM-ID paragraph to name a program HYPNOSIS.

```
         IDENTIFICATION DIVISION.
         PROGRAM-ID. HYPNOSIS.
```

12. The only required entry in the Identification Division of an ANS COBOL program is the PROGRAM-ID paragraph. You have now learned to write a complete division (although you'll learn some optional entries later). To write a complete division effectively, however, you must conform to a few rules in making up your program-name.

Rule 1. The first character must be a letter (alphabetic).

Rule 2. Any letters (A—Z), digits (0-9), or the hyphen may be used, but the hyphen may not be last.

Rule 3. Name may be as long as thirty characters, but the first eight must be unique, or different from any other program-name.

Rule 4. Name may not be a reserved word (see Appendix A). Reserved words may never be used as names in a program.

NOTE: It is customary to use what is called a self-documenting name, or one that describes what the program does.

What is wrong with each of the following program-names?

(a) WATER-RECORD- _____

(b) GA$-BILL$ _____

(c) 789-CODE _____

(d) RECORDS-FOR-TERMINATING-PASTDUE-CHARGE-ACCOUNTS
    _____

- - - - - - - - - - - - - - - - - -

(a) ends with a hyphen
(b) $ is not a letter, digit, or hyphen
(c) does not begin with a letter
(d) contains more than thirty characters

13. Refer to the rules on making up a program-name. Could you name two programs PRACTICE-PROGRAM-1 and PRACTICE-PROGRAM-2?

_____

- - - - - - - - - - - - - - - - - - -

No. The first eight characters are the same in both (Rule 3). We will study name-forming in more detail later.

14. Examine the Identification Divisions reproduced below. Which, if any, are correct?

(a) ```
IDENTIFICATION DIVISION.
     PROGRAM-ID. EVERY-NIGHT.
```

(b) ```
IDENTIFICATION DIVISION.
PROGRAM-ID. NEVERMORE?
```

(c) ```
IDENTIFICATION DIVISION
PROGRAM-ID. FOREVER.
```

(d) ```
IDENTIFICATION DIVISION.
PROGRAM-ID. EVERMORE.
```

_____

- - - - - - - - - - - - - - - - - -

d (In a, the paragraph-name does not begin in area A. In b, the symbol ? is not allowed in a program-name. In c, no period follows the division header.)

ENVIRONMENT DIVISION ENTRIES

15. The second division in every COBOL program is the Environment Division. This division describes the environment, or equipment, on which the program will be run. Your entries in this division, as indicated in the Introduction, will vary depending on the computer available to you. Coding of any division header:

   (a) must begin in which margin? _____

   (b) must end with a _____

- - - - - - - - - - - - - - - - -

   (a) A; (b) period

16. The Environment Division contains sections. The section header would begin in which margin? _____

A

17. The Configuration section is sometimes used to specify the type of computer system to be used.

```
7 8   12    16    20    24    28    32    36    40    44    48
 ENVIRONMENT DIVISION.
 CONFIGURATION SECTION.
 SOURCE-COMPUTER.  IBM-370.
 OBJECT-COMPUTER.  IBM-370.
```

The fragment above shows sample coding for the Configuration Section of the Environment Division. This section includes two:

(a) additional division headers.
(b) paragraph-names.
(c) section headers.

_____

---

b (Remember that statements begin in margin B, as do entries such as IBM-370. Division headers and section headers must always be written on separate lines. Paragraph-names need not be on separate lines.)

18. The entire Configuration Section is optional with some systems, but when used it must be in the format below.

> CONFIGURATION SECTION.
> SOURCE-COMPUTER. computer-name entry.
> OBJECT-COMPUTER. computer-name entry.

The computer-names you use in the Environment Division are not optional or created by you—you must enter the official name of the computer you will be using. For example, your installation may be an IBM-370-135 or IBM-360 or 6600 or H-200 or NCR-315. You will most likely use the same entries in this section for all of your programs. Now write the division and section headers, along with the two paragraphs to compile a program on a Honeywell 200 (source computer) and then execute it on an IBM System/360 Model 40 (IBM-360-40).

```
ENVIRONMENT DIVISION.
CONFIGURATION SECTION.
SOURCE-COMPUTER.  H-200.
OBJECT-COMPUTER.  IBM-360-40.
```

(Remember the periods. Don't worry if you didn't use the right computer names. Even though we will use a variety in the sample programs you write in this book, in practice the environment will be constant in programs for the same installation.)

The Environment Division of a COBOL program describes the computers used; it also is used to describe the input/output equipment requirements— the card readers, tapes, printers, and such. As mentioned earlier, we are sticking to very simple statements in these early chapters. Later in this guide you will study files and expand your knowledge of the Environment Division to include the Input-Output Section.

DATA DIVISION ENTRIES

19. The third division of the COBOL program describes the data to be used in the final division. Input data, output data, and working data must all be described. Which of the following items might be described in the Data Division?

    (a) the name of the program
    (b) the equipment needed to run the program
    (c) the type of input information you will use

---

c

20. The Data Division includes the File Section and the Working-Storage Section. We are concerned only with the Working-Storage Section now.

14 ANS COBOL

(a) The division header for the Data Division must begin in which margin? _____

(b) The section header for the Working-Storage Section must begin in which margin? _____

- - - - - - - - - - - - - - - - - - -

(a) A; (b) A

21. In the Working-Storage Section you can describe independent data items (items which are not subdivided), and also items that are subdivided. An example of an independent data item is a social security number: this item would not be subdivided. A group item might be a name, subdivided into elementary items—first, middle, and last names; or an address subdivided into street, city, state, and zip.

    Elementary items are subdivisions of a group, while independent items stand alone. Independent and elementary items are treated similarly in the COBOL program after they are described. You describe the independent and elementary items by giving each item: (1) a level number; (2) a data-name; and (3) a PICTURE description which tells how many characters, and what kind of characters, it has. (Independent data items are coded before group items and their elementary subdivisions.)

    Independent data items (not subdivided) are always given level number 77, which must be entered in the A margin. Which of the following are correct as independent data items?

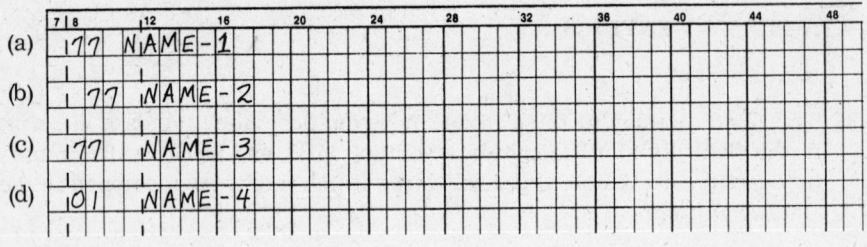

- - - - - - - - - - - - - - - - - - -

b, c   (In a, the data-name does not begin in the B margin. In d, the level number is not 77, thus it is not an independent data item.)

22. Data-names, like program-names, must be formed following certain rules. First and foremost, they must be unique—that is, each data item in a program must be distinguishable from every other data item.

    Rule 1. A data-name must be unique. (You will learn later how to circumvent this rule.)

Rule 2. A data-name must have thirty or fewer characters.
Rule 3. A data-name may contain combinations of letters, digits, and hyphens. No spaces are allowed within names.
Rule 4. A data-name must not begin or end with a hyphen.
Rule 5. A data-name must contain at least one letter.
Rule 6. No reserved words may be used.

Decide if each data-name below is valid. If not, tell what is wrong with it.

(a) -7-ARROW _____

(b) STRAIGHT ARROW _____

(c) 455-1781 _____

(d) AREA-415 _____

(e) CODE _____

- - - - - - - - - - - - - - - - - - - -

(a) begins with hyphen; (b) contains a space; (c) does not contain a letter; (d) valid; (e) reserved word

23. As we said earlier, describing data means specifying a level number, giving a data-name, and giving a PICTURE description. The PICTURE clause tells the computer how many characters are in the data item, and what kind of characters they are. As you go through this book, you will learn many different pictures that can be used. The most useful all-purpose Picture character is X, which is used to tell the computer that the corresponding character in the data item might be anything—at least any character in the standard character set (see Appendix B). Thus when you write PICTURE XX you tell the computer the data item is two characters long and both of them are standard characters—numbers, letters, $, or any of the special characters.

    77 CODE-1 PICTURE XXX.

In this example:

(a) the level number is _____.

(b) the data-name is _____.

(c) How long is the data item? _____.

- - - - - - - - - - - - - - - - - - - -

(a) 77; (b) CODE-1; (c) three characters
(Notice the period following the PICTURE clause. One space follows the data-name here. Any place one space may appear, any number of spaces may appear.)

24. Which of the following could be a value of CODE-1, based on the data description in the preceding frame?

(a) 973
(b) A-OK
(c) A-1
(d) $200.00

---

a, c   (b and d require more than three characters.)

25. Write a Working-Storage Section entry below for an independent data item named MAXIMUM-RATING, which is seven characters long.

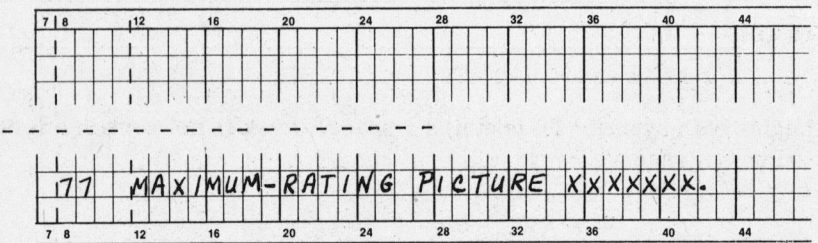

(The 77 must be in area A; the data-name must begin in the B margin. A period must follow the PICTURE clause. However, more spaces may be used before or after PICTURE.)

A few useful shortcuts in writing a COBOL program come into play here. The letters PIC may be used as an abbreviation for PICTURE. And the XXXXXXX may be replaced by X(7). Both of these alternatives are recognized by virtually all ANS COBOL compilers, and they can save you a great deal of time in writing your programs. Later you will be able to write more specific pictures, but the "repetition factor" may always be used in such clauses. We will use the short forms in answers given in this book, but the longer forms are always correct, if you choose to use them.

26. Identify what, if anything, is wrong with the Working-Storage entries below.

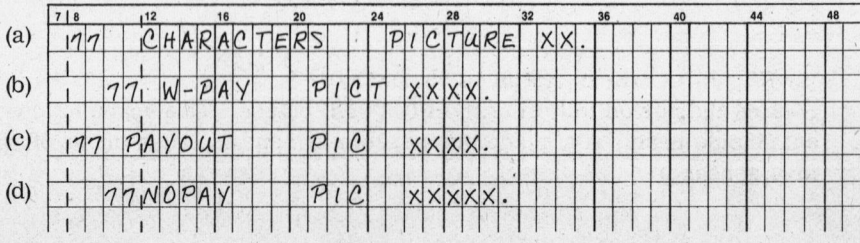

(a) CHARACTERS is a reserved word; (b) PICT is not a valid shortcut; (c) data-name begins in A margin; (d) no space after 77

27. In this format, the level number and PIC are required parts and must be used as specified. The programmer furnishes the data-name and the actual picture.

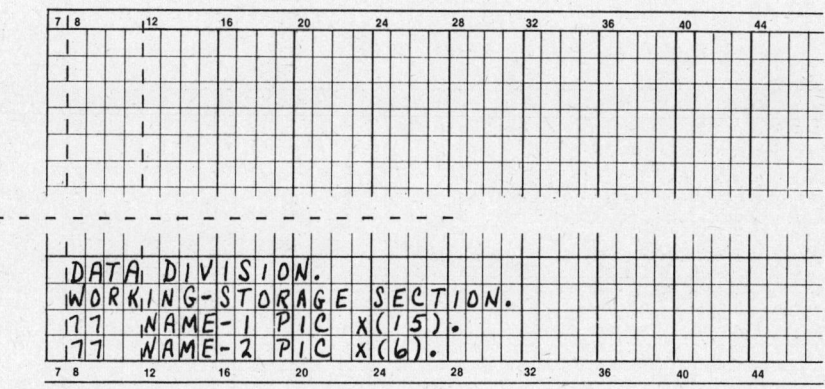

77 data-name PIC picture.

Write entries to describe independent data items called NAME-1 and NAME-2. NAME-1 will be fifteen characters long and NAME-2 will be six. Include the appropriate division and section headers.

- -

```
DATA DIVISION.
WORKING-STORAGE SECTION.
77  NAME-1  PIC X(15).
77  NAME-2  PIC X(6).
```

28. List the first three division headers required in an ANS COBOL program.

- - - - - - - - - - - - - - - - - - - -

Identification Division
Environment Division
Data Division

29. Suppose you want to write a program called OPTIONS. You will then compile it on a Honeywell 200 (H-200) and execute it on an IBM System/370 Model 135 computer (IBM-370-135). You expect to use three independent data items in your program: LAST-NAME, twelve characters; GPA, four characters; and COURSE-LOAD, two characters long. Write the first three divisions for such a program.

```
IDENTIFICATION DIVISION.
PROGRAM-ID.  OPTIONS.
ENVIRONMENT DIVISION.
CONFIGURATION SECTION.
SOURCE-COMPUTER.  H-200.
OBJECT-COMPUTER.  IBM-370-135.
DATA DIVISION.
WORKING-STORAGE SECTION.
77   LAST-NAME PIC X(12).
77   GPA PIC X(4).
77   COURSE-LOAD PIC XX.
```

PROCEDURE DIVISION ENTRIES

You have now written the minimum essentials of the first three divisions of an ANS COBOL program. In the next section of this chapter we shall discuss the Procedure Division. The procedural part of programming is more complex; that is the part in which you tell the computer exactly how to solve a problem.

30. Write a header for the Procedure Division.

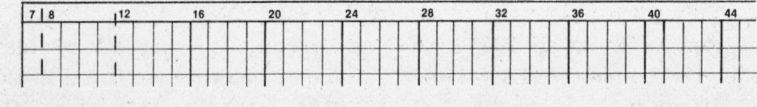

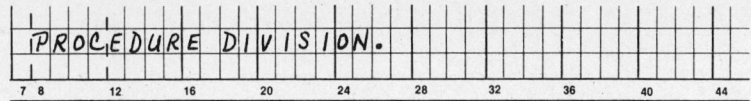

31. The Procedure Division contains statements and sentences grouped into paragraphs.

    (a) Paragraph-names begin in which margin? _____

    (b) Statements begin in which margin? _____

- - - - - - - - - - - - - - - - - -

(a) A; (b) B
(Advanced programmers may use sections in the Procedure Division also; we will not cover that in this guide.)

32. When you write a program, you must create paragraph-names for the Procedure Division. These paragraph-names may be referred to in your program, or they may be used for documentation—to explain the program to a reader. In any event, the names must conform to the same rules as do data- and program-names, except they may contain all digits. Usually we try to use descriptive names to produce a self-documenting program—that is, a program that specifies what it is doing so humans can read and understand what it does. Paragraph-names must be unique—different from data-names and other paragraph-names. Which of these might be a valid paragraph-name for the Procedure Division?

    (a) FIRST PARAGRAPH
    (b) -THE-FIRST
    (c) PREPARATION

    _____

- - - - - - - - - - - - - - - - - -

c   (a includes a space; b begins with a hyphen.)

33. Like division and section headers, paragraph-names must end with a period. At least one space must follow the period, as usual. It is customary to use a paragraph-name immediately following the division head header. Write a paragraph-name below for the paragraph FIRST-ONE.

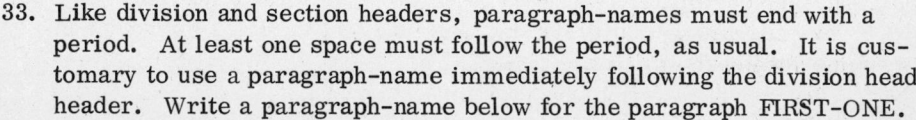

- - - - - - - - - - - - - - - - - -

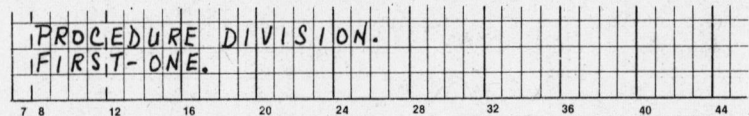

Almost any program, no matter how simple, requires some kind of input data and output data. In this chapter we will use the ACCEPT statement to handle low-volume input from either the card reader or the console keyboard, and the DISPLAY statement to handle low-volume output to either the printer or the console (typewriter or cathode ray tube). Such statements are generally used only for small amounts of data, as they are quite time-consuming to execute (even though they allow simpler writing of the programs).

Let's assume you want to write a program whose only purpose is to find out what time the computer operator runs the program. In your program you will ask the operator to enter the time of day (or night) into the computer. You will need to have a way to tell the operator what you want to be done. Then you need to have a way to get the computer to recognize the input.

34. We can use an exact value, called a literal, to put a message or other constant value on a console or printer. We do this by enclosing what we want in quotes. For example, to specify hello as a literal you write "HELLO". To specify a phone number as a literal you write "2721925". We're treating literals here as character strings. Any characters except quotation marks can be used as literals, and they may have up to thirty characters. You'll see later that numeric literals, for use in arithmetic, don't require quotes. Which of these are valid literals?

(a) "GOODNIGHT"
(b) "SAY "HELLO" TO THE COMPUTER"
(c) "PLEASE ENTER THE HOUR AND MINUTES"

---

a, c (b includes quotation marks. Some systems, notably IBM, use single quotation marks in their extensions to ANS COBOL. However, the language specifications for ANS COBOL specify double quotation marks. If you expect to use an IBM computer, use single quotes for your non-numeric literals.)

DISPLAY STATEMENT

35. Below is the format for a DISPLAY statement.

> DISPLAY $\begin{Bmatrix} \text{literal} \\ \text{data-name} \end{Bmatrix}$ [UPON CONSOLE]

Restrictions:

1. Brackets [ ] indicate optional clause.

2. Braces { } indicate choose one.

3. Literal must be exactly what you want displayed, enclosed in quotes.

4. Data-name must have been described in Data Division.

The DISPLAY statement causes either the literal or the value of the data-name to be printed as output from the computer. With the UPON CONSOLE option, as above, DISPLAY will cause the message to be printed on the console typewriter or be displayed on the cathode ray tube, depending on the setup. Without the option, the message or value is printed on the standard printer as one line. Which of the following might cause output to be produced on the console typewriter?

(a) DISPLAY FIRST-NAME UPON CONSOLE.
(b) PRODUCE OUTPUT UPON CONSOLE.
(c) DISPLAY FIRST-NAME.
(d) DISPLAY "NAME?" UPON CONSOLE.

----

a, d   (b is the wrong format; c would cause the output to be produced on the printer.)

36. Write a statement that will cause the message WHAT IS YOUR NAME? to be displayed on the console typewriter. Begin the statement in the B margin.

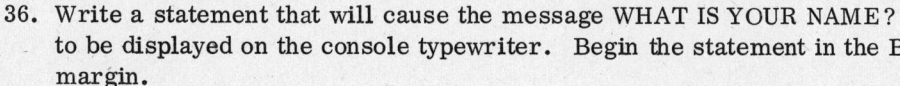

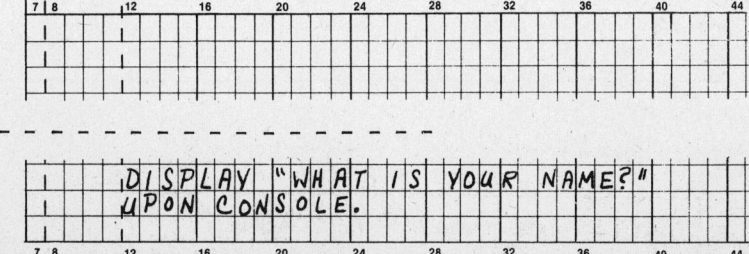

22 ANS COBOL

(On a full-size coding form this statement would be written as a single line. However, statements may always be divided between words, or wherever a space occurs. Just be certain that the statement is entirely within the B margin.)

37. Suppose you have defined a level 77 item (an independent, not subdivided, data item) called NAME. You can show its current value by coding

   DISPLAY NAME UPON CONSOLE.

   You can, in fact, combine literals and data names:

   DISPLAY NAME "HOW OLD ARE YOU" UPON CONSOLE.

   Write DISPLAY statements to produce the following outputs on the system printer.

   (a) Put the value of data-name EMPLOYEE

   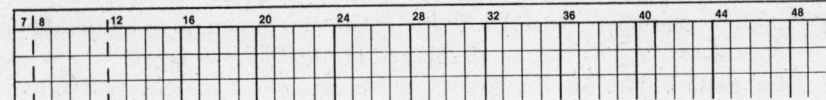

   (b) Print the message "The social security number is" and the data-item "SSNO".

   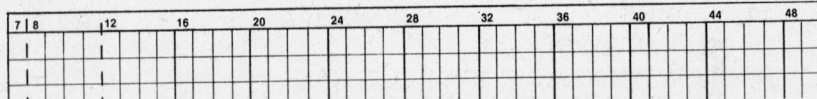

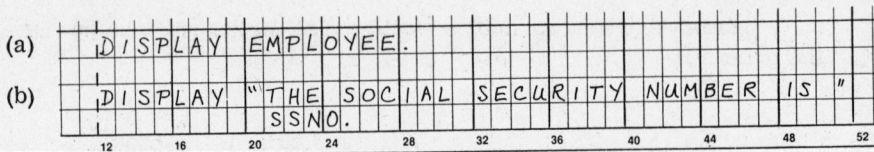

(a) DISPLAY EMPLOYEE.
(b) DISPLAY "THE SOCIAL SECURITY NUMBER IS" SSNO.

ACCEPT STATEMENT

38. Below is the format for the ACCEPT statement.

   ACCEPT data-name [FROM CONSOLE]

Restrictions:

1. Brackets indicate optional phrase.
2. Data-name must have been described in the Data Division.

The ACCEPT statement instructs the computer to receive input information. When the FROM CONSOLE option is used, the data is entered through the console keyboard. Without the option, the card reader is the device used. The computer will then accept as many character positions as were specified, up to the device limitation. Follow the format above and write a statement to receive input data in the form of EXACT-TIME, which was described in the Data Division. The data will be entered at the keyboard.

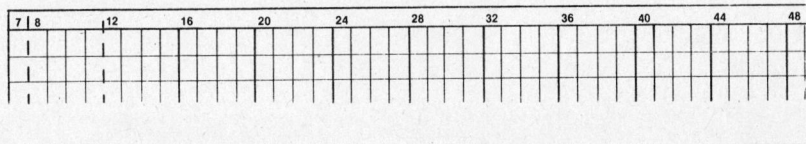

39. Suppose EXACT-TIME is described like this:

    77   EXACT-TIME   PIC   XXXXX.

When the operator enters 12:15, those five characters are placed in EXACT-TIME; they become its value. Characters are placed in EXACT-TIME starting on the left. If the operator entered 1215, the value of EXACT-TIME would be 1215∅ (∅ represents a blank). What would be the value if "twelve fifteen" were entered? _____

TWELV

40. Assume EXACT-TIME has been described as PIC XXXX. The data is entered as 10/25. The computer accepts the number of characters specified, filling the leftmost position first. What is the value of EXACT-TIME after ACCEPT is executed? _____

10/2   (Four positions are accepted and any extras are dropped. Pictures must be specified very carefully so data is not lost like this.)

24 ANS COBOL

41. As we saw earlier in the format, the DISPLAY statement can also specify a data-name. The value of that data-name would then be displayed. Write a statement now to print on the printer the EXACT-TIME which the operator has just entered in the preceding frame.

```
       DISPLAY EXACT-TIME.
7 8   12    16    20    24    28    32    36    40    44    48
```

(10/2 would be printed. If the operator had entered 1025, that would be printed.)

42. The complete Procedure Division below will instruct the computer to print on the printer the EXACT-TIME, assuming the first three divisions were correctly written.

```
PROCEDURE DIVISION.
FIRST-ONE.
    DISPLAY "ENTER EXACT TIME" UPON CONSOLE.
    ACCEPT EXACT-TIME FROM CONSOLE.
    DISPLAY EXACT-TIME.
    STOP RUN.
```

The statement DISPLAY "ENTER EXACT TIME" UPON CONSOLE puts a message on the console in the computer room. The statement ACCEPT EXACT-TIME FROM CONSOLE causes the program to wait until the operator enters something via the keyboard. The value that is entered is then printed on the system printer. Eventually, the pages from the printer make their way back to the programmer, with the time printed that the operator was running your program.

One statement above terminates execution of your program. Which one? _____

STOP RUN

43. A STOP RUN statement is used to end every program. The statement assures orderly termination and allows you to tell the computer very easily when you have finished with your instructions. What margin must STOP RUN begin in? _____

the B margin

44. An ACCEPT or DISPLAY statement can be used to receive or produce more than one item of input or output at a time. You simply list the items. For example, you could write ACCEPT ABC BCD EFT FROM CONSOLE or ACCEPT KIND PRICE. Either will then allow for receiving values of the listed data-names. Notice that the data-names are separated by spaces. You may also use a comma as a separator, followed by at least one space, as in ACCEPT ABC, BCD. A combination of literals and data-names may be displayed. For example, DISPLAY "TODAY THE PASSWORD IS ", PASSWORD UPON CONSOLE. would cause the literal and the day's password to become output. Now write a statement that will print the phrase THIS PROGRAM WAS RUN AT followed by the value of the data item EXACT-TIME. Allow for a space after AT.

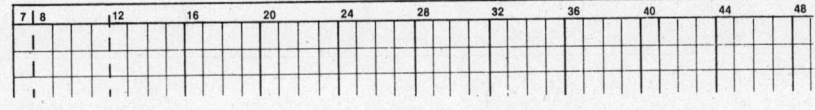

- - - - - - - - - - - - - - - - -

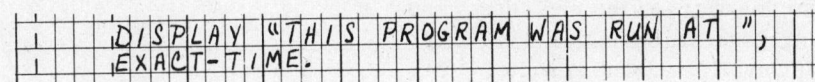

DISPLAY "THIS PROGRAM WAS RUN AT ",
EXACT-TIME.

(The comma could be omitted.)

45. Write a statement to receive two data items called PASSWORD and CODE-7 from the console.

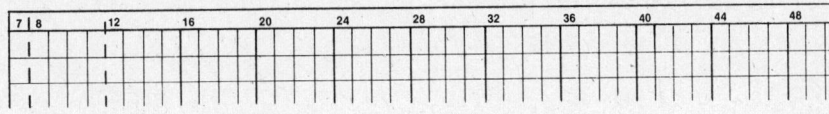

- - - - - - - - - - - - - - - - -

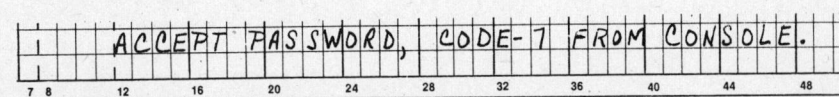

ACCEPT PASSWORD, CODE-7 FROM CONSOLE.

(The comma is optional.)

REVIEW

46. In the Procedure Division, the first entry after the header is usually a _____.

- - - - - - - - - - - - - - -

paragraph-name   (This is not required, but it is customary.)

47. The statement that terminates execution of a COBOL program is
    _____.

- - - - - - - - - - - - - - - - - - - -

STOP RUN

48. In which margin must each of the following entries begin?
    (a) division headers _____   (d) statements _____
    (b) section headers _____   (e) level number 77 _____
    (c) paragraph-names _____

- - - - - - - - - - - - - - - - - - - -

(a) A; (b) A; (c) A; (d) B; (e) A

49. The flowchart on the right describes a program called NAME-DISPLAY, which you are about to write. This program will be compiled and run on a 6800 system. The only data item is NAME, which is twenty characters long. Use ONLY-PARA as the paragraph-name in the Procedure Division. Write the program on the coding sheet on the next page.

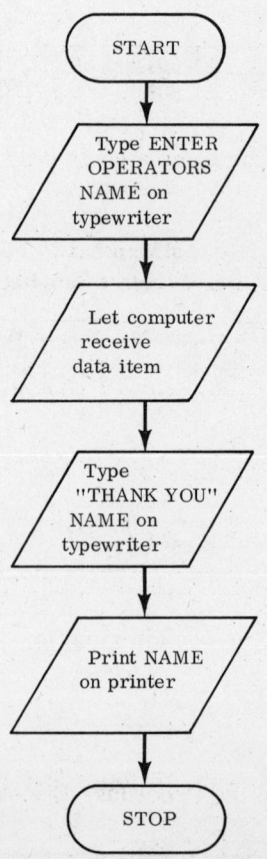

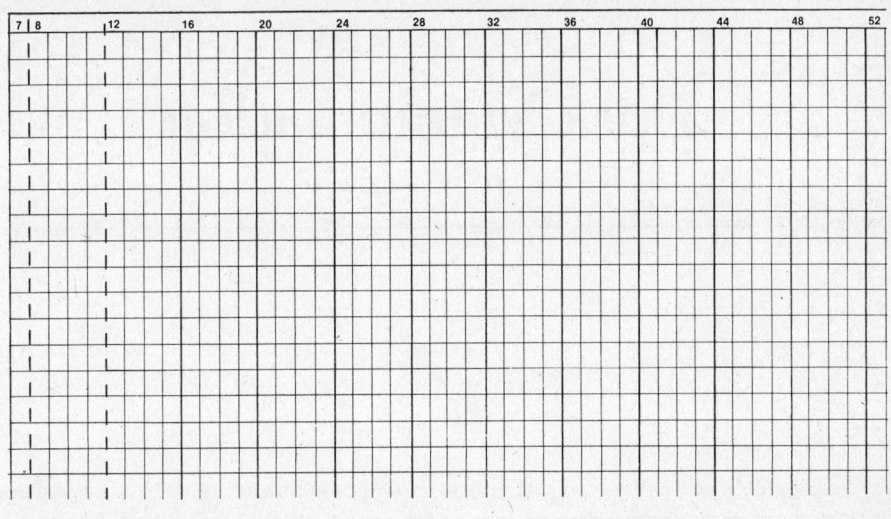

```
IDENTIFICATION DIVISION.
PROGRAM-ID.  NAME-DISPLAY.
ENVIRONMENT DIVISION.
CONFIGURATION SECTION.
SOURCE-COMPUTER.  6800.
OBJECT-COMPUTER.  6800.
DATA DIVISION.
WORKING-STORAGE SECTION.
77  NAME PIC X(20).
PROCEDURE DIVISION.
ONLY-PARA.
    DISPLAY "ENTER OPERATORS NAME"
    UPON CONSOLE.
    ACCEPT NAME FROM CONSOLE.
    DISPLAY "THANK YOU", NAME UPON CONSOLE.
    DISPLAY NAME.
    STOP RUN.
```

You have now written a complete program in ANS COBOL, and are ready to go on to bigger and better programs!

CHAPTER TWO
Data Manipulation

In Chapter 1, you learned to write a simple program using only a few options. In this chapter you will learn to use a few more entries. You will learn to use three additional entries in the Identification Division to document your program. You will also learn to describe group, or subdivided, data items, and to move data from one location to another within your program.

After you complete this chapter you will write a program to demonstrate your ability to use the following ANS COBOL entries:

- Identification Division entries
    AUTHOR paragraph
    DATE-WRITTEN paragraph
    DATE-COMPILED paragraph
    REMARKS paragraph

- Data Division entries
    01 and 02 level numbers

- Procedure Division entries
    MOVE statement

OPTIONAL IDENTIFICATION DIVISION ENTRIES

The Identification Division of a COBOL program identifies the program to the computer and to the reader. It is analogous to the title page in a book, which gives additional information to whomever cares to look. There is quite an assortment of optional paragraphs to use in the Identification Division. We will consider four of these: the AUTHOR, DATE-WRITTEN, DATE-COMPILED, and REMARKS paragraphs.

The format for an Identification Division with optional identification entries is shown on the next page.

DATA MANIPULATION   29

> IDENTIFICATION DIVISION.
> PROGRAM-ID. program-name.
> [AUTHOR. comment-entry.]
> [DATE-WRITTEN. comment-entry.]
> [DATE-COMPILED. comment-entry.]
> [REMARKS. comment-entry.]

1. The optional entries are in brackets and must be in the order shown (for most compilers). Which of the examples below uses the entries in the correct order?

   (a)
   ```
   IDENTIFICATION DIVISION.
   AUTHOR. RUTH ASHLEY.
   DATE-WRITTEN. APRIL 17, 1979.
   ```

   (b)
   ```
   IDENTIFICATION DIVISION.
   PROGRAM-ID. SPECIMEN.
   REMARKS. THIS PROGRAM IS JUST AN
            EXAMPLE AND DOESN'T REALLY
            DO ANYTHING.
   ```

   (c)
   ```
   IDENTIFICATION DIVISION.
   DATE-WRITTEN. APRIL 30, 1979.
   PROGRAM-ID. SPECIMEN.
   ```

----

b   (a omits the required entry; c is out of order.)

2. If you use any of the optional Identification Division entries, you must use a comment-entry. This entry can be composed of any combination of characters accepted by ANS COBOL. The comment-entry must be entirely contained in the B margin, but may take as many lines as seems appropriate. What would be an appropriate comment-entry for the AUTHOR paragraph?

----

your name

3. What would be an appropriate comment-entry for the DATE-WRITTEN paragraph? _____

----

the date the program was written

4. Most comment-entries are stored with the program but are not affected by it. However, in the DATE-COMPILED paragraph, a comment-entry may be replaced with the actual date of compilation by the COBOL compiler. Write an appropriate DATE-COMPILED paragraph for a program compiled today.

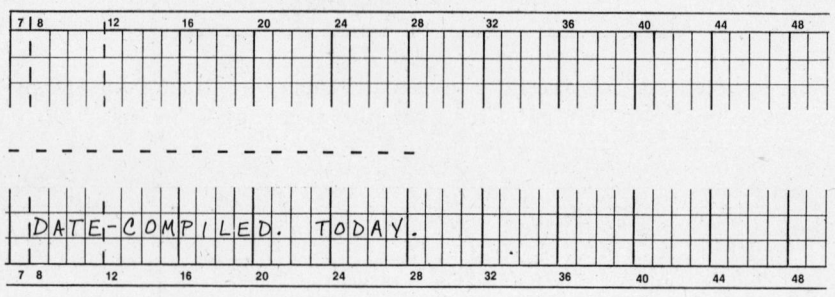

- - - - - - - - - - - - - - - - - -

DATE-COMPILED. TODAY.

- - - - - - - - - - - - - - - - - -

5. You might put the explanation of what the program is designed to do as the comment-entry for which Identification Division paragraph?

_____

- - - - - - - - - - - - - - - - - -

REMARKS

6. The computer ignores most of the comment-entries except that it includes them when it lists the program. Comment-entries are useful in explaining to future users what the program does and who created it. They are often required by installations to ensure at least minimal documentation of programs. Well-used comments help make the program self-documenting. According to the format at the beginning of this section, each comment-entry must end with a _____.

- - - - - - - - - - - - - - - - - -

period

7. Comment-entries must be entirely contained in which margin? _____

- - - - - - - - - - - - - - - - - -

B

8. If a comment-entry requires more than one line, it may be continued on the next line. (As we noted earlier, a single space may be replaced by many spaces, therefore a line need not be completely filled before a new

DATA MANIPULATION 31

one is begun.) When starting a second line, what is the leftmost permissible column? _____

- - - - - - - - - - - - - - - - - - -

12

9. The optional paragraph entries in the Identification Division must begin in which margin? _____

- - - - - - - - - - - - - - - - - - -

A

10. List four optional Identification Division entries in order.

_____

_____

_____

_____

- - - - - - - - - - - - - - - - - - -

AUTHOR.
DATE-WRITTEN.
DATE-COMPILED.
REMARKS.
(They must be in this order.)

11. Must the required paragraph in the Identification Division come before or after any optional entries? _____

- - - - - - - - - - - - - - - - - - -

before

Additional optional Identification Division paragraphs are listed in the complete format in Appendix C. These will not be described here, as they are largely self-explanatory.

DATA DIVISION ENTRIES: GROUP DATA ITEMS

In the first chapter, you learned to describe independent data items in the Data Division using level number 77 in the A margin. As you remember,

32 ANS COBOL

these were data items that were not subdivided. In this chapter you will learn to describe subdivided data items, where one data-name refers to a group of several items. These are called group items.

12. The entries below show how a data item could be described as either an independent data item or as a group data item.

```
7│8    │12    16    20    24    28    32    36    40    44
│77│ │E│X│A│C│T│-│T│I│M│E│ │P│I│C│ │X│X│X│X│.│
│  │ │ │ │ │ │ │ │ │ │ │ │ │ │ │ │ │ │ │ │ │ │
│0│1│ │E│X│A│C│T│-│T│I│M│E│-│2│.│
│  │ │0│2│ │H│O│U│R│S│ │P│I│C│ │X│X│.│
│  │ │0│2│ │M│I│N│U│T│E│S│ │P│I│C│ │X│X│.│
```

Here EXACT-TIME-2 is subdivided into HOURS and MINUTES. Study the example. Level number 01 is used to refer to the highest level of a data item. This level number is coded in which margin? _____

- - - - - - - - - - - - - - - - - -

A

13. Secondary level numbers can range from 02 to 49 in a group item, but they must be kept in order. We will use them in sequence, from 02 to whatever we need. In practice, you could use 05, 10, 12, for example, as long as the levels increase. In this chapter we will use only two levels, 01 and 02. Level number 02 must be coded in which margin?

_____

- - - - - - - - - - - - - - - - - -

B

14. The lowest level data items in our example above use level number 02. These items are not further subdivided and are elementary data items. Since they are small parts of a larger item, we cannot call them independent data items, although they act independently when on the same level. Refer to the example in frame 12 and write independent or elementary after each of the data items listed below.

   (a) HOURS _____

   (b) EXACT-TIME _____

   (c) MINUTES _____

- - - - - - - - - - - - - - - - - -

(a) elementary; (b) independent; (c) elementary
(EXACT-TIME-2 is a group item. A level 01 item is actually a record, but this will be discussed later.)

15. A data item that is subdivided is called a group item. Group items do not have PICTURE clauses. A data item that has a PICTURE clause would be:

    (a) an independent data item.
    (b) an elementary data item.
    (c) either an elementary or independent data item.

    ---

    c

16.
```
77   FIRST-NAME      PIC X(12).
77   INITIAL         PIC X.
77   LAST-NAME       PIC X(12).

01   WHOLE-NAME.
     02  FIRST-NM    PIC X(12).
     02  INIT        PIC X.
     02  LAST-NM     PIC X(12).
```

The examples above show two ways of describing the same data. Suppose you have described it as in the first example. Write a statement to print the full name on the printer.

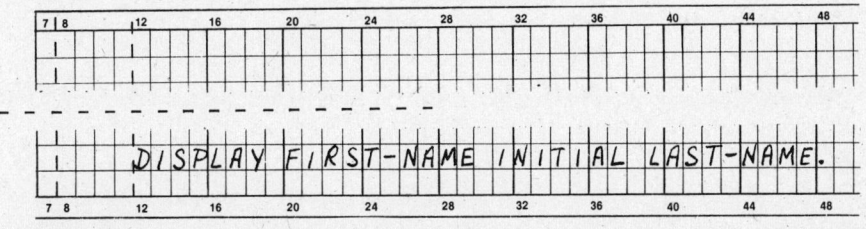

```
            DISPLAY FIRST-NAME INITIAL LAST-NAME.
```

(Commas could be used to separate the data names. Each comma must be followed by a space.)

17. Suppose you had described your data as shown in the second example in the preceding frame. A reference to the group item refers to all elementary data items within the group. Write a statement to print the full name on the printer on the coding sheet portion on the next page.

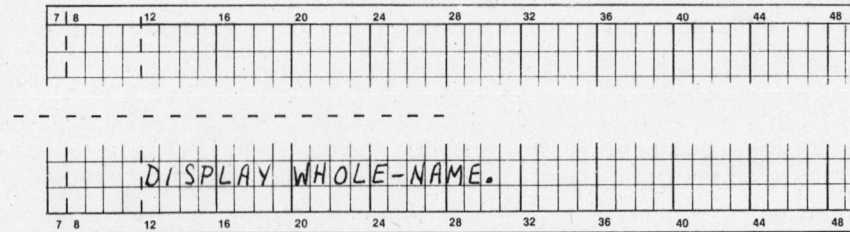

(DISPLAY FIRST-NM INIT LAST-NM is correct, but unnecessarily cumbersome. Also, the spacing will be different, since three data items are named. Exact DISPLAY spacing may vary with the system.)

18. Suppose you have the data described by the group item WHOLE-NAME in your computer. Write a statement to display the last name only on the console.

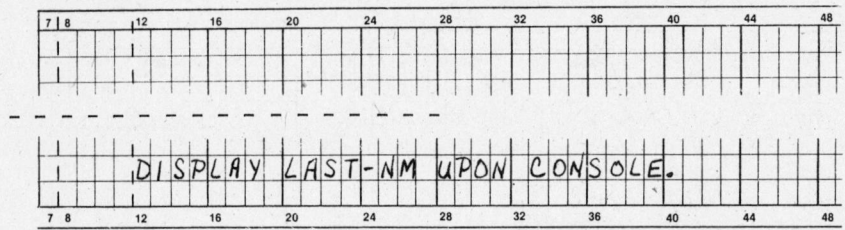

19. A variable you will use in a program is to be called TODAYS-DATE. This is to be subdivided into MONTH, which is three characters long, DAYX, which is two characters long, and YEARX, which is four characters long. Write group and elementary items to describe this variable. (Do not describe them as independent data items.)

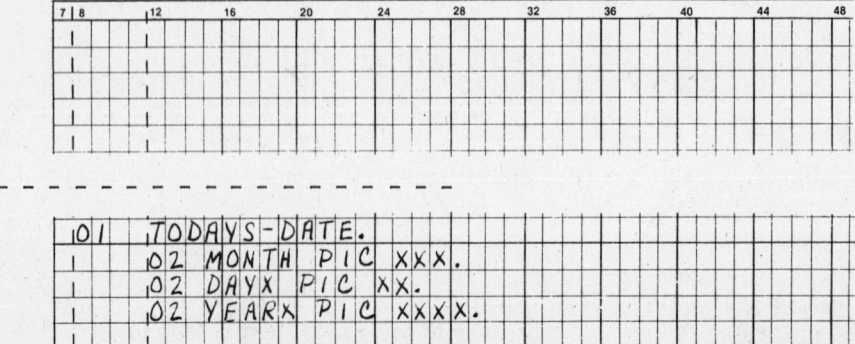

DATA MANIPULATION 35

20. Now write Working-Storage Entries to describe the following.

    STOCK-ITEM is subdivided into a CODE-NO that is three characters long and a DESCRIPTION that is twenty characters long.

    SYMBOL is a single item that always contains two digits then three letters.

    REORDER includes a two-digit month and a two-digit year.

    Independent data item descriptions are entered before any group items. Space is provided for your answer below.

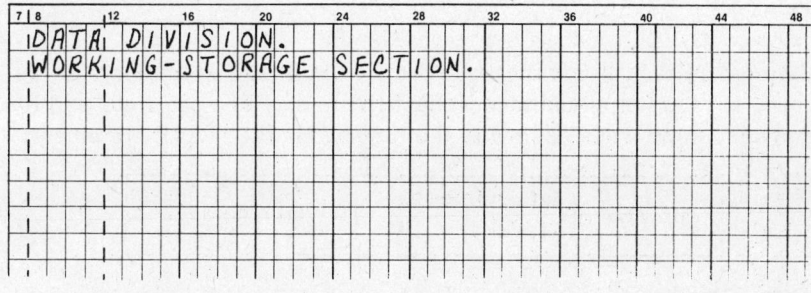

- - - - - - - - - - - - - - - - - - - -

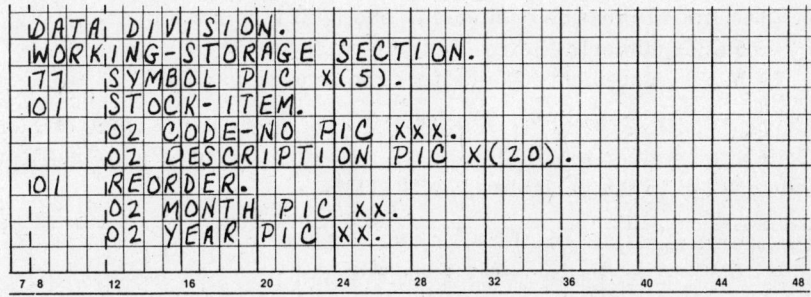

(The order of REORDER and STOCK-ITEM could be reversed.)

You are now able to describe data in group and elementary data items. In later chapters we will expand this to include more levels, but the concept remains the same.

MOVE STATEMENT

Data values can be moved around in the Procedure Division. One way to do this is to use the MOVE statement. This statement causes the data to be copied from one data location to another.

36 ANS COBOL

21. The statement MOVE ITEM-A TO ITEM-B. causes the value of ITEM-A to be copied into the data item ITEM-B. It does not change the value of ITEM-A. Suppose ITEM-A has a value of WALL, and ITEM-B has a value of HIGH. After the execution of the MOVE statement above:

    (a) ITEM-A will have the value _____.

    (b) ITEM-B will have the value _____.

- - - - - - - - - - - - - - - - - -

   (a) WALL; (b) WALL

22. Elementary data items may be specified in MOVE statements as we have seen. Group items and independent items may be specified, and literals may also be moved. Below is the format for the MOVE statement.

    MOVE {data-name-1 / literal} TO data-name-2

    Restrictions:
    1. Data-names must have been described in the Data Division.
    2. The literal must be enclosed in quotes if it is not numeric. (We will consider numeric literals in the next chapter.)
    3. A MOVE statement never alters the sending variable.

    MOVE "NONE-GIVEN" TO FIRST-NM. would cause the value of NONE-GIVEN to be given to FIRST-NM. Write a statement to give the literal value NOON to the variable EXACT-TIME.

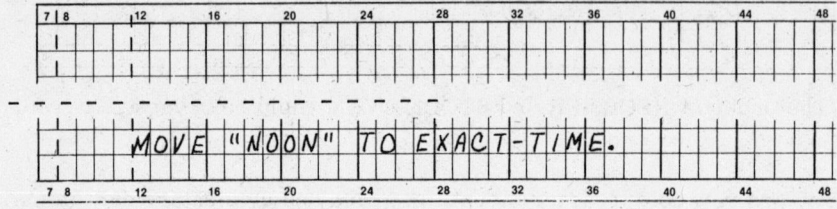

23. The MOVE statement must begin in which margin? _____

- - - - - - - - - - - - - - - -

   B   (All statements begin here.)

24. Alphanumeric data is moved in a certain way. The individual characters are placed in the receiving field (data-name-2) from left to right. If the sending field (data-name-1 or the literal) is too short, the rightmost positions in the receiving field will contain blanks. If the sending field is too long, the leftover positions will be ignored. Suppose INITIAL

DATA MANIPULATION 37

were described as a one-position field. What would be the value of INITIAL after MOVE "NONE" TO INITIAL? _____

N (The excess—three characters "ONE"—would be ignored.)

25. Suppose you write MOVE INITIAL TO FIRST-NM. when the value of INITIAL (PIC X) is Q and the value of FIRST-NM (PIC X(7)) is WILLIAM. What is the final value of FIRST-NM? _____

Qbbbbbb   (The symbol b represents a blank. The computer never prints a b, but leaves the position empty.)

26. Suppose NAME-1 has the value GEORGE and NAME-2 has the value MARVIN. Write a MOVE statement that would cause both NAME-1 and NAME-2 to have the value MARVIN.

```
        MOVE NAME-2 TO NAME-1.
```

(MOVE "MARVIN" TO NAME-1 would also solve the problem.)

27. Assume SIMPLE-S has been described as a ten-position item. What does it contain after execution of each of the following?

```
(a)     MOVE "SEVENTEEN" TO SIMPLE-S.
(b)     MOVE "TWENTY-SEVEN" TO SIMPLE-S.
(c)     MOVE "I LOVE YOU" TO SIMPLE-S.
```

(a) _____

(b) _____

(c) _____

(a) SEVENTEENb; (b) TWENTY-SEV; (c) IbLOVEbYOU

38 ANS COBOL

28. Group items can be treated as sending or receiving variables. In either case, the group item would be considered to have as many positions as all of its elementary items, in the order they occur in the elementary items.

```
 7|8    12      16      20      24      28      32      36      40      44      48
17 7    SYMBOL  PIC X(5).
10 1    STOCK-ITEM.
        02 CODE-NO PIC XXX.
        02 DESCRIPTION PIC X(20).
```

In the example above:

(a) STOCK-ITEM has how many character positions? _____

(b) MOVE "DRESSES" TO STOCK-ITEM. results in what value for
    CODE-NO? _____

- - - - - - - - - - - - - - - - - - -

(a) 23
(b) DRE   (DESCRIPTION has the value "SSES" followed by sixteen blanks.)

29. Assume the data items described in the preceding frame have the following values:

SYMBOL is AB123
CODE-NO is 798
DESCRIPTION is BASKETBALLbEQUIPMENT

Give the value of the receiving variable after each of these. (Consider the values as above prior to each MOVE.)

```
 7|8    12      16      20      24      28      32      36      40      44      48
(a)     MOVE DESCRIPTION TO SYMBOL.
(b)     MOVE CODE-NO TO SYMBOL.
(c)     MOVE SYMBOL TO STOCK-ITEM.
(d)     MOVE "SYMBOL" TO STOCK-ITEM.
```

(a) _____

(b) _____

(c) _____

(d) _____

- - - - - - - - - - - - - - - - - - -

(a) SYMBOL has the value BASKE
(b) SYMBOL has the value 798ØØ
(c) STOCK-ITEM has the value AB123 followed by eighteen blanks
(d) STOCK-ITEM has the value SYMBOL followed by 17 spaces
(Remember that the sending variable is never altered when a MOVE statement is executed.)

30. Assume the same beginning data as in the preceding frame. What is the value of the receiving variable after execution of MOVE STOCK-ITEM TO SYMBOL? _____

- - - - - - - - - - - - - - - - - - - -

798BA

31.
```
DATA DIVISION.
WORKING-STORAGE SECTION.
77  CLASS-NUMBER PIC X.
01  STUDENT-LISTING.
    02  S-NAME PIC X(14).
    02  S-NUMBER PIC X(19).
    02  CLASS-NR PIC X.
```

Suppose you have a batch of data cards with the data in group item STUDENT-LISTING shown above punched into the first part of each card. You want to read each card, transfer the value in CLASS-NR to CLASS-NUMBER, then print only the class number. Write the three statements that could accomplish this for one card.

- - - - - - - - - - - - - - - - - - - -

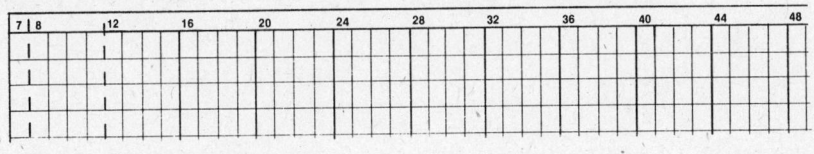

```
ACCEPT STUDENT-LISTING.
MOVE CLASS-NR TO CLASS-NUMBER.
DISPLAY CLASS-NUMBER.
```

(ACCEPT accesses an entire card. The first 34 columns are assigned to STUDENT-LISTING. The appropriate value is assigned to CLASS-NR.)

REVIEW

32. Suppose you want to write a program called DATA-MANIPULATE. This program will display several messages, asking for responses, which will then be accepted and moved around by the computer before part of the information is printed. This program should use the optional Identification Division paragraphs you learned in this chapter, with appropriate comment-entries. You may omit the Configuration Section, but use the required division header. Use two independent data items, LAST-NAME, which is twelve characters long, and SOCIAL-SEC, which is nine characters long. You will also need two group items as shown below.

FIRST-NAME	
INIT	REST-OF-NAME
1 char.	8 characters

STUDENT-RECORD		
STUDENT-NO	STUDENT-NAME	S-INIT
9 char.	12 char.	1 char.

Now follow the flow chart on the following page as you write a complete COBOL program.

DATA MANIPULATION 41

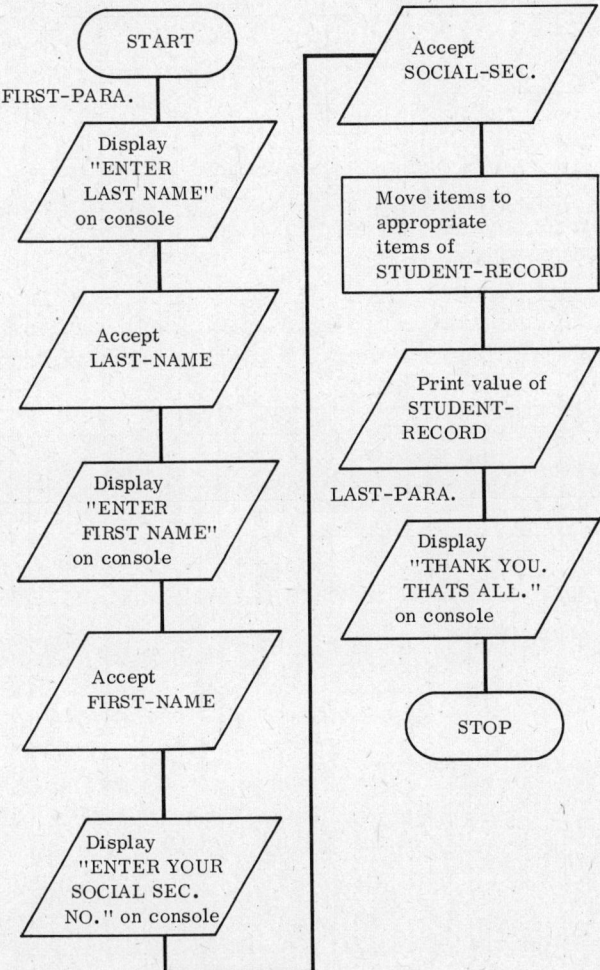

On the next page is space for writing your program. The correctly written program is on page 43.

```
       7 8   12     16      20      24      28      32      36      40      44      48      52
        IDENTIFICATION DIVISION.
        PROGRAM-ID. DATA-MANIPULATION.
        AUTHOR.  RUTH ASHLEY.
        DATE-WRITTEN. APRIL 19, 1979.
        REMARKS.  THIS IS A SAMPLE PROGRAM TO BE
            WRITTEN AFTER CHAPTER TWO COMPLETED.

        ENVIRONMENT DIVISION.
        DATA DIVISION.
        WORKING-STORAGE SECTION.
        77   LAST-NAME PIC X(12).
        77   SOCIAL-SEC PIC X(9).
        01   FIRST-NAME.
             02 INIT PIC X.
             02 REST-OF-NAME PIC X(8).
        01   STUDENT-RECORD.
             02 STUDENT-NO PIC X(9).
             02 STUDENT-NAME PIC X(12).
             02 S-INIT PIC X.

        PROCEDURE DIVISION.
        FIRST-PARA.
            DISPLAY "ENTER LAST NAME" UPON CONSOLE.
            ACCEPT LAST-NAME FROM CONSOLE.
            DISPLAY "ENTER FIRST NAME" UPON CONSOLE.
            ACCEPT FIRST-NAME FROM CONSOLE.
            DISPLAY "ENTER YOUR SOCIAL SEC. NO."
            UPON CONSOLE.
            ACCEPT SOCIAL-SEC FROM CONSOLE.
            MOVE SOCIAL-SEC TO STUDENT-NO.
            MOVE LAST-NAME TO STUDENT-NAME.
            MOVE INIT TO S-INIT.
            DISPLAY STUDENT-RECORD.
        LAST-PARA.
            DISPLAY "THANK YOU. THATS ALL." UPON
            CONSOLE.
            STOP RUN.
```

In checking your program, be sure that the following items are correctly placed and that they contain the proper information.

In A margin: division headers, section headers, paragraph-names, level 77, and level 01.

In B margin: everything else.

Comment-entries: may include almost anything.

Working-Storage Section: level 77 items must precede group items, but the order isn't otherwise important.

Spacing: blank lines may be left where desired.

Procedure Division: paragraph-names are nice but not necessary; the order is not critical in the MOVE statements; in the last DISPLAY statement, there must be no apostrophe in THATS; there must be no quotes of any kind in literals. More than one statement may be written on a line in the Procedure Division.

CHAPTER THREE
Arithmetic Coding

In this chapter you will learn to describe data in more detail for more efficient storage within the computer. You will learn to program the computer to perform arithmetic operations, and to round the result or notify you if the result is too large for the space you specified for it. You will also learn to transfer control within a program to any paragraph, to set up a loop, and to test the computer to get it out of a loop.

The specific COBOL entries you will learn to use are:

- Data Division
    Picture character A
    Picture character 9
    Picture character V
    USAGE clause

- Procedure Division
    ADD statement
    SUBTRACT statement
    MULTIPLY statement
    DIVIDE statement
    COMPUTE statement
    ROUNDED, ON SIZE ERROR, and GIVING options
    GO TO statement
    IF statement

We will continue using the same input and output statements as before as you gain experience with these new COBOL features.

PICTURE CHARACTERS

1. In Chapter 1 we described independent data items using:

    (a) level number _____

    (b) Picture character _____

46 ANS COBOL

    (a) 77; (b) X

2. In Chapter 2 we also used Picture character X to describe:

    (a) group items.
    (b) elementary data items.
    (c) both of these.

- - - - - - - - - - - - - - - - -

   b

3. Which of the data values below might be described with Picture character X?

    (a) WILLIAM∅JOHNSON   (c) 1873∅3rd∅Street
    (b) JOHN∅O'HANLON   (d) 1927

- - - - - - - - - - - - - - - - -

all of them   (Remember, X can be used for <u>any</u> character.)

4. Data items, independent and elementary, can also be described in other ways. For instance, a variable that will contain only letters and spaces is said to be alphabetic. It could be described with Picture character A. Which of the items below might be described with a picture of all A's?

    (a) DAVISON   (c) 1928
    (b) O'HANLON   (d) BILL III

- - - - - - - - - - - - - - - - -

a, d   (b contains an '; c contains digits.)

5. The PICTURE clause of a data item must describe any value that might be given to that data item. Below are three sets of values for three different data items. Write a PICTURE clause for each set.

    (a) CARSON
        DAY
        O'HARE _____

    (b) AAA
        BC7
        DDD _____

(c) WILLIAM
   SUZANNE
   TUESDAY _____

- - - - - - - - - - - - - - - - - - - -

(a) PIC X(6) or PICTURE XXXXXX
(b) PIC XXX or PICTURE X(3)
(c) PIC A(7) or PICTURE AAAAAAA   (In c, X(7) would also be correct, but less precise.)

6. Any data item that contains only the digits 0 through 9 may be described with the Picture character 9. In fact, any data item to be used in arithmetic operations <u>must</u> be described with 9's. Thus PIC 9(6) could accommodate a number of six digits, such as 000123. No spaces are permitted, but leading zeros are all right. Which of the following values could be described by 9(6)?

   (a) 13789ɓ   (d) 12.98
   (b) 000000   (e) ɓɓ27
   (c) 020000

_____

- - - - - - - - - - - - - - - - - - - -

b, c   (The decimal point in d is not a digit; a and e contain spaces.)

7. Write the PICTURE clause for a data item that will accommodate values such as 1372.

   _____

- - - - - - - - - - - - - - - - - - - -

PIC 9(4) or PICTURE 9999

8. Write 9, A, or X after each of the following. Use X only if neither 9 nor A is correct.

   (a) BOSTON _____   (c) 2.98 _____
   (b) 376402495 _____   (d) MALE _____

- - - - - - - - - - - - - - - - - - - -

(a) A; (b) 9; (c) X; (d) A
(In practice, any of these could be described with X. The use and other possible values determine which picture you select.)

9. Often, data items have decimal points that are very important in the calculations the computer will perform. You must remember not to include the decimal point as a digit, as we have seen in frame 6. For these cases we use a special Picture character V. The V represents an implied decimal point, not a character position. It saves space, and allows the system to use the value in calculation while keeping track of the decimal places. Thus if a data item were described as PIC 999V99, a value could be entered as 13995. The computer would consider it as 13995, noting internally the correct location of the point, two places from the right. Suppose you describe a data item as 77 PRICE PIC 9V99. This item could contain values from 000 to 999. If you want to input PRICE through an INPUT statement, however, the input data must not contain a decimal point since the V does not stand for a character. Which of the following might be an acceptable value for PRICE?

(a) ∧123   (c) 12∧5
(b) 1∧24   (d) 1∧2

----

b (The symbol ∧ is used throughout this guide to represent an implied decimal point in an internal value.)

10. Numeric data items are described using the Picture character _____.

9

11. The Picture character V represents a(n):

(a) character position.
(b) actual decimal point.
(c) implied decimal point.

----

c

The rules below apply to the V character:

Rule 1: A picture can contain only one V.
Rule 2: The V cannot be at the extreme right.
Rule 3: The V is not a character position.
Rule 4: The V may be used only with 9.

Rule 1 makes sense when you consider that a number can contain only one decimal point. Rule 2 reflects the fact that if no V is included, the number is considered a whole number, hence it has a decimal place at the extreme right.

12. The numeric data items below have incorrect descriptions. What is wrong with each picture?

	PICTURE	Value	What is Wrong?
Example:	V9V	₫2	Only one V is permitted.
(a)	XXVX	12₫6	_____
(b)	999V	127₫	_____
(c)	99V99	12.34	_____
(d)	9V999	₫876	_____

- - - - - - - - - - - - - - - - - - -

(a) V cannot be used with X
(b) V cannot be at the extreme right
(c) V doesn't represent an actual decimal point
(d) a 9 does not represent a blank position

13.

Data Type	Picture Char.	Allowable Characters
alphanumeric	X	letters, digits, spaces, and special characters
alphabetic	A	letters and spaces only
numeric	9	digits 0-9 only
numeric	V	not a character position; implied decimal point

The chart above summarizes the Picture characters studied so far. Refer to it as necessary as you write PICTURE clauses to reflect each value below.

(a) 13₫98   PIC _____

(b) 40.0   PIC _____

(c) PETER-GEORGE   PIC _____

(d) CORSONI   PIC _____

(e) 376401495   PIC _____

- - - - - - - - - - - - - - - - - - -

(a) 99V99
(b) X(4)   (99V9 is not correct because the . is an actual character.)
(c) X(12)   (A(12) is not correct because of the hyphen.)
(d) A(7) or X(7)
(e) 9(9) or X(9)

14. When the V Picture character is not included in a picture of 9's, the decimal is assumed to be placed at the extreme right of the picture. Below are listed several pictures for numeric data items. Write the value of each if the input value is 123456. (Use $\wedge$ for implied decimal points.)

    (a) 9999V99 _____   (c) V999999 _____

    (b) 9V99999 _____   (d) 9999999 _____

- - - - - - - - - - - - - - - - - - - -

(a) 1234$_\wedge$56; (b) 1$_\wedge$23456; (c) $_\wedge$123456; (d) 123456$_\wedge$

15. Write pictures for the values below. Use the most specific pictures you can.

    (a) 1984 _____

    (b) RAPID HARDWARE _____

    (c) 14998 _____
          $^\wedge$

    (d) $_\wedge$2 _____

- - - - - - - - - - - - - - - - - - - -

(a) 9(4); (b) A(14); (c) 999V99 or 9(3)V99; (d) V9

16.

CUSTOMER-DATA			
CUSTOMER	C-NAME	C-ADDRESS	C-BALANCE
all digits	letters, spaces	digits, letters, spaces	value like 1973$_\wedge$24
7 char.	17 char.	28 char.	6 char.

Write the Data Division entries for the group and elementary items indicated above. Use level numbers and the appropriate picture clauses.

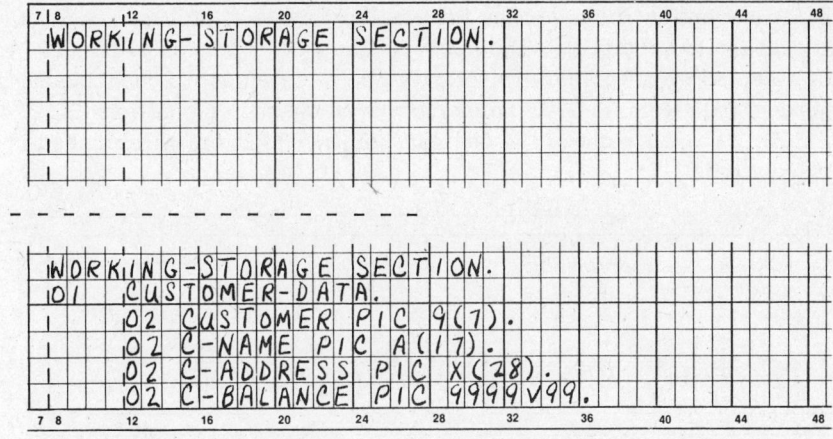

(CUSTOMER and C-NAME could also have been described with X.)

USAGE CLAUSE

One reason for using different pictures is that data items are used in different ways. One variable may be used as a display item and treated as a string of characters in moving or comparing. Another variable may be used in arithmetic. The meaning of each variable is very relevant. We can write more efficient programs if we can instruct the computer in advance how the variables will be used, and we can specify this with a USAGE clause in the Data Division.

17. The entry on the coding sheet below specifies that computations will be performed on BALANCE throughout the program. Thus the computer will store the value of BALANCE in a more efficient way. This will save both computer time and storage space.

```
   02  BALANCE  PIC  999  USAGE  COMPUTATIONAL.
```

USAGE COMPUTATIONAL can be specified only for numeric data items since only such items can be used in computations. For which of the items described below could USAGE COMPUTATIONAL be specified?

(a) X(7)
(b) 999
(c) AAAAA
(d) V9999

---

b, d

18. The alternative to USAGE COMPUTATIONAL is USAGE DISPLAY. The DISPLAY option, however, is the standard mode of storage, so it is never necessary to specify it. The abbreviation COMP for COMPUTATIONAL is accepted by all compilers. Now write a statement to describe an independent data item TOTAL which has seven character positions, four of which are to the right of the decimal point. This item will be used in calculations.

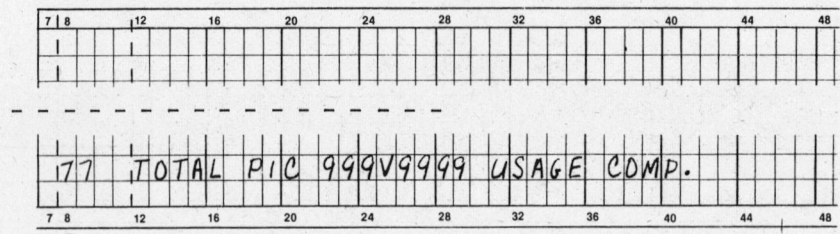

(9(3)V9(4) is also correct.)

Several compilers have additional USAGE options, including COMP-1, COMP-2, COMP-3. Of these, COMP-3 is the most common. Information about these can be obtained from the reference manuals at installations where these compilers are in use. All USAGE options specify methods of storing data. The standard way (DISPLAY) is at one character per byte. For more information on internal storage, refer to another Self-Teaching Guide, Introduction to Data Processing, second edition, by Martin Harris.

You can now describe numeric data items and specify that they will be used in arithmetic operations. Now you will learn to specify the arithmetic operations.

NUMERIC LITERALS

19. In the arithmetic operation of addition, the values of two data-names may be added together, or the value of a data-name may be added to a numeric literal. Unlike non-numeric literals, numeric literals are not written with quotes. A numeric literal is a value such as 17 or 19.98. The numeric literal may contain a single actual decimal point, but—as with an implied decimal point—it may not appear at the extreme right. Which of the following might be a numeric literal?

(a) "12.50" (c) 143.
(b) 7   (d) 99.98

---

b, d (a includes quotes; c has the decimal point at the extreme right.)

ARITHMETIC CODING 53

20. Match the following:

　　_____ (a) PARTIAL-SCORE　　1. data-name
　　_____ (b) 1938.255　　　　　2. non-numeric literal
　　　　　　　　　　　　　　　　　　　 3. numeric literal
　　_____ (c) "37892"
　　_____ (d) "PARTIAL"
　　_____ (e) SCORE73

- - - - - - - - - - - - - - - - - -

(a) 1; (b) 3; (c) 2; (d) 2; (e) 1

21. Another use of numeric literals is in MOVE statements. The statement MOVE 12.98 TO PPRICE is valid if PPRICE has been described as 99V99. The numeric literal value is then assigned to PPRICE with the actual decimal point aligned with the implied decimal point. After execution of the statement above, the value of PPRICE will be _____.

- - - - - - - - - - - - - - - - - -

12ˬ98

22. For each of the numeric literals and data-name pictures listed below, give the value of data-name after execution of the statement MOVE numeric-literal TO data-name.

Numeric-literal	Picture of Data-Name	Value of Data-Name
1.98	99V99	(a) _____
21.9	99V99	(b) _____
1.973	9V99	(c) _____
746	999V9	(d) _____

- - - - - - - - - - - - - - - - - -

(a) 01ˬ98; (b) 21ˬ90; (c) 1ˬ97; (d) 746ˬ0
(Leading or trailing zeros are inserted by the computer.)

23. Write a statement to assign the value 348ˬ50 to INITIAL-COST, described as PIC 999V99.

- - - - - - - - - - - - - - - - - -

54 ANS COBOL

ARITHMETIC OPERATIONS

24. The formats for arithmetic operations are very straightforward, and the four standard ADD, SUBTRACT, MULTIPLY, and DIVIDE statements are very similar. Either numeric data-names or numeric literals can be specified in these four statements. Which of these entries is a valid numeric literal?

(a) 19̭98
(b) 111.222.333.444
(c) 12.

(d) .35
(e) 3.14159

---

d, e   (a has an implied decimal point; b contains more than one decimal point; c has its decimal point at the extréme right.)

25. This is the ADD statement format:

$$\text{ADD} \begin{Bmatrix} \text{data-name} \\ \text{num-literal} \end{Bmatrix} \begin{Bmatrix} \text{data-name} \\ \text{num-literal} \end{Bmatrix} \text{GIVING data-name.}$$

Write a statement that would cause the value of PRICE to be added to 1.03 to produce the result ADJUSTED.

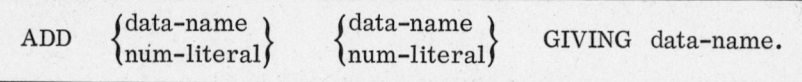

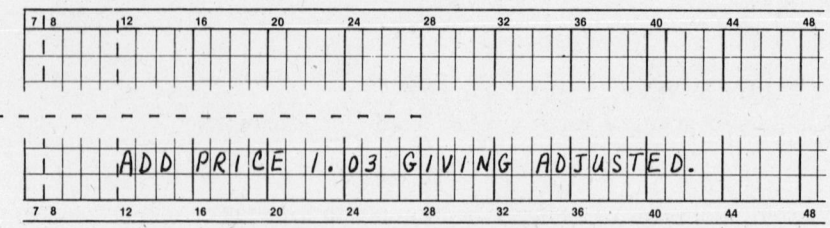

(You may include a comma to separate PRICE and 1.03.)

26. This is the format for the SUBTRACT statement:

$$\text{SUBTRACT} \begin{Bmatrix} \text{data-name} \\ \text{num-literal} \end{Bmatrix} \text{FROM} \begin{Bmatrix} \text{data-name} \\ \text{num-literal} \end{Bmatrix} \text{GIVING data-name.}$$

Write a statement to cause the value .50 to be subtracted from the value of COST. The difference will be the value of NEW-COST.

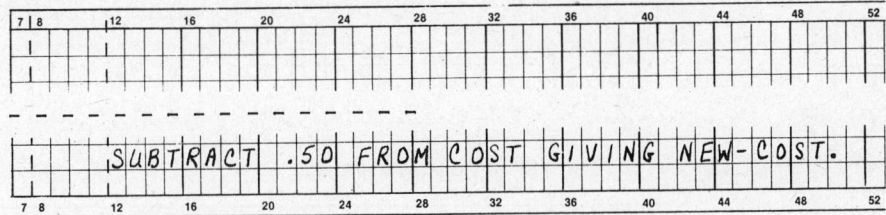

27. Write a statement to solve each of the following:

    (a) 17 + 193.1 = SUMX

    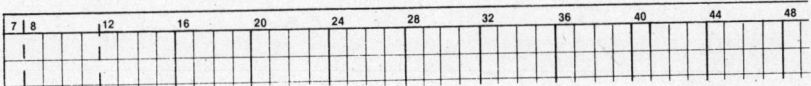

    (b) 19.98 - 4.6 = DIFF

    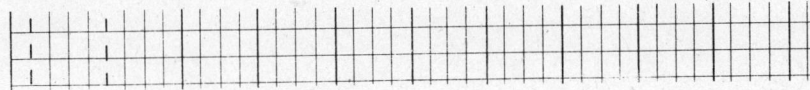

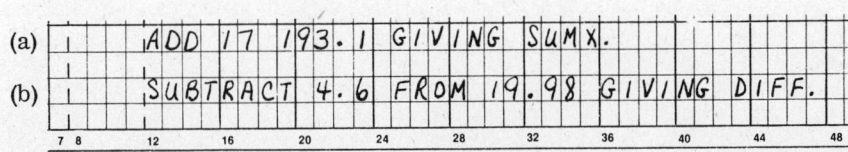

28. This is the format for the MULTIPLY statement:

    MULTIPLY {data-name / num-literal} BY {data-name / num-literal} GIVING data-name.

    Write a statement to calculate 15 percent of INTEREST and store the amount in RATE.

    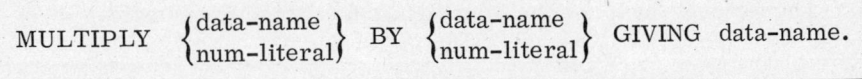

56 ANS COBOL

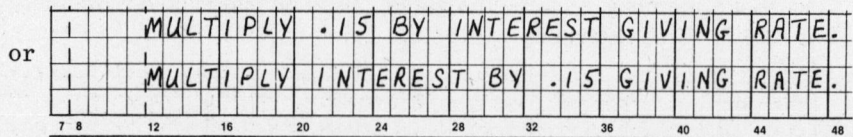

29. This is the format for the DIVIDE statement:

DIVIDE {data-name / num-literal} {BY / INTO} {data-name / num-literal} GIVING data-name.

The DIVIDE statement differs from the other arithmetic statements in that either BY or INTO can be used depending on the division required.

DIVIDE PRI INTO 7 GIVING NOW. = PRI/7
DIVIDE PRI BY 7 GIVING NOW.   = 7/PRI

The word you use sets up the order in which the operation is carried out. In this guide, the word INTO is used most of the time. Write a statement to cause the operation:

$\dfrac{\text{SCOUT}}{9/173}$

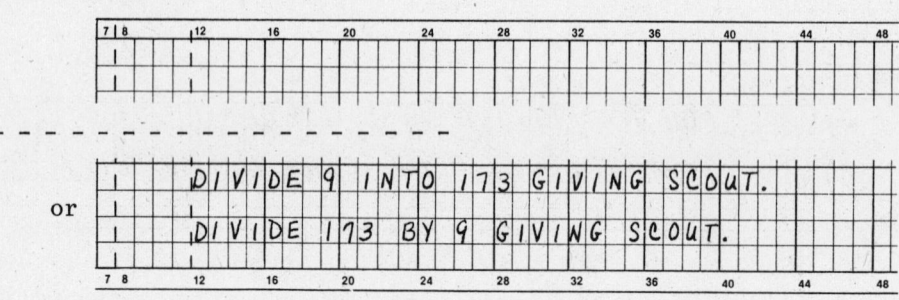

The format, then, for the four standard arithmetic operations is:

ADD
SUBTRACT
MULTIPLY   {data-name-1 / numeric-literal}   FROM / BY / INTO or BY   {data-name-2 / numeric-literal}   GIVING   data-name-3
DIVIDE

Restrictions:
1. Data-names must be numeric.
2. Numeric-literals may have up to eighteen characters and may include a decimal point.
3. Decimal point may not be rightmost character.

30. Determine which of the following are correct.

    (a) ADD HOURS BONUS GIVING 149.50.
    (b) SUBTRACT LOST-TIME HOURS GIVING FINAL.
    (c) MULTIPLY HOURS BY 3.75 GIVING GROSS.
    (d) DIVIDE 5 INTO SALARY GIVING DAILY.

---

c, d   (a uses a numeric literal following GIVING; b omits the required word FROM.)

31. When these formats are used, the operation specified is performed and the result is stored as data-name-3. No change occurs in the values of any other data-names in the statement. Suppose the value of HOURS is 40$_\wedge$; the value of WAGES is 3$_\wedge$50. After execution of the statement MULTIPLY HOURS BY WAGES GIVING GROSS, what is the value of:

    (a) HOURS _____

    (b) WAGES _____

    (c) GROSS _____

(a) 40$_\wedge$;   (b) 3$_\wedge$50;   (c) 14000$_\wedge$

32. Write a statement to perform the operation represented by WEEKLY-PAY divided by 5 equals DAILY-PAY.

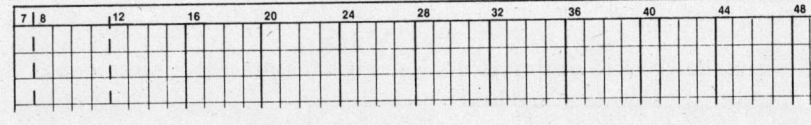

---

or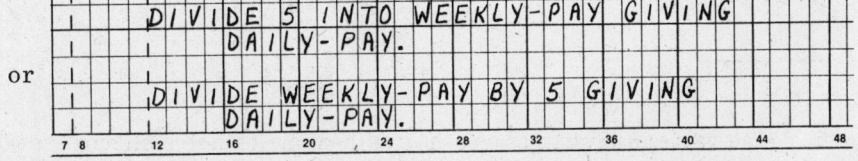

The basic arithmetic statement formats shown below do not include the GIVING option, although the option can be used at any time.

$$\begin{Bmatrix} \text{ADD} \\ \text{SUBTRACT} \\ \text{MULTIPLY} \\ \text{DIVIDE} \end{Bmatrix} \begin{Bmatrix} \text{data-name-1} \\ \text{numeric-literal} \end{Bmatrix} \begin{Bmatrix} \text{TO} \\ \text{FROM} \\ \text{BY} \\ \text{INTO} \end{Bmatrix} \{\text{data-name-2}\}$$

33. One difference in the format shown above is that a second numeric literal may not be used. Another difference is apparent in which statement?

_____

- - - - - - - - - - - - - - - - - -

ADD   (The word TO is required when GIVING is not used.)

34. When a format without GIVING is used, the arithmetic operation is performed and the result is stored in data-name-2. In which variable is the result stored in each of the following?

   (a) DIVIDE 3 INTO TOTAL-SCORE. _____

   (b) ADD LENGTH TO WIDTH. _____

   (c) SUBTRACT A FROM B GIVING C. _____

   (d) MULTIPLY 4 BY QUARTER. _____

- - - - - - - - - - - - - - - - - -

   (a) TOTAL-SCORE; (b) WIDTH; (c) C; (d) QUARTER

The decision of whether or not to use the GIVING option in any arithmetic statement is left to the programmer. You must decide if your purpose is to change the value of a variable or to maintain the variable values intact while storing new values in new variables.

35. When the GIVING option is not used in an arithmetic statement, the resulting value is stored in:

   (a) data-name-1   (c) numeric-literal-2
   (b) data-name-2   (d) data-name-3

_____

- - - - - - - - - - - - - - - - -

   b   (The value is always stored in a data-name, since numeric literals have a constant value.)

ARITHMETIC CODING 59

36. Write a statement to subtract the value of ADJUSTMENT from the value of GROSS-INCOME and store the result in GROSS-INCOME.

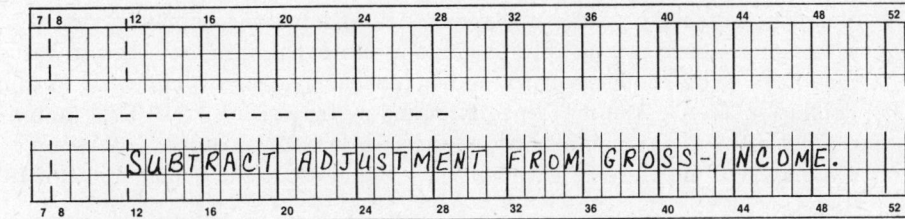

SUBTRACT ADJUSTMENT FROM GROSS-INCOME.

37. Refer to the formats as necessary and write what is wrong with each of the following.

   (a) ADD 7 TO AGE GIVING ADJUSTED-AGE.
   _____

   (b) SUBTRACT AGE FROM 21.
   _____

   (c) MULTIPLY HOURS TIMES WAGES GIVING GROSS.
   _____

- - - - - - - - - - - - - - - - - -

   (a) TO is not used in ADD statements when GIVING is specified
   (b) data-name must be specified following FROM because the GIVING option is not used   (Always use GIVING to subtract from a literal.)
   (c) the word BY must be used in a MULTIPLY statement

   Two additional entries that may be specified in any arithmetic statement are ROUNDED and ON SIZE ERROR. The ROUNDED option is used when the result is expected to be too large for the allotted space to the right of the decimal place. The ON SIZE ERROR option is used when there is not enough space to the left of the decimal place.

38. Normally, values are placed in a numeric item working outward from the decimal point. When the value is too large (has too many characters) for the data item, extra characters will just be dropped. A value of 1498̭375 assigned to a data item described as 999V99 would normally be stored as 498̭37. Several data descriptions are listed below. Give the stored result for each if the intended value is 2798̭1275.

   (a) 9999V99 _____   (c) 9V9999 _____

   (b) 99V999 _____   (d) 9999V9 _____

- - - - - - - - - - - - - - - - - -

(a) 2798͜12; (b) 98͜127; (c) 8͜1275; (d) 2798͜1

39. You can ordinarily predict the exact size of input and output variables, although you may not be able to judge the internal values. Certain values may have to be rounded off to the nearest penny, for example, or to four decimal places. You may specify rounding by writing ROUNDED immediately after the variable in which the result is to be stored. Write a statement to multiply HOURS by WAGES and store the rounded result in SALARY.

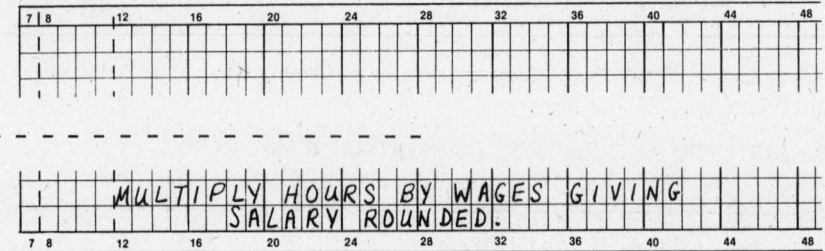

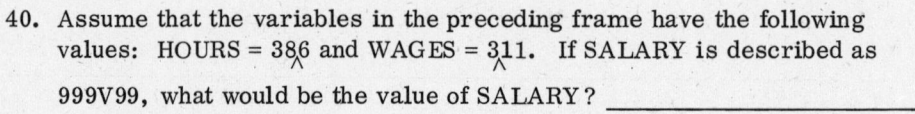

40. Assume that the variables in the preceding frame have the following values: HOURS = 38͜6 and WAGES = 3͜11. If SALARY is described as 999V99, what would be the value of SALARY? _____

120͜05 (120͜046) (If you are not sure what "rounded" means, you might want to review another Self-Teaching Guide, <u>Background Math for a Computer World</u> by Ruth Ashley, before continuing in this guide.)

41. The ON SIZE ERROR option tells the computer what to do when there are too many digits to the left of the decimal point. In this case, the most important digits of a number would be dropped and could seriously affect the validity of the program. The option is usually included at the end of the arithmetic statement, and is followed by a statement to be executed only when the ON SIZE ERROR occurs. Such a statement might be DIVIDE X-1 INTO X-2 ON SIZE ERROR DISPLAY "ERROR ON DIVIDE". Any time both ROUNDED and ON SIZE ERROR are used, the ROUNDED option must be written first, immediately following the data-name in which the result is stored.
   Write an arithmetic statement that will find the products of HOURS and WAGES, store it in SALARY, and transfer control to TOO-BIG if any positions on the left are truncated.

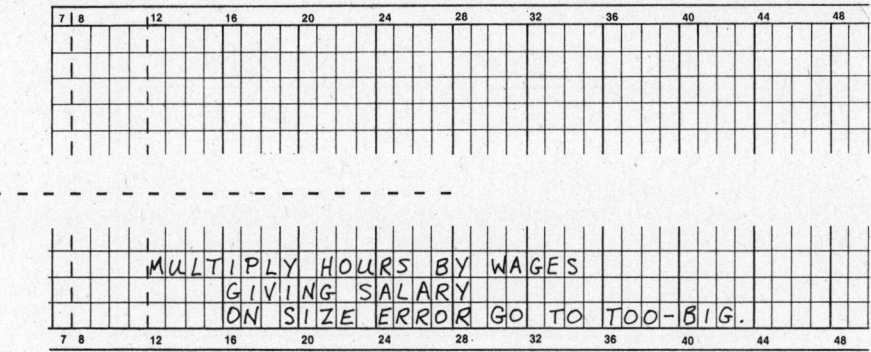

You have now learned to write four arithmetic statements. You know where results are stored and can specify whether to round the result. You have seen what to do when a result may be too large for the data item. One arithmetic statement remains. It doesn't do anything the prior four don't do, but it can save you a great deal of writing and often will also save steps for the computer.

COMPUTE STATEMENT

The COMPUTE statement has several uses. It can be used in much the same way as the other arithmetic statements you have studied so far. Below are several examples of the use of the COMPUTE statement:

    COMPUTE SUM = ANUMBER + BNUMBER.
    COMPUTE DIFF = ANUMBER - BNUMBER.
    COMPUTE PRODUCT = ANUM * BNUM.
    COMPUTE QUOTIENT = ANUM / BNUM.
    COMPUTE RESULT = PRICE - (RATE * PRICE) * .04.
    COMPUTE VOLUME = PI * (R**2) * LENGTH.

Any of the operators in Table 1 (on the next page) can be used in the COMPUTE statement. You must leave a space before and after each operator, however. A receiving variable on the left is set equal to the value of the expression on the right by the COMPUTE statement.

62 ANS COBOL

Table 1. Arithmetic Operators

symbol	meaning	example
+	addition	5 = 2 + 3
-	subtraction	4 = 3 - 1
*	multiplication	10 = 2 * 5
/	division	2 = 10 / 5
**	exponentiation	9 = 3 ** 2 (3^2)

42. Write a COMPUTE statement that will have the same effect as DIVIDE FIELD1 INTO FIELD2 GIVING FIELD3.

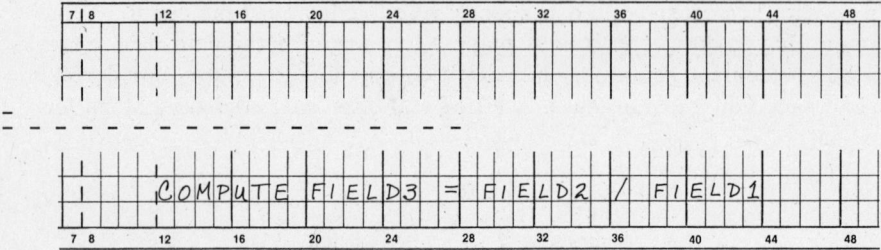

    COMPUTE FIELD3 = FIELD2 / FIELD1

43. Write a COMPUTE statement that will have the same effect as MULTIPLY PONE BY PTWO.

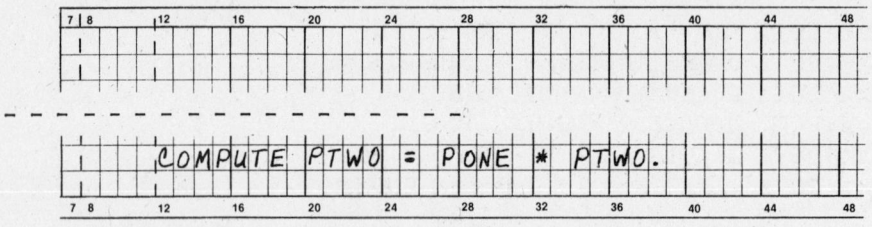

    COMPUTE PTWO = PONE * PTWO.

(In this MULTIPLY statement, the result was stored in PTWO.)

44. This is the format for a COMPUTE statement:

$$\text{COMPUTE data-name-1} = \begin{Bmatrix} \text{data-name-2} \\ \text{numeric-literal} \\ \text{arithmetic-expression} \end{Bmatrix}$$

The COMPUTE statement has several uses. It can be used to set one data item equal to another. COMPUTE HOURS = REGULAR has the same effect as MOVE REGULAR HOURS. In a COMPUTE statement which side of the equal sign contains the receiving variable? _____

---

left   (This is always true.)

45. The COMPUTE statement can also be used to give a specific value to a variable. Write a statement to set the value of OVERTIME-PAY at 1.5.

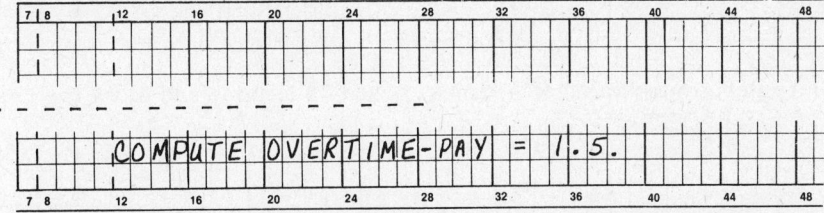

(Remember that a decimal point may be used in numeric literals.)

46. When you use more than one operator in a COMPUTE statement, the usual order is **, then * and /, then + and -. You may use parentheses to modify the usual order. Refer to Table 1 for arithmetic operators and give the value of each of the following.

   (a) 7 + 4 / 2 _____   (c) 4 * 3 ** 2 _____
   (b) (7 + 4) / 2 _____   (d) (4 * 3) ** 2 _____

(a) 9; (b) 5.5; (c) 36; (d) 144
(The sole purpose of this exercise is to focus your attention on the parentheses. Use extra parentheses if you are in doubt, but be sure the number of opens equals the number of closes in each expression.)

If the symbols used in arithmetic expressions bother you, just write out the individual statements whenever operations are needed. Even exponentiation can be handled with the MULTIPLY statement. If you stick with COBOL, you will be exposed to the symbols and soon will become accustomed to the COMPUTE statement. The expressions in the COMPUTE statement can decrease the number of statements you write, as well as the number of intermediate variables for subtotals you must define.

47. According to the COMPUTE format, the data-name on the left can be set equal to an arithmetic expression. Expressions are made up using the operators shown in Table 1. Given the statement COMPUTE HOURS = (MON + TUES + WED) / 3., if MON = 8, TUES = 9, and WED = 10, what would be the value of HOURS? _____

---

48. Write a COMPUTE statement to:

    (a) set COUNTER equal to 0.

    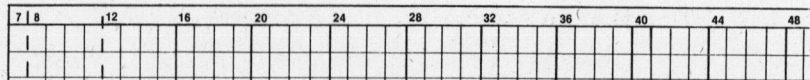

    (b) set the values of X-1 and X-2 equal to the current value of X-1.

    (c) calculate the value of A times B, add 75 to this, and store the result in DEPOSIT.

    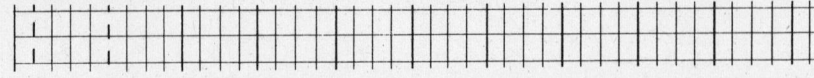

(a) `COMPUTE COUNTER = 0.`
(b) `COMPUTE X-2 = X-1.`
(c) `COMPUTE DEPOSIT = A * B + 75.`

(Hyphens in data-names are not confused with minus signs, since a space must precede and follow each operator.)

49. The area of a triangle is calculated as one half the base times the height. Assume that the data items HEIGHT, BASE, and TRI-AREA have been described. Write a COMPUTE statement (using .5 as one half) to find the area of a triangle.

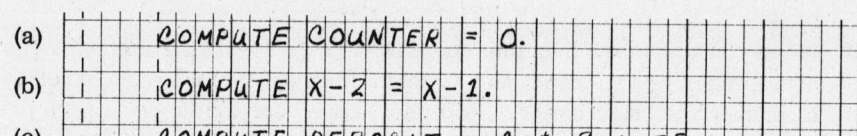

`COMPUTE TRI-AREA = .5 * BASE * HEIGHT.`

(The order of items to the right of the equal sign may be different.)

50. Like the other arithmetic statements, COMPUTE may be written using the ROUNDED or ON SIZE ERROR options. As in the other statements, the word ROUNDED must be written:

    (a) at the beginning of the statement.
    (b) following the last word in the statement.
    (c) directly following the data-name in which the result is stored.

---

c

51. Write a statement to calculate the product of T-BAL and DURATION and divide that by MONTHS. Store the rounded result in FINAL-B.

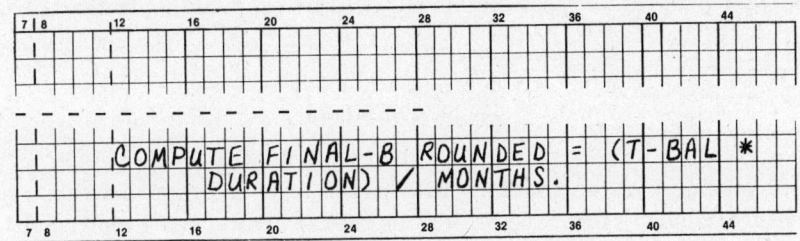

(The parentheses here could have been omitted.)

52. The ON SIZE ERROR option, as before, is written at the end of the statement when a size error is likely to occur. When it is included, the resulting size is checked and the computer follows your directions when an error exists. Write a statement to calculate the average of SCORE1, SCORE2, and SCORE3, then display "SIZE ERROR ON AVERAGE" on the console if an error exists.

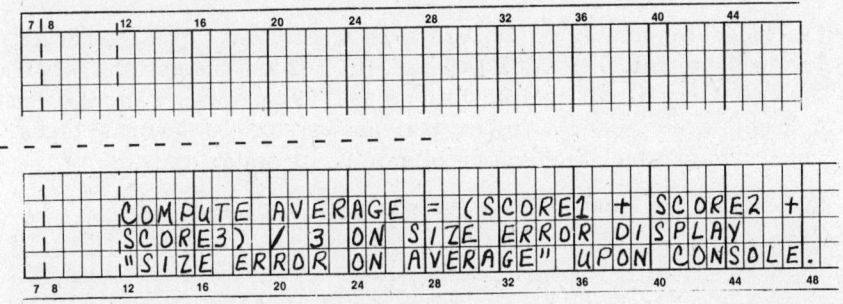

53. Which option would you use if the result might have too many digits to the right of the decimal place? _____

- - - - - - - - - - - - - - - - -

ROUNDED

54. Which option would you use when the result might have too many digits to the left of the decimal place? _____

- - - - - - - - - - - - - - - - -

ON SIZE ERROR

Up to this point, you have had to write separate statements for each time an operation was to be performed. In the next section you will learn to create a loop in your program so that statements will be executed more than one time.

GO TO STATEMENT

55. Let's assume you are helping a fifth-grade teacher prepare an answer sheet for a quiz. You have offered to get the answers to twenty multiplication problems. The teacher gives you the information as shown below.

Numbers	Result
17 20	_____
19 18	_____
. .	_____
. .	_____
. .	_____

It includes two numbers which are to be multiplied to give the result. You decide to call them MULT-1 and MULT-2 and the result ANSWER. The variables will all be described as 999V99 in Working Storage, and the pupils are expected to round their answers to two decimal places. You decide to attack the first problem. Write statements to:

(a) ACCEPT the appropriate values from the console.

(b) perform the arithmetic operation.

(c) print the result on the printer.

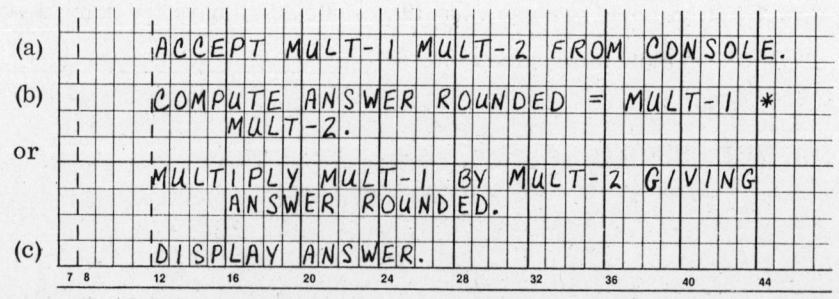

(a) ACCEPT MULT-1 MULT-2 FROM CONSOLE.
(b) COMPUTE ANSWER ROUNDED = MULT-1 *
         MULT-2.
or
     MULTIPLY MULT-1 BY MULT-2 GIVING
         ANSWER ROUNDED.
(c) DISPLAY ANSWER.

56. You could of course simply rewrite those three lines to solve the second problem, but that could very easily get out of hand. The flowchart at the right shows the problem, and also how to solve it, if you can cause control to loop back to the beginning of the three statements. The COBOL programming for this flowchart is shown below.

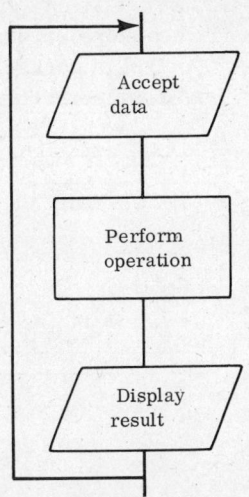

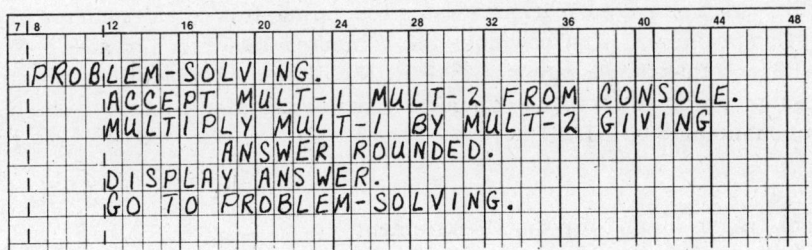

The GO TO statement specifies a paragraph-name to which control is transferred. Here the paragraph-name is _____.

- - - - - - - - - - - - - - - - - - - -

PROBLEM-SOLVING

57. This is the format for the GO TO statement:

> GO TO paragraph-name.

Suppose you want control to pass to a paragraph named ERROR-ROUTINE. Write a statement to cause this.

- - - - - - - - - - - - - - - - - - - -

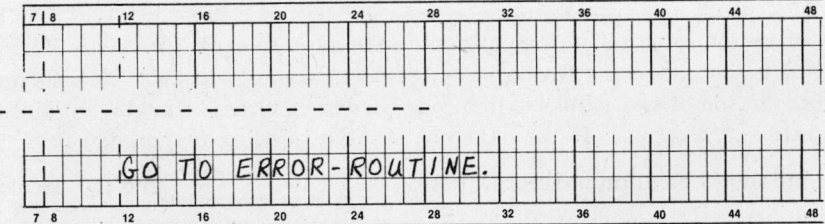

58. The GO TO statement is often used to transfer control to an error routine when some error occurs. On the next page write an option to transfer control to paragraph GOOFED-AGAIN when a size error occurs during an arithmetic operation.

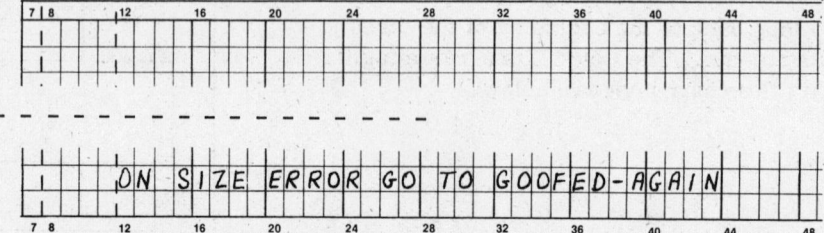

- -

ON SIZE ERROR GO TO GOOFED-AGAIN

IF STATEMENT

The flow chart on page 67 demonstrates the calculation of any number of multiplication problems. But how does the computer know when to stop? You already know that the statement STOP RUN will cause termination of a program, but how do you tell the computer when to transfer control to the paragraph containing STOP RUN?

59. This is the format for the IF statement:

             IF   condition   statement

example: IF MULT-1 = 999.99   GO TO END-PARA.

The IF statement is often used to test a condition and specify an action to be taken if the condition is true. In the example above the condition is _____ and the statement to be executed if the condition is true is _____.

- - - - - - - - - - - - - - - - - - - -

MULT-1 = 999.99; GO TO END-PARA
(A value of all 9's is frequently used as an end-of-job (EOJ) indicator.)

60. A condition in an IF statement could take any of several forms. The one used in the preceding frame is called a relation condition. This is the comparison of two values which may be data-names, literals, or arithmetic expressions. In the example in the preceding frame, the first value in the relation condition is a(n)_____ and the second value is a(n)_____.

- - - - - - - - - - - - - - - -

data-name; numeric literal

In relation conditions, two values may be compared in one of six ways. The six, with symbols, are shown below. We'll see more comparison types later.

Relation Condition Operators

relational operator	symbol
GREATER THAN	>
NOT GREATER THAN	NOT >
LESS THAN	<
NOT LESS THAN	NOT <
EQUAL TO	=
NOT EQUAL TO	NOT =

Restriction: Operator must be preceded by and followed by a space. Use the symbols if you are already familiar with them. You may use the words instead.

---

61. The two values specified in a relation condition are compared, and the computer decides if the relation is true or false. Suppose M-1 = 27 and M-2 = 16. Determine whether each of the following is true or false.

    (a) M-1 GREATER THAN M-2 _____

    (b) M-2 NOT EQUAL TO M-1 _____

    (c) M-2 < 15 _____

- - - - - - - - - - - - - - - - - - -

(a) true; (b) true; (c) false

---

62. Suppose you want control transferred to a paragraph named NEGATIVE-AMOUNT whenever the value of AMOUNT is negative. Write an IF statement to accomplish this.

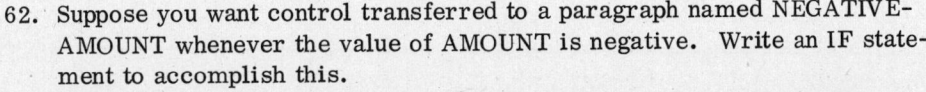
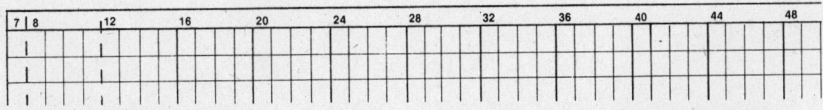

- - - - - - - - - - - - - - - -

70 ANS COBOL

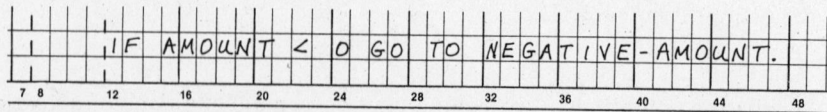

63. IF statements may include more than one statement to be executed if the condition is true. A period will appear only after the last statement within the range of the IF.

Modify the statement in the preceding frame to set the value of a variable named MESSAGE1 to "ERROR ON AMOUNT" before transferring control.

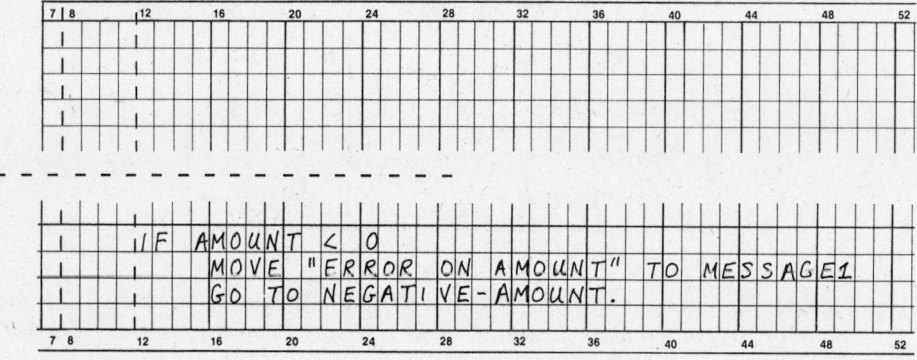

64. The IF statement can also include an ELSE clause to be executed when the condition is false.

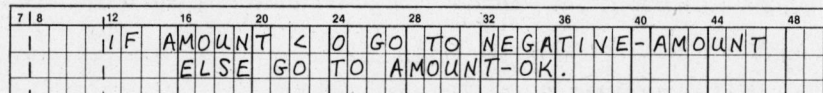

Write a statement to set MESSAGE-OUT to "AMOUNT BELOW REORDER POINT" if the value of AMOUNT is less than the value of REORDER. Otherwise, "AMOUNT ON HAND OK" should be moved to MESSAGE1.

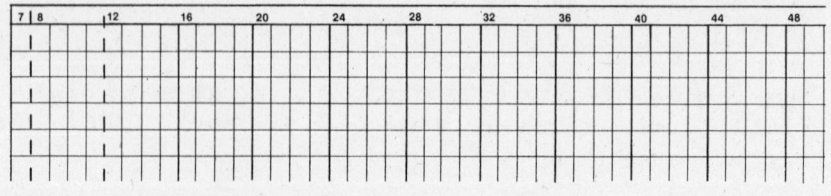

ARITHMETIC CODING 71

```
 IF AMOUNT < REORDER
    MOVE "AMOUNT BELOW REORDER POINT"
       TO MESSAGE1
    ELSE MOVE "AMOUNT ON HAND OK"
       TO MESSAGE1.
```

65. When an IF statement is executed, the appropriate statement will be executed. Control then passes to the statement following the IF period. If no GO TO appears with IF or ELSE, the statement following the IF will be executed next.

```
 IF AMOUNT < REORDER
    MOVE "AMOUNT BELOW REORDER POINT"
       TO MESSAGE1
    ELSE MOVE "AMOUNT ON HAND OK"
       TO MESSAGE1
 DISPLAY MESSAGE1
```

The set of statements above includes no periods.

(a) Where would you place period(s) to cause MESSAGE1 to be displayed in both cases? _____

(b) Where would you place period(s) to cause MESSAGE1 to be displayed only if the condition were false? _____

(c) How could you modify this to cause MESSAGE1 to be displayed only if the condition were true? _____

- - - - - - - - - - - - - - - - - -

(a) before the DISPLAY statement and after it
(b) after the DISPLAY statement
(c) move "DISPLAY MESSAGE1" to before ELSE, put period only following ELSE clause

66. Now to return to our problem of getting the answers to a quiz. Let's say you have decided that you will enter 99999 for MULT-1 after the twenty are finished. Use the flowchart on the next page as a guide and write a complete Procedure Division for the problem. Sample paragraph-names are noted on the flowchart.

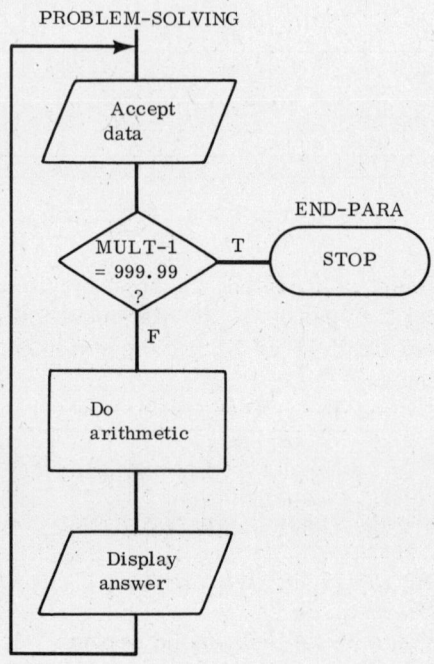

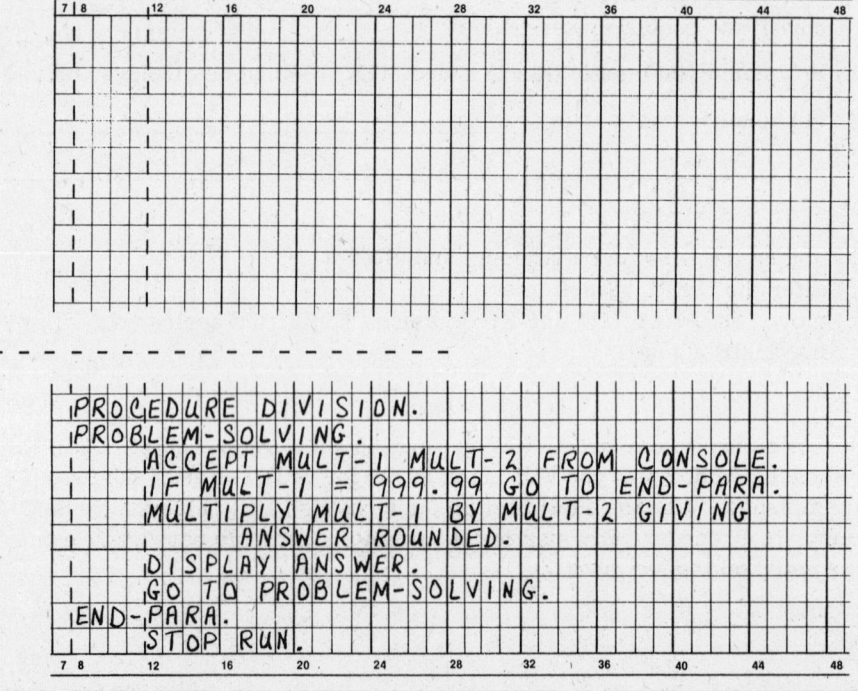

67. Write a statement to compare MULT-1 and MULT-2 and display MULT-1 on the console if it is the larger of the two.

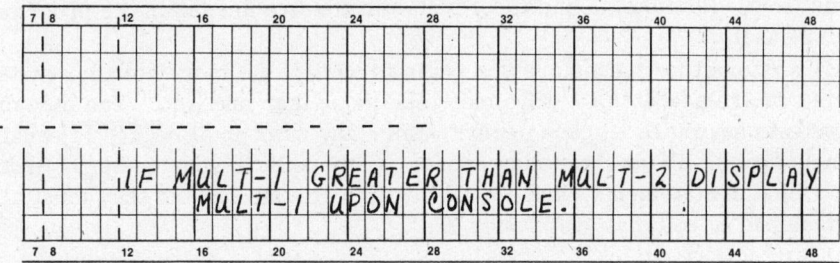

(The symbol > could be used instead of GREATER THAN.)

68. Write a statement that will compare MULT-1 and MULT-2, then add them together if they are not equal, storing the result in ANSWER.

or

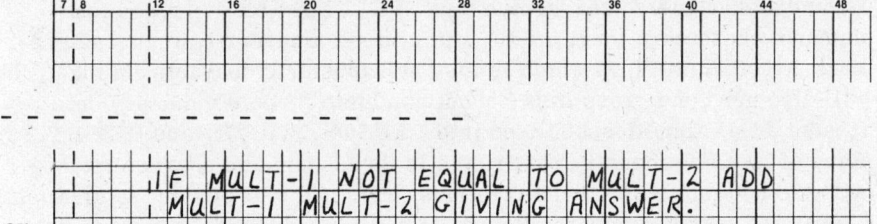

(In COBOL, the value rather than the format of a numeric item determines equality. Thus 123 = 123̂00 = 00123.)

Both condition and statement in an IF statement may be vastly more complex than the ones you have seen in this chapter. In later chapters you will use more sophisticated conditions and options with the IF statements. Even in the very simple forms, however, the IF statement is one of the programmer's more powerful tools.

REVIEW

Before you proceed to write a program, a few points should be emphasized. Statements are executed normally in a program in exactly the same order as you write them. You have learned to alter this normal sequence with a GO TO statement, which branches control to a specified paragraph-name. You learned to use an IF statement to branch under a certain condition; the computer tests this condition each time it reaches the IF statement, but the branch (or other action) is executed only when the condition is true. If an ELSE clause is included, an action to be taken when the condition is false may be included. Both the IF and GO TO statements are needed in the program you will write.

A matter of format before you begin to write: the more complex statements you are now able to write may take more than one line. You may divide statements anywhere a space occurs, since any number of spaces is equal to a single space. Blank lines may appear at any point in your coding. Procedure Division statements need not all begin in column 12, but they must all be contained in columns 12 through 72.

69. Now you are going to write a program using what you have learned in this chapter. Call your program ARITHMETIC-PRACTICE, and use any of the optional Identification Division entries you like. You may omit the Configuration Section.

    You will need four independent data items: INPUT-VARIABLE which is nine alphanumeric characters long, VOLUME which is nine alphanumeric characters long, AREA which is six alphanumeric characters long, and PERIMETER which is four alphanumeric characters long. You will also need one group item, subdivided into three elementary data items: DIMENSIONS subdivided into LENGTH, WIDTH, and HEIGHT. Each of these elementary data items is three numeric characters long, with the decimal point at the rightmost end. All will be used in arithmetic operations. Now, using the flowchart and coding sheet segment on the following pages, write the program.

ARITHMETIC CODING 75

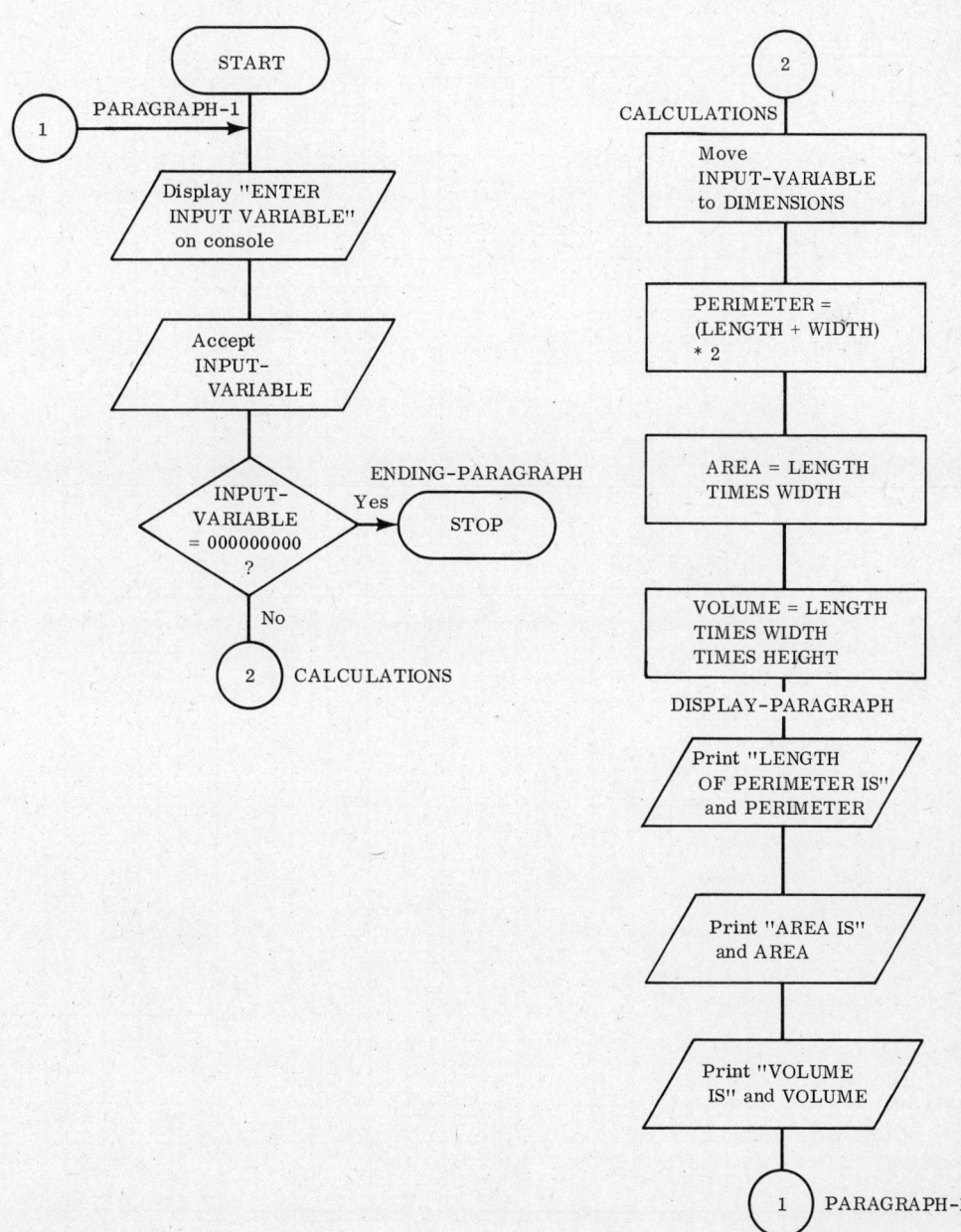

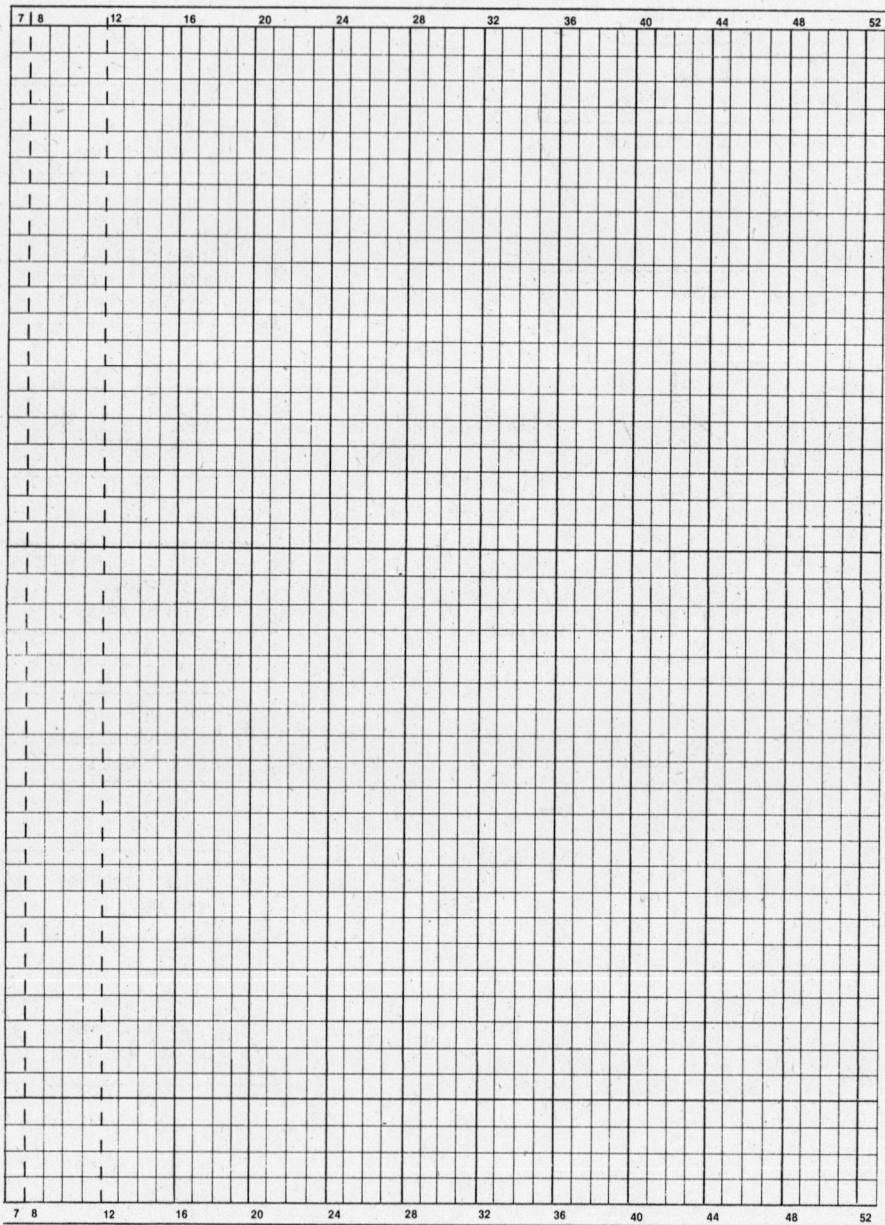

```
       IDENTIFICATION DIVISION.
       PROGRAM-ID.  ARITHMETIC-PRACTICE.
       ENVIRONMENT DIVISION.
       DATA DIVISION.
       WORKING-STORAGE SECTION.
       77  INPUT-VARIABLE PIC 9(9).
       77  VOLUME PIC X(9).
       77  AREA PIC X(6).
       77  PERIMETER PIC X(4).
       01  DIMENSIONS.
           02 LENGTH PIC 999 USAGE COMP.
           02 WIDTH PIC 999 USAGE COMP.
           02 HEIGHT PIC 999 USAGE COMP.
       PROCEDURE DIVISION.
       PARAGRAPH-1.
           DISPLAY "ENTER INPUT VARIABLE" UPON
           CONSOLE.
           ACCEPT INPUT-VARIABLE FROM CONSOLE.
           IF INPUT-VARIABLE EQUAL TO 000000000
               GO TO ENDING-PARAGRAPH.
       CALCULATIONS.
           MOVE INPUT-VARIABLE TO DIMENSIONS.
           COMPUTE PERIMETER = (LENGTH + WIDTH) * 2.
           MULTIPLY LENGTH BY WIDTH GIVING AREA.
           COMPUTE VOLUME = LENGTH * WIDTH * HEIGHT.
       DISPLAY-PARAGRAPH.
           DISPLAY "LENGTH OF PERIMETER IS"
               PERIMETER.
           DISPLAY "AREA IS" AREA.
           DISPLAY "VOLUME IS" VOLUME.
           GO TO PARAGRAPH-1.
       ENDING-PARAGRAPH.
           STOP RUN.
```

CHAPTER FOUR
Card Files

COBOL is a business oriented language designed for use in processing the masses of data critical to business and commercial operations. Large amounts of input and output are standard features of COBOL-based procedures. This data is ordinarily handled with files, stored as computer cards, printed reports, magnetic tapes, or the more complex mass-storage devices, of which the most common is the magnetic disk pack.

In this chapter, you will learn to process card files to be used as either input or output for your programs. The specific ANS COBOL features you will use as you write programs involving input and output files are:

- Environment Division
    INPUT-OUTPUT Section
    FILE-CONTROL paragraph
    SELECT clause
    ASSIGN clause

- Data Division
    FILLER entry
    03 level in record description
    FILE SECTION
    FD entry
    LABEL RECORDS clause
    DATA RECORD clause

- Procedure Division
    OPEN statement
    INPUT and OUTPUT options of OPEN statement
    CLOSE statement
    READ statement with AT END option
    WRITE statement

CARD FILES 79

DATA DESCRIPTION ENTRIES

1. As you learned in earlier chapters, the ACCEPT statement may be used to receive input from a punched card. This statement is used only for low-volume data. For which of the cards described below would you not want to use an ACCEPT statement?

    (a) a card containing the day's date
    (b) a deck of cards, each containing the credit history of a particular customer

    ----

    - - - - - - - - - - - - - - - - - -

    b

2. A collection of cards, each containing the credit history of a particular customer, may be considered a file. In a file the data must be in the same format in each record, or card. Within the record or card, each field, or elementary data item, must be described. You have already learned to write level 01 and level 02 entries. Level 01 always represented a record. Level 02, then, might represent a:

    (a) file.
    (b) field.

    - - - - - - - - - - - - - - - - - -

    b

3. A group of records makes up a:

    (a) field.
    (b) file.
    (c) statement.

    - - - - - - - - - - - - - - - - - -

    b

4. A record may be subdivided into:

    (a) fields.
    (b) files.
    (c) independent data items.

    - - - - - - - - - - - - - - - - - -

a   (Independent data items are level 77; these are neither subdivided nor subdivisions. Elementary items are the smallest divisions of a record.)

5.
```
01  EMPLOYEE-RECORD.
    02  EMPLOYEE-NUMBER  PIC 9(9).
    02  EMPLOYEE-NAME    PIC X(25).
    02  FILLER           PIC X(46).
```

The data description entry above shows that the record name is _____. The names of the fields (elementary data items) within the record are _____.

EMPLOYEE-RECORD
EMPLOYEE-NUMBER, EMPLOYEE-NAME, and FILLER

6. By adding up the total number of characters in the PICTURE clauses associated with a record, you can determine the record length. What is the record length of EMPLOYEE-RECORD in the preceding frame?

_____

80

7. Every record in a card file must have 80 characters. If each card in your file contains only one entry, a field described as PIC 99V99, the data description must account for _____ additional characters.

----

76   (Remember, V does not represent a character position, but a space does.)

8. The COBOL word FILLER can be used in a data description entry to name character positions that are not referred to in the program. Since you will most likely not refer to blank card columns, you may use the FILLER entry to account for these positions. The FILLER entry is considered an elementary data item and, as such, requires:

(a) level 77.
(b) USAGE clause.
(c) PICTURE clause.

───────────

c

- - - - - - - - - - - - - - - - - -

9. Suppose you have a card containing a nine-digit ID-NUMBER in the first nine columns and a five-letter ID-CODE in the last five columns. Write a data description entry for this ID-RECORD.

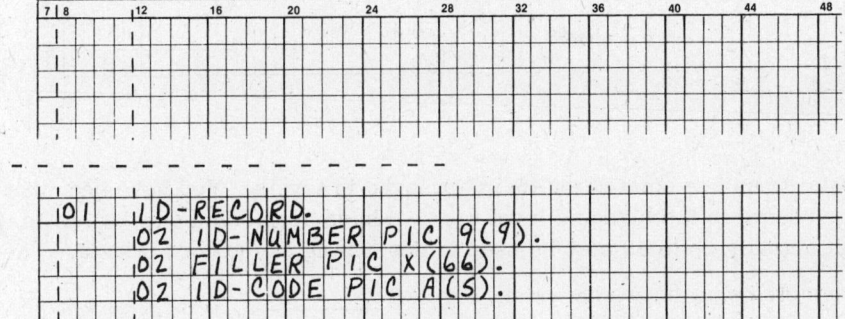

```
01  ID-RECORD.
    02  ID-NUMBER  PIC 9(9).
    02  FILLER     PIC X(66).
    02  ID-CODE    PIC A(5).
```

(The pictures for ID-NUMBER and ID-CODE might also have been described as X. FILLER could also have been described as A.)

10.
```
01  ID-RECORD.
    02  ID-NUMBER   PIC 9(9).
    02  FILLER      PIC X(6).
    02  ID-NAME     PIC X(25).
    02  ID-ADDRESS  PIC X(25).
    02  FILLER      PIC X(15).
```

The record description entry above indicates that FILLER can be used more than once in a data description entry. In fact, FILLER can be used as often as necessary in describing data. However, it can never be referred to in the Procedure Division of a program.

Suppose you have input cards prepared which are to include a five-digit EMPLOYEE-NUMBER in the first five columns, spaces in the next five, REGULAR hours in the next three columns with an implied decimal point for tenths of hours. Three columns are left blank, then OVERTIME hours are entered in the same way as regular ones. The remaining columns of the card are blank. Write a record description entry to describe this data as WORK-REC. Use FILLER to account for unused areas.

82 ANS COBOL

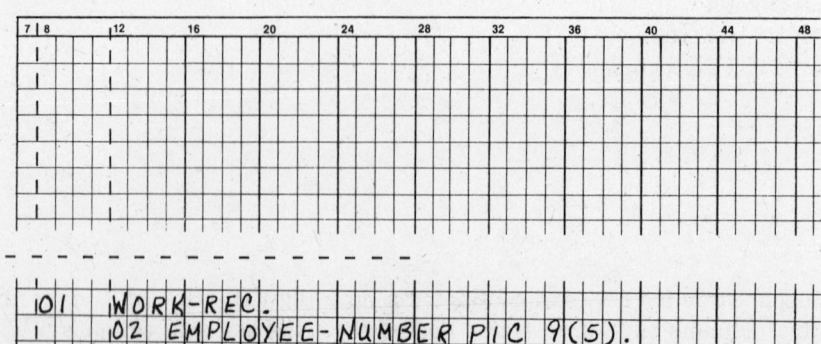

11. Data items are considered to be arranged in levels. You have seen that the record is the highest, level 01. We have been using only two levels, but actually up to 49 may be used in describing any record of data. The example below shows how many levels? _____

WORK-REC					
E-NUMBER	E-NAME		HOURS		FILLER
	E-LAST	E-FIRST	REGULAR	OVERTIME	
5 digits	12 char.	12 char.	99V9	99V9	

- - - - - - - - - - - - - - - - - -

three

12. Write a record description entry for the data record shown in the preceding frame. All level numbers other than 01 must begin in the B margin. Remember that PICTURE clauses are used for elementary data items only.

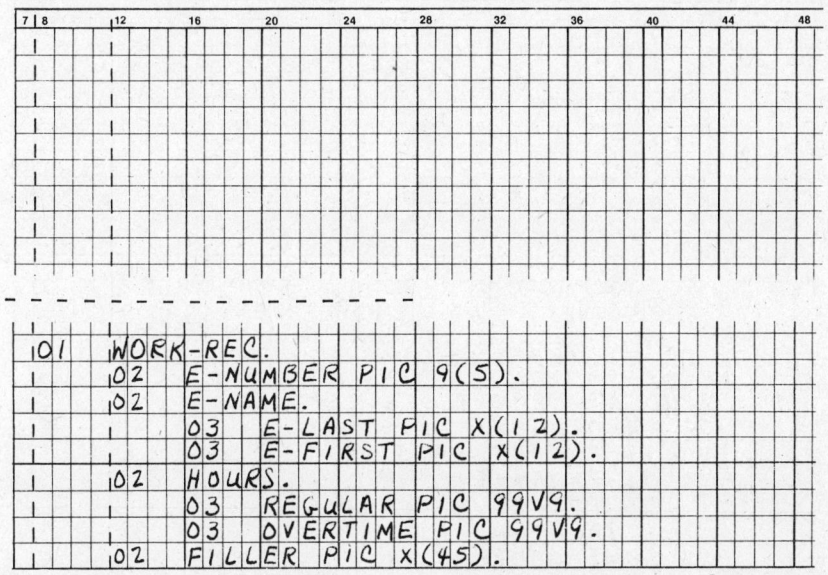

(Indentation is for readibility only. All level numbers from 02 through 49, with the data-names and pictures, must be contained in the B margin. E-LAST and E-FIRST could be described as A if you are certain no names contain any special character, such as an apostrophe or hyphen.)

13. The record description entry you wrote in the preceding frame contains a record-name, two group items that are subdivided, and how many elementary data items? (Ignore FILLER.) _____

---

five

14. Write a data description entry for the data described below. Assume that the data will be punched into cards.

STUDENT-RECORD								
ENROLLMENT-DATE			STUDENT-NO	HOME-ADDRESS				
E-MONTH	E-DAY	E-YEAR		STREET	CITY	STATE	ZIP	spaces
2 digits	2 digits	2 digits	9 digits	15 char.	10 char.	2 char.	5 digits	

```
01  STUDENT-RECORD.
    02  ENROLLMENT-DATE.
        03  E-MONTH PIC 99.
        03  E-DAY PIC 99.
        03  E-YEAR PIC 99.
    02  STUDENT-NO PIC 9(9).
    02  HOME-ADDRESS.
        03  STREET PIC X(15).
        03  CITY PIC X(10).
        03  STATE PIC XX.
        03  ZIP PIC 9(5).
    02  FILLER PIC X(33).
```

You have seen now how to describe a record. Each file in a program must have at least one record description, and every record of data in that file must adhere to a given format. The file itself must also be described. In this section you will learn to describe files in the Environment and Data Division and associate each with a record.

ENVIRONMENT DIVISION ENTRIES

15. When files are used in a COBOL program, the physical environment of the program changes. Thus additional entries must be made in the Environment Division and in the Data Division. Which section have you already studied in the Environment Division? _____

- - - - - - - - - - - - - - - - - - -

Configuration Section

16. The Input-Output Section must be included in the Environment Division whenever files are used in the program. This section must follow the

Configuration Section. Like all section headers, INPUT-OUTPUT SECTION must begin in which margin? _____

- - - - - - - - - - - - - - - - -

A

17. The Input-Output Section includes the File-Control paragraph, which, in turn, includes SELECT and ASSIGN clauses for each file to be used in the program.

    INPUT-OUTPUT SECTION.
    FILE-CONTROL.
        SELECT clause.
        ASSIGN clause.

(a) The File-Control entry begins in which margin? _____

(b) The SELECT and ASSIGN clauses begin in which margin? _____

(c) A program that will use four files would use _____ File-Control paragraph(s) and _____ SELECT clause(s).

- - - - - - - - - - - - - - - - -

(a) A; (b) B; (c) one, four

18. This is the format for a SELECT clause:

> SELECT file-name

The file-name specified in the SELECT clause must be the one you will call the file in your program. Write a SELECT clause for file INPUT-ONE.

- - - - - - - - - - - - - - - - -

    SELECT INPUT-ONE

(This is a partial entry, so no period is used.)

19. The ASSIGN clause describes to the computer exactly what physical equipment is required for the file. This is the general format:

> ASSIGN system-name

86 ANS COBOL

This clause may vary drastically from one system to another. The specific format below reflects one IBM implementation of ANS COBOL:

> ASSIGN class-organization-name

For class, card files use UR (for Unit Record). Organization is S for sequential files; card files are always sequential. The name in the ASSIGN clause is not the same as the file-name; this name refers to the external name of the file, the one that you use on job control cards as determined by the installation where you work. This name can have from one to eight characters. Now write an ASSIGN clause for a file to be used for card input (a reading device) with external name CARDX.

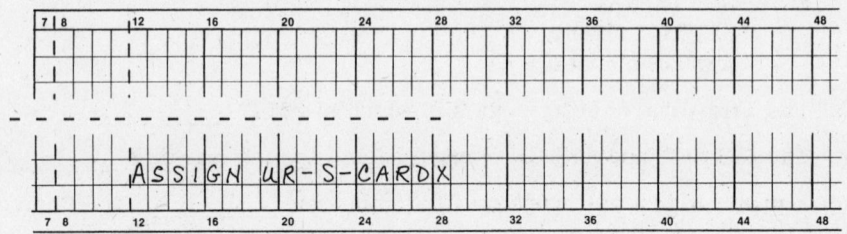

(The actual system-name will be determined by where you are running the program. We will use several common ones in this guide. This particular ASSIGN format is typical of many IBM systems.)

The control cards of a system may give most of the information needed about a file. In the cases given here, the ASSIGN clause requires only an external name, or system-name. Thus ASSIGN READ1 would be an adequate ASSIGN clause for a typical Control Data Corporation (CDC) system. Since this entry may be different for the machine you are preparing to program, you will not be asked to construct ASSIGN clauses. Be sure to include the given system-names as you code programs, however.

20. Write the Input-Output Section for a program to use one input card file named IN-DATA with the system-name ENTRIES.

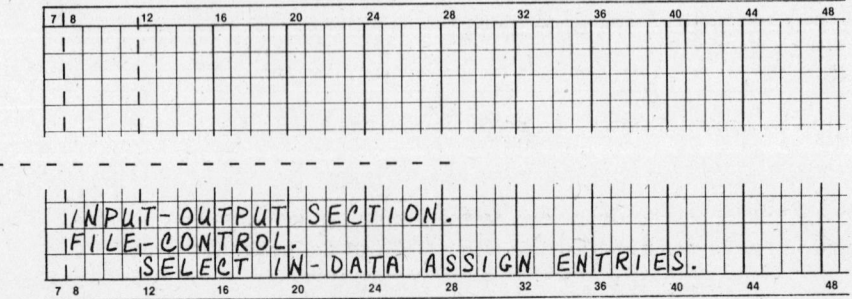

(The ASSIGN clause may begin on a separate line, as long as it begins in the B margin. When the entry is quite short, as here, only one line is ordinarily used.)

21. Many files can be described in the Environment Division, but a SELECT and an ASSIGN clause are required for each. Refer to the descriptions which follow, and write Environment Division entries for these two files. Include the section header and paragraph-name.

    Input cards are INFILE; system-name is UR-S-INXT.

CREDIT-DATA			
NUM	CREDIT		OTHER-DATA
	HISTORY	CODX	
9 digits	18 char.	3 digits	50 char.

    Output cards are OUTFILE; system-name is UR-S-OUTXT.

SUMMARY			
NUMBRR		C-CODE	
9 digits	31 spaces	3 digits	all spaces

```
       INPUT-OUTPUT SECTION.
       FILE-CONTROL.
           SELECT INFILE ASSIGN UR-S-INXT.
           SELECT OUTFILE ASSIGN UR-S-OUTXT.
```

FILE DESCRIPTION ENTRIES

22. The Data Division of a COBOL program is also divided into sections: the Working-Storage Section, which you already know how to write, and the File Section. The File Section always precedes the Working-Storage

88 ANS COBOL

Section and includes descriptions of all files and their associated records. A File Section header would begin in which margin? _____

A

23.
```
 7|8   12    16    20    24    28    32    36    40    44    48
 DATA DIVISION.
 FILE SECTION.
 FD  STUDENT-FILE
     LABEL RECORDS ARE OMITTED
     DATA RECORD IS S-RECORD.
 01  S-RECORD.
```

The coding above shows sample entries for starting out in the Data Division. The FD (File Description) entry includes the file-name, the LABEL RECORDS clause, and the DATA RECORD clause. The file-name is the same one specified in the SELECT clause. Notice that a period occurs only at the end of the complete FD entry.

We will first consider the file-name. The rules for forming file-names are the same as those for forming data-names. Which of the following are valid file-names?

(a) INPUT FILE   (c) S-1974
(b) 2345678   (d) CUSTOMERS

----

c, d   (a includes an embedded blank; b does not contain a letter.)

We have said that a file consists of many records of data in identical formats. For many types of files special records are used to label the file; both header (at the beginning) and trailer (at the end) label records may be included. The records may be created by the programmer; they may be in a standard format, in which case they are created by the system; or they may be omitted in some files. Unit record files, which include card files since each card is treated as an individual, or unit, record, cannot use label records.

24. This is the format for an FD entry with a LABEL RECORDS clause:

> FD   file-name
>   LABEL RECORDS ARE $\begin{Bmatrix} \text{OMITTED} \\ \text{STANDARD} \end{Bmatrix}$

Write a LABEL RECORDS clause for a card file.

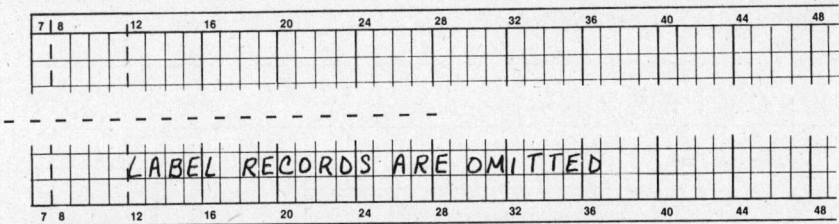

25. Every FD entry must include a LABEL RECORDS clause. Many files use labels to communicate to the computer where the particular file begins and ends. These records may be unique to that file, they may be standard, or in some files they may be omitted. For unit record files, such as card files or printer files, the label clause reads LABEL RECORDS ARE OMITTED. The DATA RECORD clause specifies the record name associated with the file being described.

Refer to the example in frame 23. Write an FD entry for a file named MEDICAL-FILE that will be stored on cards. The associated data record will be named PATIENT-DATA. Remember to place a period after the last clause.

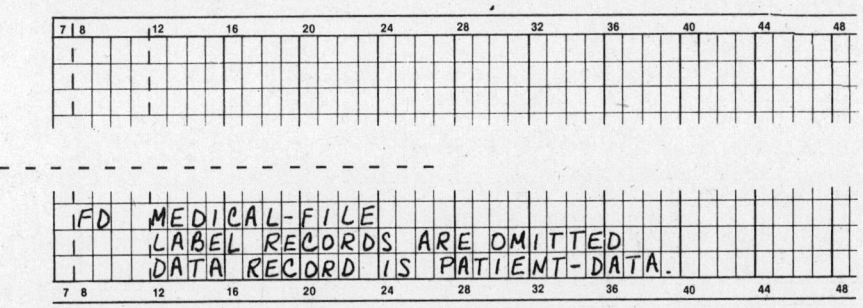

The order of the LABEL and DATA clauses does not matter, but the file-name must be first. The spacing is also flexible; FD must begin in the A margin, the rest in the B margin. Another correct way to write the entry is:

    FD   MEDICAL-FILE LABEL RECORDS ARE OMITTED DATA
          RECORD IS PATIENT-DATA.

Commas are optional as usual.

The DATA RECORD clause is not required in most computer systems, since the description of the associated data record must directly follow each FD entry. This entry is always permitted, however, even when it is not required. The LABEL RECORDS clause is always required for every FD entry.

26. The data record illustrated below is to be associated with a file called INPUT-ONE. Write the FD and data description entries.

CARD-DATA (level 01)				
LAST-NAME	ADDRESS1		SYMBOL	FILLER
	STREET	CITY-STATE		
16 char.	20 char.	20 char.	4 digits	20 char.

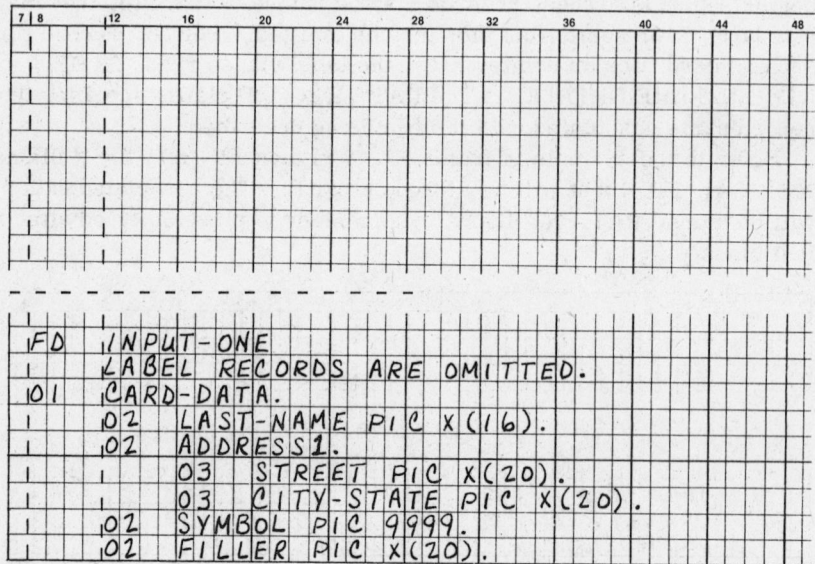

```
FD  INPUT-ONE
    LABEL RECORDS ARE OMITTED.
01  CARD-DATA.
    02  LAST-NAME PIC X(16).
    02  ADDRESS1.
        03  STREET PIC X(20).
        03  CITY-STATE PIC X(20).
    02  SYMBOL PIC 9999.
    02  FILLER PIC X(20).
```

(The DATA RECORD clause could also be included.)

27. The File Section of a COBOL program will usually include many file description entries. Each FD is followed by its associated clauses, then by the record description entry for its associated record. The files can be described in any order. Assume a program uses one input file and creates two output files. The File Section would include descriptions of _____ files.

- - - - - - - - - - - - - - - - - - - -

three   (but in any order)

28. Assume the card files are FILEIN, FILE01, and FILE02. The associated records are RECIN, REC01, and REC02. The DATA RECORD clause is to be specified for RECIN only. The files are described in the order given below. Indicate the sequence in which these entries would be written.

_____ (a) FD   FILEIN

_____ (b) FD   FILE01

_____ (c) FD   FILE02

_____ (d) LABEL RECORDS ARE OMITTED

_____ (e) 01   RECIN

_____ (f) 01   REC01

_____ (g) 01   REC02

_____ (h) DATA RECORD clause

(a) 1; (b) 5; (c) 8; (d) 2, 6, 9; (e) 4; (f) 7; (g) 10; (h) 3
(The order is a, d, h, e, b, d, f, c, d, g; d and h could be reversed.)

29. As we saw earlier, all files must be described in the File Section of the Data Division. The FD and record description entries for one file are completed, then the entries for the next file begin. Refer back to frame 21, and write Data Division entries for the files described there.

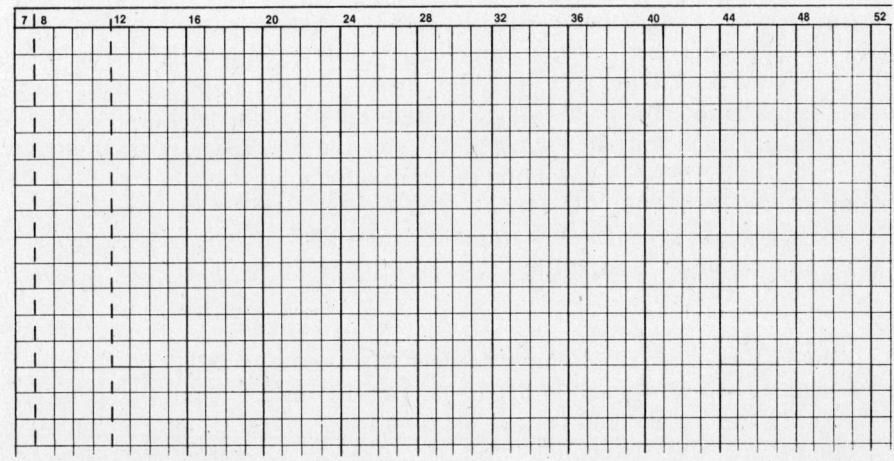

```
       7 8   12      16      20      24      28      32      36      40      44      48
       FILE SECTION.
       FD  INFILE
               LABEL RECORDS ARE OMITTED.
       01  CREDIT-DATA.
           02  NUM PIC 9(9).
           02  CREDIT.
               03  HISTORY PIC X(18).
               03  CODX PIC 999.
           02  OTHER-DATA PIC X(50).
       FD  OUTFILE
               LABEL RECORDS ARE OMITTED.
       01  SUMMARY.
           02  NUMBRR PIC 9(9).
           02  FILLER PIC X(31).
           02  C-CODE PIC 999.
           02  FILLER PIC X(37).
```

(The file descriptions could be in either order; the DATA RECORD clause could be included. Spacing and indenting can vary.)

PROCEDURE DIVISION ENTRIES

In the Procedure Division, card files are accessed or created. They are used as input to a program to give it data to work with or as output to give back to the programmer the computer's solution to the problem. Before a file can be used, the computer must be told it is ready. To do this you write an OPEN statement to alert the computer, specifying either INPUT or OUTPUT. You use a READ or a WRITE statement, depending on whether the computer needs to know what is punched into the card, or whether it must do the punching. Then you tell the computer you are finished. To do this you CLOSE the file. Between execution of these statements the ones you learned earlier are used—MOVE, GO TO, IF, and the arithmetic statements. We will now cover file processing statements of OPEN, CLOSE, READ, and WRITE as they apply to card files.

30. Files are selected in the Environment Division, described in the Data Division, and processed in the Procedure Division. Before processing of a file can begin, however, it must be made ready by the computer. You instruct the computer to make a file ready by writing an OPEN statement that also indicates how the file will be used. A simplified format for an OPEN statement is included below:

> OPEN [INPUT file-name] [OUTPUT file-name].

Which of the OPEN statements below seems to be in the correct format?

(a) OPEN OUTPUT INPUT TIME-FILE.
(b) OPEN INPUT CARD-FILE.
(c) OPEN CARD-FILE.

---

b (a includes both OUTPUT and INPUT; c includes neither OUTPUT nor INPUT.)

31. The OPEN statement must begin in which margin? _____

B (All statements are contained within the B margin.)

32. An OPEN statement may be used to prepare more than one file for use in a program. The statement OPEN INPUT CARDFILE, TAPEFILE, OUTPUT PRINTFILE., for example, opens two files for input and one for output. (All commas may be omitted, but you may add them for readability.) Write a single OPEN statement to prepare INFILE for use as input data and OUTFILE for use as output.

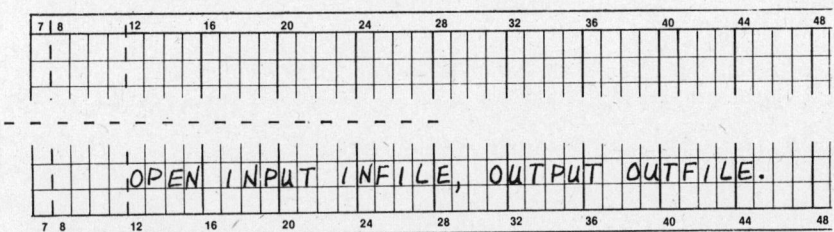

---

33. Write a statement to prepare CARDFILE for input use and two files named MISTEAKS and EXTRAS for output.

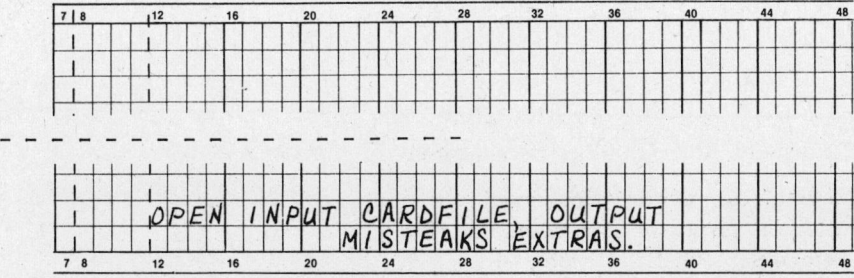

34. Just as files must be prepared before use, so they must be closed or put away after use but before the end of the program. This is done with a CLOSE statement. It is not necessary to specify the use of the file in a CLOSE statement. This is the format for the CLOSE statement:

> CLOSE file-name.

Write a CLOSE statement to put away a file named DATA-C.

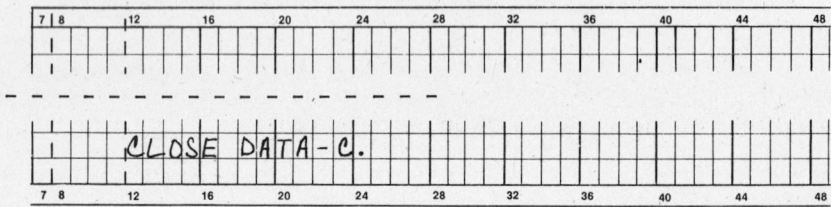

35. More than one file may be closed in a single statement by listing the names of the files to be closed. Write a statement to close MISTEAKS, EXTRAS, and CARDFILE.

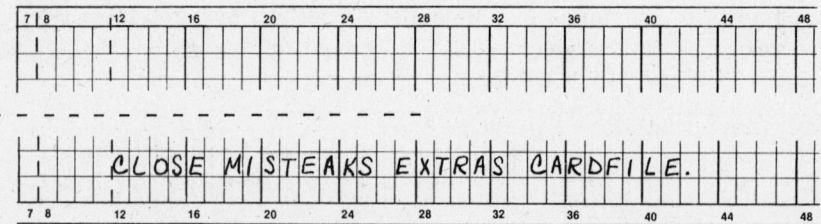

(Commas may be used for separation or ease of reading.)

36. Write a statement to close the files opened in frame 32.

37. In a program, the CLOSE statement must be executed.
    (a) before a file can be processed.
    (b) after the program is terminated.
    (c) before STOP RUN is executed.

---

c

Between the execution of the OPEN statement for a file and its CLOSE statement, processing of the data in the file takes place. In order for this to occur, the computer must be instructed to access the input records and to produce output records. These instructions are communicated to the computer with READ and WRITE statements.

READ STATEMENT

38. This is the format for the READ statement:

> READ file-name AT END statement.

   example: READ INFILE AT END GO TO ENDING-PARA.

   As shown in the format and example above, the READ statement includes the AT END clause. AT END functions rather like an IF statement: if the end of the file has been reached, the statement following AT END is executed. A card file has a final card that contains / * in columns 1 and 2. This end-of-file (EOF) card signals the computer to execute the AT END clause. Write a statement to read a record from MEDICAL-FILE and transfer control to END-PARA at the end of the file.

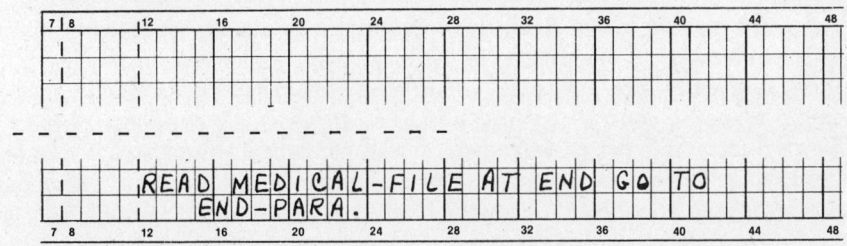

39. Each time a READ statement is executed, the next record in a card file is made available for processing. When you write a READ statement, you specify the:

   (a) file-name.
   (b) record-name.
   (c) elementary data name.

   _____

   - - - - - - - - - - - - - - - - - -

   a

40. Write a statement to access the next record (INREC) in an input file called ACCOUNTS and display TOTAL-BILLED when the EOF card is reached.

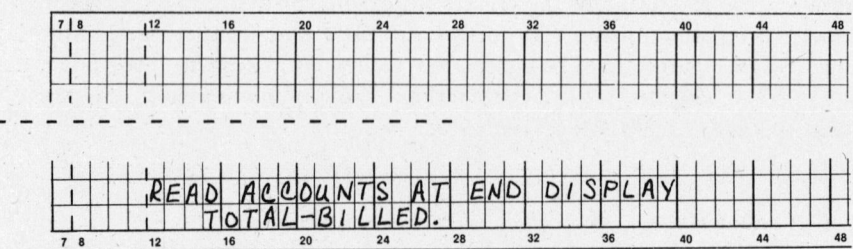

41. Two OPEN statements may not be executed for the same file, unless it is first closed. Since opening and closing are inefficient, these statements are almost never included in a loop. When you write a program that includes a loop, you would need to include a paragraph-name:

   (a) after CLOSE.   (c) following the loop.
   (b) after OPEN.   (d) after each READ.

   ---

   b   (to avoid including OPEN in the loop)

42. Paragraph-names in the Procedure Division are usually created by the programmer. It is customary to write a paragraph-name immediately following the division header. You need a paragraph-name when you wish to transfer control to some point, as in a GO TO statement. It is also permissible, and encouraged, to use paragraph-names as documentation, to tell someone reading the program what each group of statements accomplishes. Look at the flowchart in Figure 4-1 (page 98). In writing this program, you would probably use at least _____ paragraphs.

   ---

   three   (one at the beginning, one at each right-pointing arrow)

43. On the following page is a flowchart and an ANS COBOL program to solve it. Look these over and answer the questions which follow the program entries.

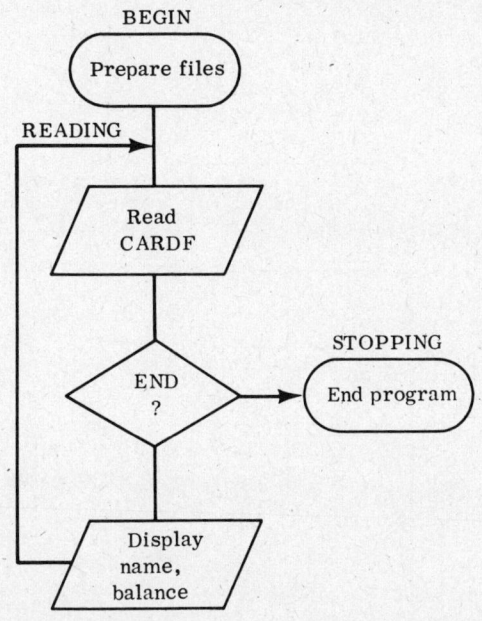

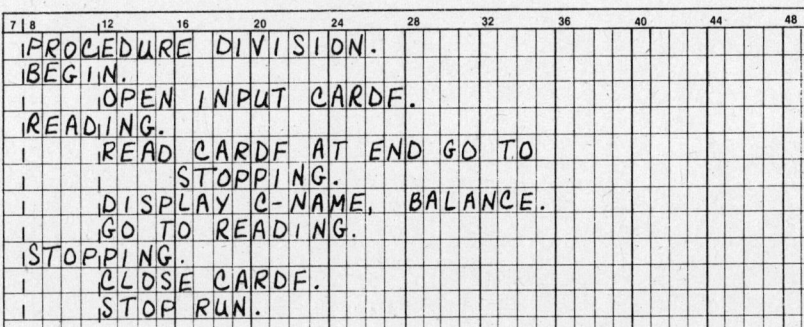

(a) Which paragraph is not referred to in a GO TO statement?

_____

(b) If CARDF contains seven record cards, plus an end-of-file card, how many times will each paragraph be completely executed?

BEGIN _____

READING _____

STOPPING _____

- - - - - - - - - - - - - - - - - -

(a) BEGIN; (b) once, seven, once

44. The flowchart in Figure 4-1, on the next page, represents a procedure for counting cards in an input file and displaying the result on the console.

98 ANS COBOL

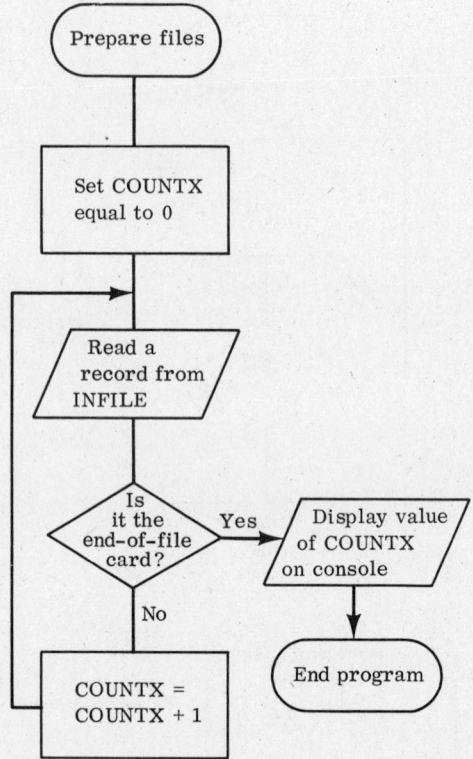

Figure 4-1

We count in COBOL by initially setting the value of a variable to zero, then adding 1 to it for each item to be counted. This can be done with COMPUTE (COUNTER=COUNTER + 1) or ADD (ADD 1 TO COUNTER). Study the flow chart, then write the Procedure Division to perform the operations. Use paragraph-names PREPARE, PROCESS, and ENDING. The Data Division is shown below.

CARD FILES 99

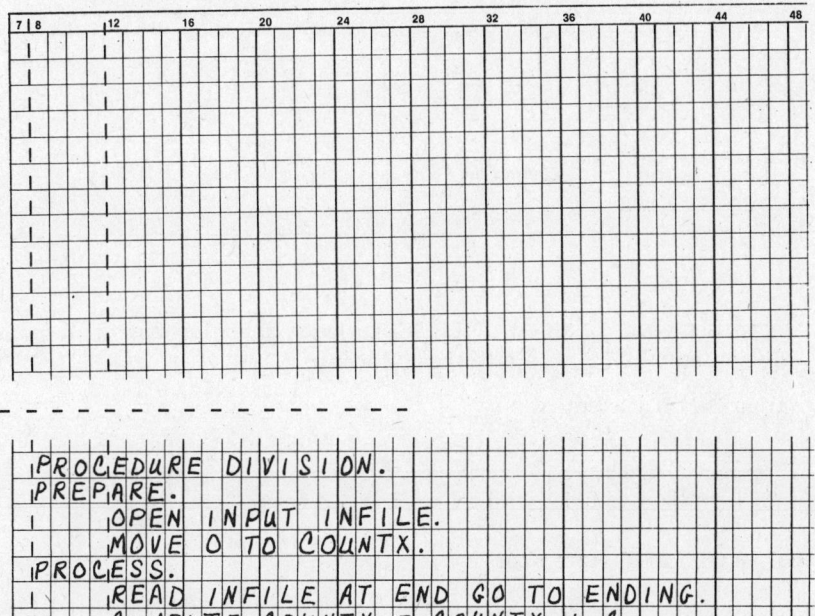

(MOVE 0 TO COUNTX could have been accomplished with COMPUTE COUNTX = 0. The COMPUTE statement in the program could have been replaced with an ADD statement.)

WRITE STATEMENT

45. Here is a format for the WRITE statement:

> WRITE record-name.

example: WRITE STUDENT-RECORD.

After an output card file has been opened, a WRITE statement can cause the computer to punch a card in the format specified in the data description entries for that file. You have already written the Environment and Data Division entries shown in Figure 4-2 (page 101). Write the OUTPUT statement you would use to produce the output file described.

100 ANS COBOL

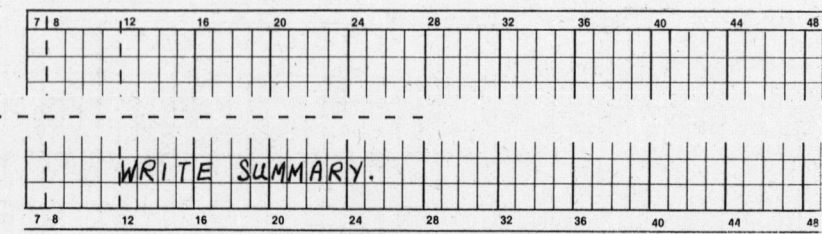

46. Suppose a record named OUTREC has been associated with an output file named OUTFIL. Write the following:

    (a) an OPEN statement

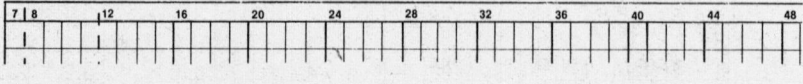

    (b) an OUTPUT statement

- - - - - - - - - - - - - - - - - -

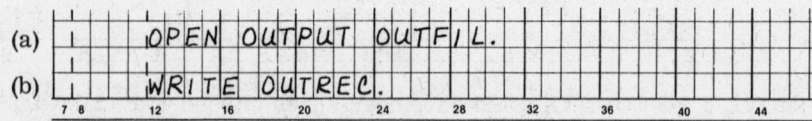

(You would, of course, have to assign values to variables in OUTREC before the output statement is executed.)

47. Which of the following statements require you to write the name of the record associated with the file?

    (a) OPEN   (c) READ
    (b) CLOSE   (d) WRITE

_____

- - - - - - - - - - - - - - - - - -

    d   (WRITE is the only one that uses a record-name; all the others use file-names in the statement.)

48. Study the three divisions in Figure 4-2 on the facing page. Notice that the input record contains several variables, but only two are to be included in the output record. Now write a Procedure Division to read the input data, move the appropriate fields to the output record, and punch cards containing the output data. Use any paragraph-names.

```
 IDENTIFICATION DIVISION.
 PROGRAM-ID. SUMMARY-CARDS.
 ENVIRONMENT DIVISION.
 CONFIGURATION SECTION.
 SOURCE-COMPUTER. IBM-370.
 OBJECT-COMPUTER. IBM-370.
 INPUT-OUTPUT SECTION.
 FILE-CONTROL.
     SELECT INFILE ASSIGN UR-S-INXT.
     SELECT OUTFILE ASSIGN UR-S-OUTXT.
 DATA DIVISION.
 FILE SECTION.
 FD  INFILE
     LABEL RECORDS ARE OMITTED.
 01  CREDIT-DATA.
     02  NUM PIC 9(9).
     02  CREDIT.
         03  HISTORY PIC X(18).
         03  CODX PIC 999.
     02  OTHER-DATA PIC X(50).
 FD  OUTFILE
     LABEL RECORDS ARE OMITTED.
 01  SUMMARY.
     02  NUMBRR PIC 9(9).
     02  FILLER PIC X(31).
     02  C-CODE PIC 999.
     02  FILLER PIC X(37).
```

Figure 4-2

```
 PROCEDURE DIVISION.
 BEGIN-PARA.
     OPEN INPUT INFILE OUTPUT OUTFILE.
 PROCEDURE-PARA.
     READ INFILE AT END GO TO END-PARA.
     MOVE NUM TO NUMBRR.
     MOVE CODX TO C-CODE.
     WRITE SUMMARY.
     GO TO PROCEDURE-PARA.
 END-PARA.
     CLOSE INFILE OUTFILE.
     STOP RUN.
```

REVIEW

49. The diagrams below contain all the information you need to write a program called CREDIT-FILES. During execution of this program the computer will punch out the names and credit limits of all customers whose limits are less than $200. During the process of writing this program you will use most of the features you studied in this chapter. Look at the flowchart and item descriptions in the figure and write your program in the space provided on page 103. Use INFI and INFO as your system-names. A sample correct program appears on page 104.

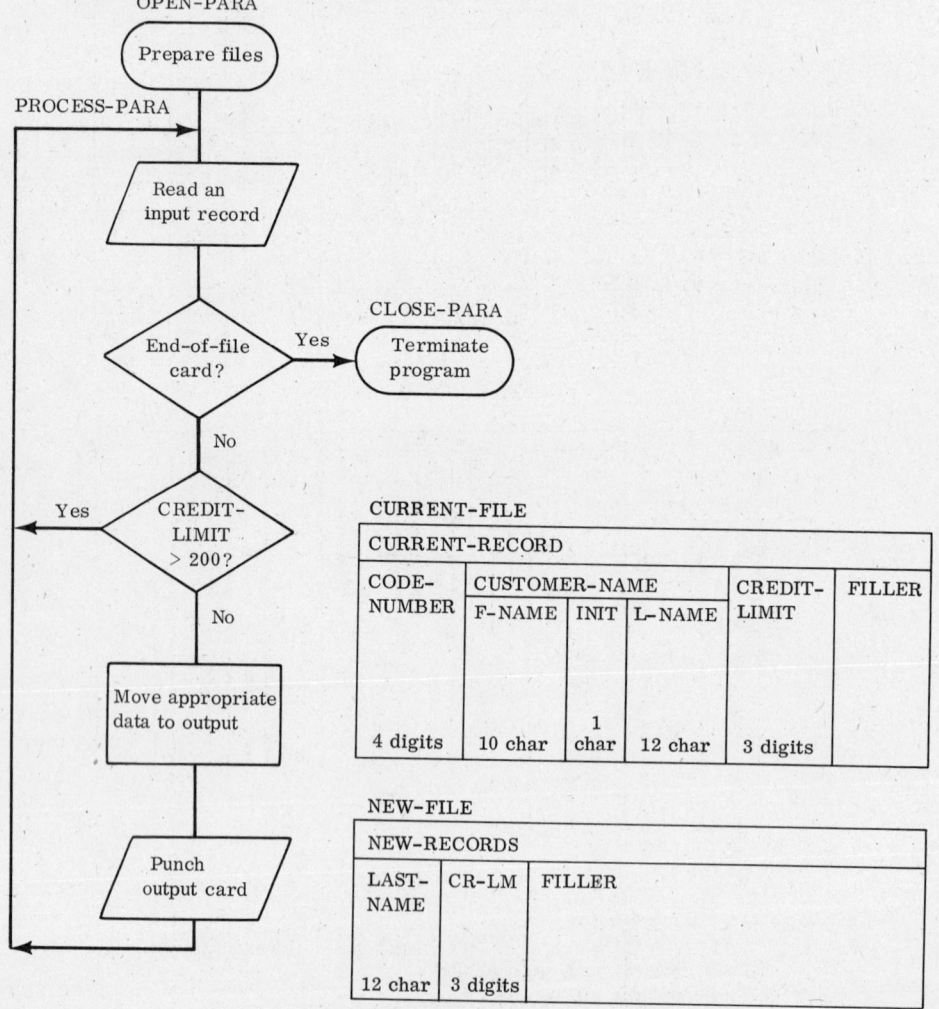

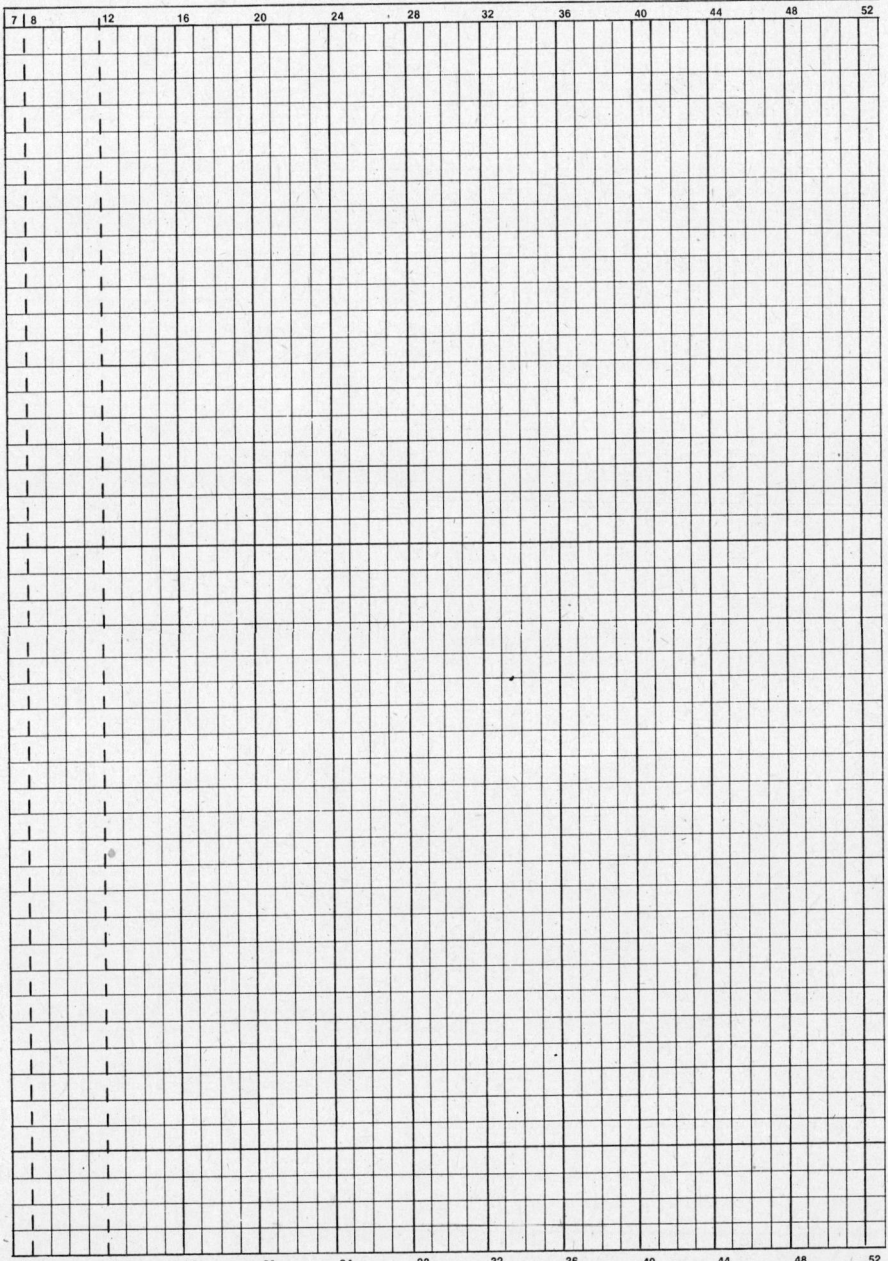

```
       IDENTIFICATION DIVISION.
       PROGRAM-ID. CREDIT-FILES.
       ENVIRONMENT DIVISION.
       INPUT-OUTPUT SECTION.
       FILE-CONTROL.
           SELECT CURRENT-FILE ASSIGN INF1.
           SELECT NEW-FILE ASSIGN INFO.
       DATA DIVISION.
       FILE SECTION.
       FD  CURRENT-FILE
           LABEL RECORDS ARE OMITTED.
       01  CURRENT-RECORD.
           02  CODE-NUMBER PIC 9(4).
           02  CUSTOMER-NAME.
               03  F-NAME PIC X(10).
               03  INIT PIC X.
               03  L-NAME PIC X(12).
           02  CREDIT-LIMIT PIC 999.
           02  FILLER PIC X(50).
       FD  NEW-FILE
           LABEL RECORDS ARE OMITTED.
       01  NEW-RECORDS.
           02  LAST-NAME PIC X(12).
           02  CR-LM PIC 999.
           02  FILLER PIC X(65).
       PROCEDURE DIVISION.
       OPEN-PARA.
           OPEN INPUT CURRENT-FILE OUTPUT NEW-FILE.
       PROCESS-PARA.
           READ CURRENT-FILE AT END GO TO
                CLOSE-PARA.
           IF CREDIT-LIMIT GREATER THAN 200
                GO TO PROCESS-PARA.
           MOVE L-NAME TO LAST-NAME.
           MOVE CREDIT-LIMIT TO CR-LM.
           WRITE NEW-RECORDS.
           GO TO PROCESS-PARA.
       CLOSE-PARA.
           CLOSE CURRENT-FILE NEW-FILE.
           STOP RUN.
```

Spacing and commas are arbitrary in this program as indicated earlier. One space within an area is equivalent to dozens of spaces within that same area. As you check over your coding, note the entries that pertain to files. The complete Input-Output Section of the Environment Division and the File Section of the Data Division take up almost half the program. Four different statements that relate only to files, OPEN, CLOSE, READ, and WRITE, are included in the Procedure Division. Files and their usage are a critical part of most COBOL programs. The rest of the programs in this guide all use files, and rely heavily on the entries and statements you have begun to use in this chapter.

CHAPTER FIVE
Print Files

In the last chapter you learned to use card files for recording input and output data for a COBOL program. In this chapter you will learn to use the output printer file, another unit record device, in which each line represents one record. Specific ANS COBOL features you will study include:

- Environment Division entries
    ASSIGN clause for printer files

- Data Division entries
    VALUE clause
    SPACES figurative constant
    Editing Picture characters
        .
        ,
        $
        Z

- Procedure Division entries
    FROM option of the WRITE statement
    CORRESPONDING option of the MOVE statement
    Qualified names of data items

In the last chapter you learned to write many entries and statements that were needed for card file processing. These entries are needed, in fact, when any file is used, no matter what the device. In the Environment Division of any COBOL program using files, you must include the Configuration Section and the Input-Output Section. In the Input-Output Section, the FILE-CONTROL paragraph must include a SELECT clause and ASSIGN clause for each file. In the Data Division, the File Section must include an FD entry for each file with associated record description entries. All files must be opened and closed. READ and WRITE are the basic input and output statements of COBOL. We will now continue to build on the skeleton of file usage by adding features peculiar to printer files, also known as printed reports.

ENVIRONMENT DIVISION ENTRIES

1. A printer file is always an output file; the typical computer cannot, as yet, accept print as input. The standard print device number is 1403. Each line of print is a discrete record. Which of the program entries below could be an adequate ASSIGN clause for a printer file connected to an IBM system?

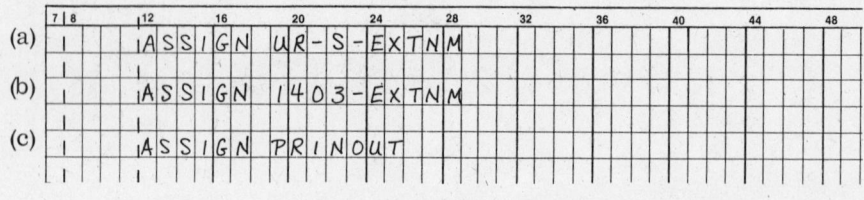

---

    a (c would be correct for a CDC system.)

As with card files, ASSIGN clause requirements vary with the system. Therefore the general format for ASSIGN is not terribly specific:

> ASSIGN system-name.

The system-name for any file may range from a five-section description of the file to a simple external name given to the file by the control system. The system-name will be given to you in programs or segments that you write during your study of this guide.

2. System flow charts often give all the information you need for writing the Environment Division entries for a program. Write the entire Environment Division for the program represented by the system flow chart below.

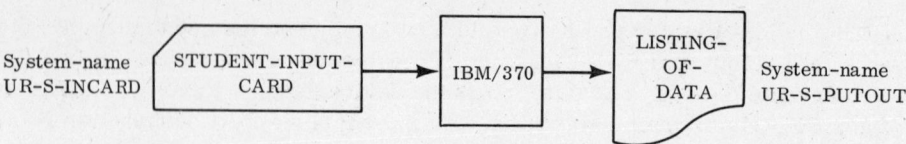

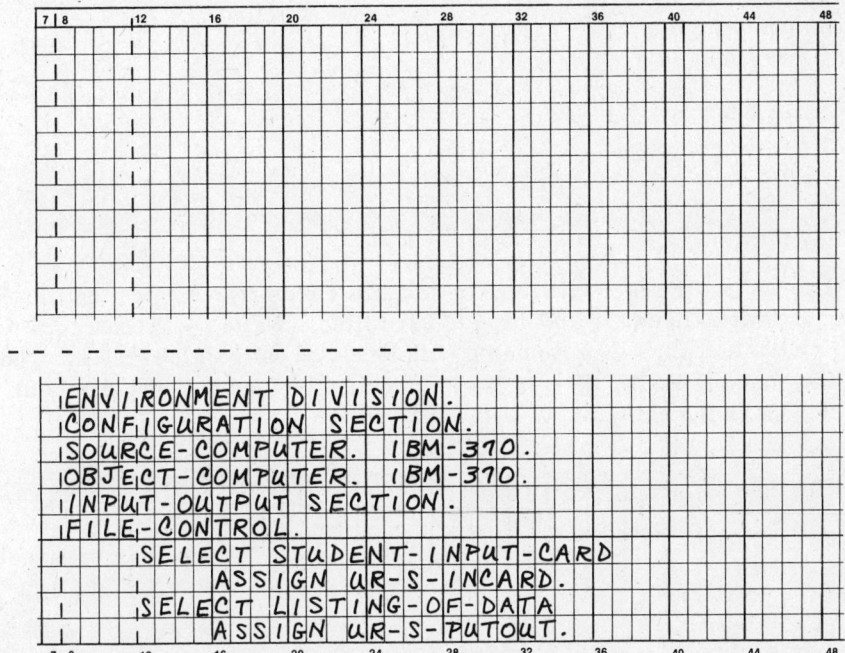

DATA DIVISION ENTRIES

An FD entry must be included in the File Section for each file. The entry must include FD with the file-name, a LABEL RECORDS clause, and may include a DATA RECORD clause.

3. You learned in the last chapter that the LABEL RECORDS clause for unit record files must be written in what way?

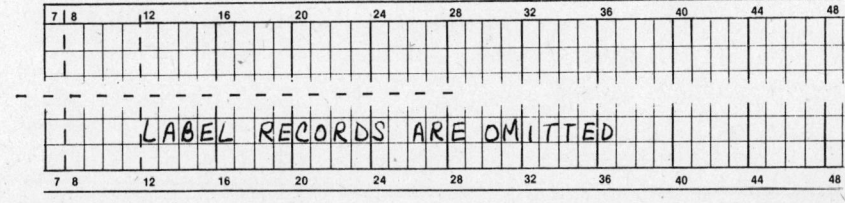

4. Each card is a discrete record. Each line on a printed report is also a discrete record. Specifically, then, label records must be omitted from:

(a) card files.
(b) printer files.
(c) all files.

---

a, b

5. The DATA RECORD clause is optional in FD entries for printer files, just as it is in entries relating to card files. Write an FD entry for a printer file which is associated with a record called LIST-LINE. The file-name is PRINTER-FILE. Remember to place the period only at the end of the entry.

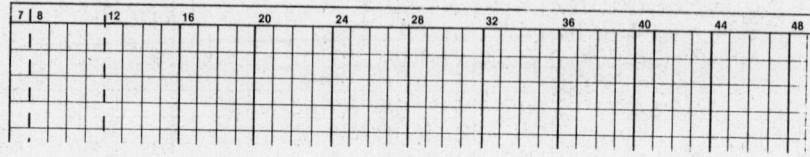

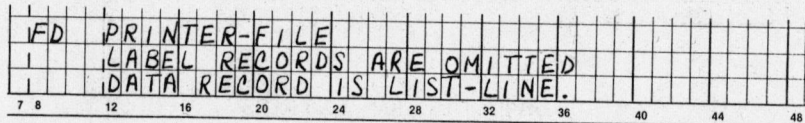

```
FD  PRINTER-FILE
    LABEL RECORDS ARE OMITTED
    DATA RECORD IS LIST-LINE.
```

(The DATA RECORD clause may be omitted.)

6. EACH-LINE is a record to be associated with a file named PRINTOUT. The system-name of this printer file is PRINT2. Write the following (put each clause on a separate line):

(a) Environment Division entries

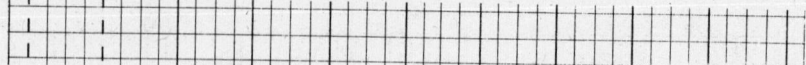

(b) Data Division entries

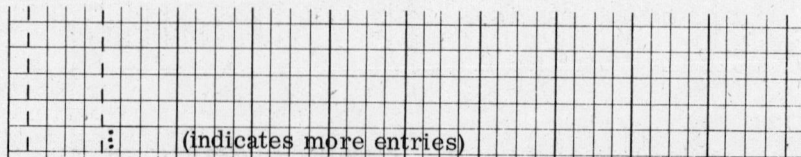

(indicates more entries)

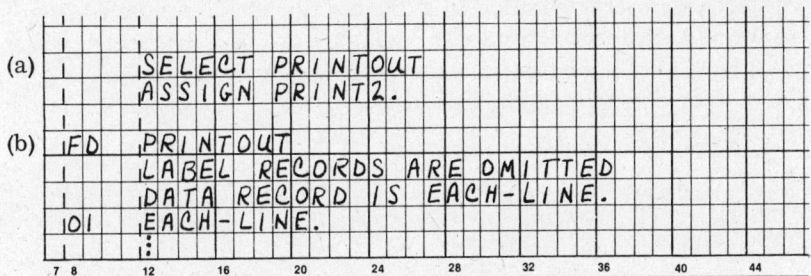

RECORD LENGTH IN FILES

7. The length in characters of a record within a file is ordinarily consistent, or fixed, within that file. The length of a card record is _____ characters.

- - - - - - - - - - - - - - - - -

80

The length of a record on a printer file is determined by the device type, commonly as much as 133 characters. Special pre-printed forms, such as billing forms or payroll checks, may use a different record length. The record length may also be adjusted by specifying a certain clause (RECORD CONTAINS) in the FD for the file. This requires a working knowledge of bytes of storage so we will not consider this here. For the purposes of this guide the standard record length for a printer file will be 133 characters.

8. The characters in a record must all be accounted for in a record description entry. The FILLER item can be used to refer to unused spaces in a printer file. Write a record description entry for a record called MAKE-DO, which is to contain a five-digit number (CODE-NR) beginning in position 10. Be sure to account for 133 positions.

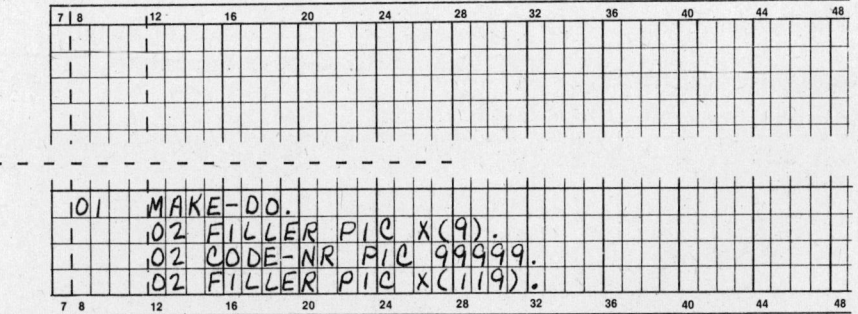

9. The first character position in a printer file is not a print position; it can be used to control vertical spacing by use of a carriage-control character. We have used a blank to indicate single spacing. Here are a few other characters that are used:

    0   skip two lines before printing

    -   skip three lines before printing

    +   skip to top of next page

Although several additional characters may be used, these are the most common ones.

(a) How many positions are available for printing output in printer file set up with a record length of 133 bytes? _____

(b) What value would you move to the first character position to cause double spacing on the printer? _____

(a) 132; (b) 0

10. Rewrite the record description entry for MAKE-DO, specifying that CODE-NR will be printed in the first available position, and that CTL-CHAR will hold the carriage control character.

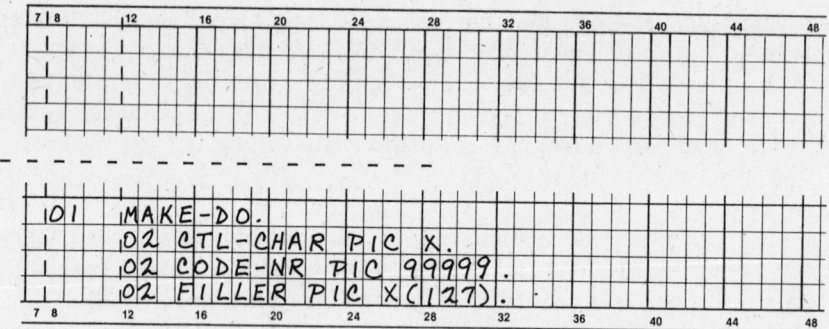

```
01  MAKE-DO.
    02  CTL-CHAR  PIC  X.
    02  CODE-NR   PIC  99999.
    02  FILLER    PIC  X(127).
```

11. Write a description of PRINT-RECORD that will result in the printing of ID-NO in positions 2 through 7 and PRICE in positions 10 through 13. Both of these data items are numeric.

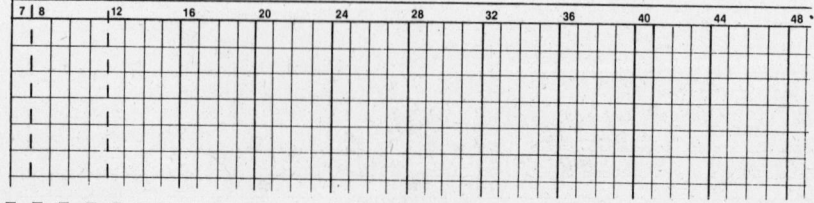

```
01  PRINT-RECORD.
    02  FILLER  PIC X.
    02  ID-NO   PIC 9(6).
    02  FILLER  PIC XX.
    02  PRICE   PIC 9999.
    02  FILLER  PIC X(120).
```

EDITING DATA FOR PRINTED REPORTS

A printed report is usually arranged on a page for easy reading. The printed data items, often called report-items, may be edited with a dollar sign, commas, an actual decimal point, and zero suppression (not printing leading zeros). The data may be arranged in columns, with blank areas described with FILLER, as you have just seen. Headings at the top of the page also contribute to the readability of a report. In this section you will learn to edit data items by inserting the characters . , and $, and suppressing leading zeros. When edited, variables can no longer be used in arithmetic except as a receiving variable.

12. Printer files are generally used for reports to be read by persons other than the programmer. The programmer will frequently wish to edit the data that appears in such reports. Editing takes place in the picture specification for a data item, in which division? _____

- - - - - - - - - - - - - - - - - -

Data

13. One of the most common editing procedures is to specify the appearance of an actual decimal point in the data item. For example, PIC 999.99 specifies that the decimal point:

(a) will appear between the third and fourth digits.
(b) will be implied only.

_____

- - - - - - - - - - - - - - - - - -

a

14. The PICTURE clause PIC 999.99 specifies that an actual decimal point will appear in the data item. Remember that every numeric item is assumed to have a decimal point—at the extreme right if nowhere else.

The value 55̭14, with the PICTURE clause specified, would be printed as 055.14. The actual decimal point will be aligned with any implied decimal point. Excess positions are dropped (no rounding) in editing, and zeros are filled in where needed. With the same picture, the value 46̭78 would appear as 004.67. Give the printed result of each of the following values, if the picture were 999.99.

(a) 777̭921 _____ (c) 1295 _____

(b) 9̭275 _____ (d) ̭5674 _____

- - - - - - - - - - - - - - - - - - - -

(a) 777.92 (excess position is dropped)
(b) 009.27 (excess position dropped and leading zeros added)
(c) 295.00 (excess position dropped and trailing zeros added)
(d) 000.56 (excess positions dropped and leading zeros added)

15. The editing character . may be used only in numeric data items, and may be used only once in each item. The actual decimal point is always printed at the position of the implied decimal point. Examine the pictures and values below. If the value may contain a ., then write the value that would be printed.

Picture	Value	Printed Result
(a) 999.9	12̭50	_____
(b) 9(5).99, or 99999.99	210̭25	_____
(c) 9.99	ACE	_____

- - - - - - - - - - - - - - - - - - - -

(a) 012.5; (b) 00210.25; (c) not a numeric item

16. The editing symbol , may be used in numeric items at the programmer's discretion. A comma appears in the edited result in the exact position the symbol appears in the picture. A data item pictured as 99,999.99 might be printed as 00,029.00 if the value 29 were assigned to it. Write the printed result after each set of picture and value below.

Picture	Value	Printed Result
(a) 99,999	48̭0	_____
(b) 9,999,999	1234567	_____
(c) 9,999,999.999	0	_____

- - - - - - - - - - - - - - - - - - - -

(a) 00,048; (b) 1,234,567; (c) 0,000,000.000

17. The . and , in a report item represent actual character positions, as they are printed in a character position. How many character positions are required for each data picture below?

(a) 9,999.9 _____

(b) 99V9 _____

(c) 99.9 _____

- - - - - - - - - - - - - - - - - -

(a) seven; (b) three; (c) four

18. The editing character Z suppresses leading zeros in a report and replaces them with blanks.

Source Value	Picture	Report Item
00870	ZZZ99	ƀƀ870
00073	ZZ999	ƀƀ073

As shown in these examples, the leading zeros are suppressed only in those positions that contain a Z. Give the report item for the following.

Source Value	Picture	Report Item
01000	ZZZZ9	(a) _____
00003	ZZZ99	(b) _____

- - - - - - - - - - - - - - - - - -

(a) ƀ1000 (result 1000)
(b) ƀƀƀ03 (result   03)

19. Since Z causes suppression of leading zeros, a Z must appear in the leading (leftmost) digit position of a picture if any Z's at all are to be used. As many Z's as desired left of the decimal place may be used, but they must be continuous. No Z may appear in a picture to the right of a 9. The comma and actual decimal point may be included in a string of Z's. Which of these pictures seems correct?

(a) 999ZZ
(b) ZZ9ZZ
(c) Z,ZZZ

_____

- - - - - - - - - - - - - - - - - -

c   (a does not begin with a Z; b has Z's to the right of a 9, and its Z's are not continous.)

20. When a comma appears in a string of Z's, it too may be replaced by a blank. If the digit position immediately to the left of the comma is suppressed, the comma is not printed. What would be printed for each source value below if the picture is ZZ,999?

(a) 01234 _____   (c) 12345 _____

(b) 00234 _____   (d) 00023 _____

- - - - - - - - - - - - - - - - - - - -

(a) ♭1,234; (b) ♭♭♭234; (c) 12,345; (d) ♭♭♭023

21. The character Z to the right of an actual decimal point must be written in all positions, if it appears at all. Why is each of the following incorrect?

(a) ZZZ9.ZZ _____

(b) ZZZ.Z9 _____

(c) 999.ZZZ _____

- - - - - - - - - - - - - - - - - - - -

(a) a 9 appears to the left of the Z's
(b) all positions to the right of the decimal point must be the same, either Z's or 9's
(c) leftmost digit positions do not contain Z's

22. A picture such as ZZZ.ZZ causes zeros to the right of the decimal point to be suppressed only when the value of the data item is zero. A source value of 00005 would be printed as ♭♭♭.05. When the source value is zero, however, even the actual decimal point is suppressed. The entire report item would contain blanks. Give the printed values for each of the following, using the picture ZZZ.ZZ.

(a) 080̭02 _____

(b) 000̭01 _____

(c) 000̭00 _____

- - - - - - - - - - - - - - - - - - - -

(a) ♭80.02
(b) ♭♭♭.01
(c) ♭♭♭♭♭♭ (Notice the blank for the decimal point position.)

23. A picture such as ZZZ.99 would produce a report item that would always be printed as at least a decimal place and two digits. Write the resulting report item for each of these source values.

(a) 002̬98 _____   (c) 000̬08 _____

(b) 000̬98 _____   (d) 000̬00 _____

(a) ƀƀ2.98
(b) ƀƀƀ.98
(c) ƀƀƀ.08
(d) ƀƀƀ.00

24. Give report items for each of the following.

Source Value	Picture	Report Item
0̬004	Z.999	(a) _____
0̬004	Z.ZZZ	(b) _____
0000	Z.999	(c) _____
0000	Z.ZZZ	(d) _____

(a) ƀ.004; (b) ƀ.004; (c) ƀ.000; (d) ƀƀƀƀƀ

25. In order for a report-item to be completely replaced by blanks in a printed report, the programmer must describe it with:

(a) no simple insertion characters, but all Z's.
(b) Z's to the left of the decimal point, but 9's in digit positions to the right of the decimal point.
(c) Z's in all digit positions.

_____

---

c   (In a, simple insertion characters could be included; they too would be suppressed. In b, the 9's to the right of the decimal place would result in 0's and the point being printed.)

26. Another frequently used editing symbol, even in very simple reports, is the dollar sign. For example, PIC $99.99 would result in the value 2̬98 being printed as $02.98. When you specify a single $ at the left of a picture, it causes:

(a) insertion of leading zeros in the data item.
(b) printing of $ at the extreme left of the item.
(c) alignment of decimal points.

_____

---

b (a and c are caused by other factors in the picture.)

27. The $ represents an actual character position. How many character positions are represented by each of the following pictures?

(a) 9999 _____

(b) 99.99 _____

(c) $99.99 _____

- - - - - - - - - - - - - - - - - - -

(a) four; (b) five; (c) six

28. Suppose you have a data item described as $9(5).99; a value such as 2̂98 would then be printed as _____.

- - - - - - - - - - - - - - - - - -

$00002.98

29. You have seen how to suppress leading zeros by specifying Z's. Another way is by using the floating dollar sign in a picture. For example, $$$$$$.99 would result in the printing of ƀƀƀƀ$2.98. Here we have four spaces to the left of the dollar sign. The editing symbol floats over to the leftmost non-zero digit when more than one $ is used. The editing symbol may be floated to any position left of the decimal point, or it may include the entire picture. Examine these examples.

	Picture	Value	Printed Result
1.	$$$9.99	̂12	$0.12
2.	$$$$.$$	̂05	$.05
3.	$$$$.$$	0	(all spaces)
4.	$$$$.99	1298	$298.00

(a) What would be the printed result in example 1 if the value were 14̂00?

_____

(b) What would be the printed result in example 2 if the value were 0?

_____

(c) What would be the printed result in example 3 if the value were 5̂7?

_____

- - - - - - - - - - - - - - - - - -

(a) $14.00
(b) nothing printed (all spaces)

(c) $5.70

(Actually, the pictures in examples 3 and 4 cause different results only when the value of the item is zero.)

30. Fill in the printed results for the items in the table below.

Picture	Value	Printed Result
(a) 9(4).9	3357	_____
(b) 99V99	1298	_____
(c) $$999	2	_____
(d) $$$.99	0	_____

- - - - - - - - - - - - - - - - -

(a) 0033.5
(b) 1298 (V does not represent a character position.)
(c) ᵇ$002
(c) ᵇᵇ$.00

31. Write a picture clause for a data item to be printed with two decimal places and four digits to the left of the decimal point. A dollar sign is to appear in the leftmost position. _____

- - - - - - - - - - - - - - - - -

$9999.99

32. Write a picture for the data item described in the preceding frame if leading zeros to the left of the decimal point are to be suppressed and the $ printed immediately to the left of the first non-zero digit or the decimal point. _____

- - - - - - - - - - - - - - - - -

$$$$$.99

33. How would you have written the picture of the preceding frame to cause nothing to be printed if the value were zero? _____

- - - - - - - - - - - - - - - - -

$$$$$.$$

118 ANS COBOL

34. Suppose you wish to have printed a CUSTOMER-NUMBER beginning in position 20 (print position 19) and a CREDIT-LIMIT beginning in column 35 on the printer page. PRESENT-BALANCE is to begin in column 45. Write a record description to specify the following:

CUSTOMER-NUMBER is eight digits long, with commas at appropriate points.

CREDIT-LIMIT has three digits and is to be preceded by a fixed dollar sign. No decimal point is necessary.

PRESENT-BALANCE has up to three digits preceding the decimal point and two digits after. The dollar sign is to be printed immediately before the first non-zero digit to the left of the point.

In writing your record description be sure to count the character positions and add FILLER items to make up to 133 positions.

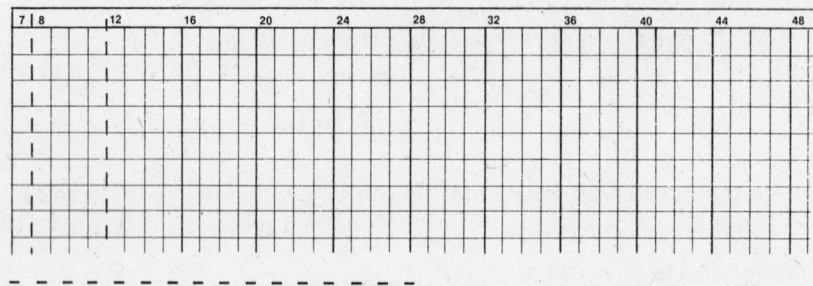

```
01   RECORD-DESCRIPTION.
     02   FILLER            PIC X(19).
     02   CUSTOMER-NUMBER   PIC 99,999,999.
     02   FILLER            PIC X(5).
     02   CREDIT-LIMIT      PIC $999.
     02   FILLER            PIC X(6).
     02   PRESENT-BALANCE   PIC $$$$.99.
     02   FILLER            PIC X(82).
```

HEADING RECORDS

When a programmer has a report printed up, he or she finds it necessary to have headings above the columns of data to tell the reader what the data means. Heading records, and data records too, may be described in the Working-Storage Section of a program, then moved to the record associated with the printer file for printing. In this part of the chapter, you will see how to specify heading records using the VALUE clause in the Data Division of your program.

PRINT FILES 119

35. Figure 5-1 shows an output record in the File Section simply as 133 spaces. Here the records for a heading and for output data are described in the _____ Section.

Working-Storage   (The File Section precedes the Working-Storage Section; this sequence must be followed in any ANS COBOL program.)

```
FILE SECTION.
FD  PRINT-FILE
    LABEL RECORDS ARE OMITTED.
01  PRINT-RECORD PIC X(133).
WORKING-STORAGE SECTION.
01  HEADING-RECORD.
    02  FILLER    PIC X(10) VALUE IS SPACES.
    02  HEADING-1 PIC A(6)  VALUE IS "NUMBER".
    02  FILLER    PIC X(12) VALUE IS SPACES.
    02  HEADING-2 PIC A(4)  VALUE IS "NAME".
    02  FILLER    PIC X(26) VALUE IS SPACES.
    02  HEADING-3 PIC A(3)  VALUE IS "AGE".
    02  FILLER    PIC X(72) VALUE IS SPACES.
01  WORKING-RECORD.
    02  FILLER    PIC X(10) VALUE IS SPACES.
    02  SYMBOL    PIC 9(4).
    02  FILLER    PIC X(14) VALUE IS SPACES.
    02  NAME      PIC A(20).
    02  FILLER    PIC X(10) VALUE IS SPACES.
    02  AGE       PIC 99.
    02  FILLER    PIC X(73) VALUE IS SPACES.
```

Figure 5-1

36. The VALUE clause may be used only in the Working-Storage Section as a rule. In Figure 5-1 you find two uses of the VALUE clause. One is to specify literals to be printed exactly as they appear in the clause. The other specifies the appearance of _____.

----

spaces   (The word IS can be omitted from any VALUE clause.)

37. The rules for literals to be used in the VALUE clause are the same as those for use in the DISPLAY statement we studied earlier. Which of the following would not be valid literals in a VALUE clause?

   (a) DISEASE
   (b) NAME OF "CLIENT"
   (c) EGG-ROLL

----

   b   (Quote marks may not be used within a literal.)

120 ANS COBOL

38. Write the necessary Working-Storage Section entries to describe the heading and data records diagrammed below.

HEADING							
4 blanks (includes carriage position)	NAME	34 blanks	ADDRESS	47 blanks	BALANCE	32 blanks

DATA-LINE							
4 blanks	C-NAME	10 blanks	C-ADDR	10 blanks	C-BAL	remainder blanks
	30 char.		40 char.			

appear as: 7 digits, 2 to right of actual decimal point, with fixed dollar sign and comma

Space is provided for your entries below.

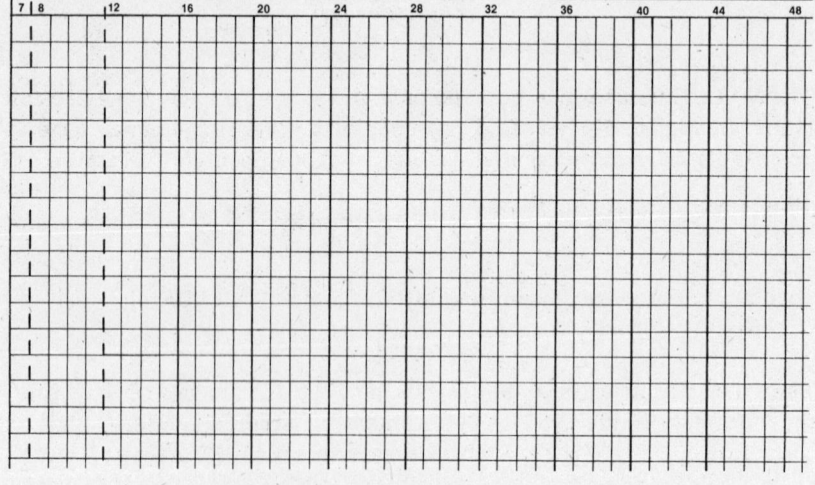

```
01  HEADING.
    02  FILLER PIC X(4) VALUE SPACES.
    02  H1 PIC X(4) VALUE "NAME".
    02  FILLER PIC X(34) VALUE SPACES.
    02  H2 PIC X(7) VALUE "ADDRESS".
    02  FILLER PIC X(47) VALUE SPACES.
    02  H3 PIC X(7) VALUE "BALANCE".
    02  FILLER PIC X(32) VALUE SPACES.
01  DATA-LINE.
    02  FILLER PIC X(4) VALUE SPACES.
    02  C-NAME PIC X(30).
    02  FILLER PIC X(10) VALUE SPACES.
    02  C-ADDR PIC X(40).
    02  FILLER PIC X(10) VALUE SPACES.
    02  C-BAL PIC $99,999.99.
    02  FILLER PIC X(29) VALUE SPACES.
```

39. The VALUE clause can be used to describe elementary data items only in which Section? _____

Working-Storage

40. Which of the following can be specified in a VALUE clause?

    (a) literal
    (b) SPACES
    (c) variable

    _____

---

a, b   (Actually, SPACES is a figurative constant. Other figurative constants, such as ZEROS, can also be specified in VALUE clauses.)

41. In order to print the heading and the first two data lines using records described in Figure 5-1, you would have to execute statements in a specific order.

```
1.     WRITE PRINT-RECORD.
2.     MOVE HEADING-RECORD TO PRINT-RECORD.
3.     MOVE WORKING-RECORD TO PRINT-RECORD.
```

Specify the order in which the statements on the preceding page would be executed to print:

(a) the heading record. _____

(b) the data record. _____

(a) 2, 1; (b) 3, 1

PROCEDURE DIVISION ENTRIES

42. The three statements of the preceding frame could be replaced by two, using a new format of the WRITE statement, which accomplishes a MOVE and a WRITE in a single ANS COBOL operation. The following is the format for the new WRITE statement:

> WRITE record-name FROM data-name.

This format accomplishes both moving of data-name to record-name and writing of the record. Rewrite the statements of the preceding frame as two WRITE...FROM statements.

```
          WRITE PRINT-RECORD FROM HEADING-RECORD.
          WRITE PRINT-RECORD FROM WORKING-RECORD.
```

43. Write a statement that will accomplish moving data from a record called MICH-DATA to an output record called STATE-DATA and print the line on the printer.

```
          WRITE STATE-DATA FROM MICH-DATA.
```

44. Suppose you wanted the report double-spaced, with headings at the top of each page.

(a) How would you have to change the record descriptions in frame 38? _____

(b) What character would cause double-spacing? _____

(c) What character would cause a skip to the top of the next page? _____

- - - - - - - - - - - - - - - - - - - -

(a) give a data-name to the first position; (b) 0; (c) +

QUALIFIED NAMES IN DATA DESCRIPTIONS

In an earlier chapter, it was stated that data-names must be unique. Actually, the elementary data items need not be unique, but must be able to be qualified to make them unique. This means that you must be able to specify a group item for each that makes it unique, for example, CUST-NUM OF IN-RECORD.

45. Figure 5-2 shows a data description entry in which some of the elementary data items are not uniquely named. What data-names appear more than once? _____

- - - - - - - - - - - - - - - - - - - -

HI and LOW

```
 01    CUSTOMER-RECORD.
       02  CUSTOMER-NUMBER  PIC X(5).
       02  PAYMENTS.
           03  HI       PIC X(5).
           03  LOW      PIC X(5).
       02  BALANCE.
           03  PRESENT  PIC X(7).
           03  HI       PIC X(7).
           03  LOW      PIC X(7).
```

Figure 5-2

46. Data-names are qualified by specifying the name of a group item or record that then makes the name unique. What might be specified to qualify HI and LOW? _____

- - - - - - - - - - - - - - - - - - - -

PAYMENTS and BALANCE (Not CUSTOMER-RECORD. Both HI's are contained in CUSTOMER-RECORD.)

47. A complete qualification of the first HI in Figure 5-2 would read HI OF PAYMENTS OF CUSTOMER-RECORD. A very adequate, unambiguous qualification would read HI OF PAYMENTS. Write an adequate qualification of the second LOW.

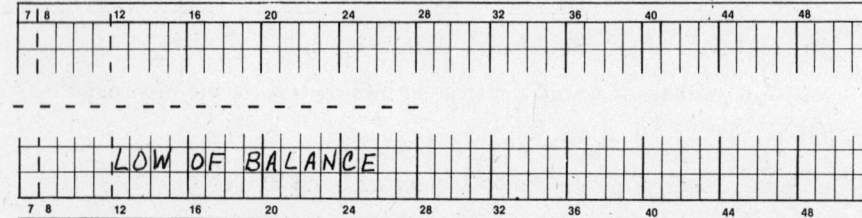

LOW OF BALANCE

48. A qualified name may be used anywhere the data-name may be used. With reference to Figure 5-2, which of the following statements may be valid?

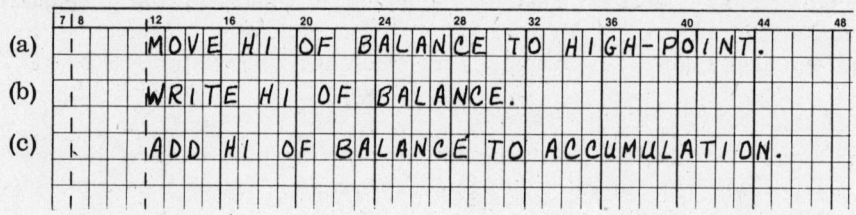

(a) MOVE HI OF BALANCE TO HIGH-POINT.
(b) WRITE HI OF BALANCE.
(c) ADD HI OF BALANCE TO ACCUMULATION.

a, c (In a WRITE statement as in b, a record-name, not an elementary data-name, must be specified.)

49. Names must be qualified enough to make them unique. Group items in which the elementary items are included must be specified in order of level hierarchy. That is, in qualifying a level 03 item, the level 02 qualifier must be specified before any level 01 qualifier is mentioned. Write a complete qualification for the second HI in Figure 5-2.

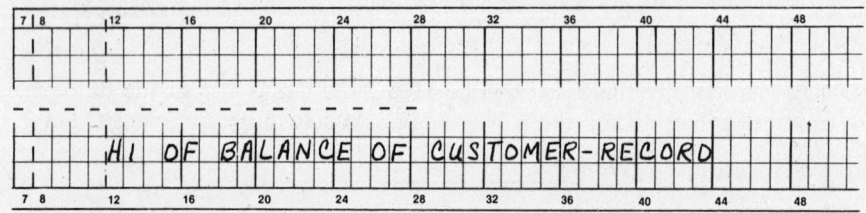

HI OF BALANCE OF CUSTOMER-RECORD

(Actually, the file-name may also be specified as one level higher than the record if necessary for complete qualification.)

50. Since qualification becomes necessary when duplicate data-names are used within a program, you may wonder why people use them. One reason is an option of the MOVE statement. When the CORRESPONDING option of the MOVE statement is specified, data is moved between variables with identical names.

INPUT-RECORD		
NAME	HOME-ADDRESS	CUSTOMER-NUMBER

WORK-RECORD					
NAME	FILLER	HOME-ADDRESS	FILLER	CUSTOMER	FILLER

In this example, the values of NAME and HOME-ADDRESS would be moved with the single statement MOVE CORRESPONDING INPUT-RECORD TO WORK-RECORD.

EMPLOYEE-RECORD		
NUMBER1	EMPLOYEE-NAME	ADDRESS1

WORKING-RECORD				
NUMBER1	FILLER	NAME	FILLER	ADDRESS1

Which variable values would be moved if you specified MOVE CORRESPONDING EMPLOYEE-RECORD TO WORKING-RECORD. ?

- - - - - - - - - - - - - - - - - -

NUMBER1 and ADDRESS1

51. How could you qualify NUMBER1 so that both data-names would be unique?

- - - - - - - - - - - - - - - -

NUMBER1 OF EMPLOYEE-RECORD
and NUMBER1 OF WORKING-RECORD

52. Suppose you wish to move the complete contents of EMPLOYEE-RECORD to WORKING-RECORD as one item. How would you write the MOVE statement?

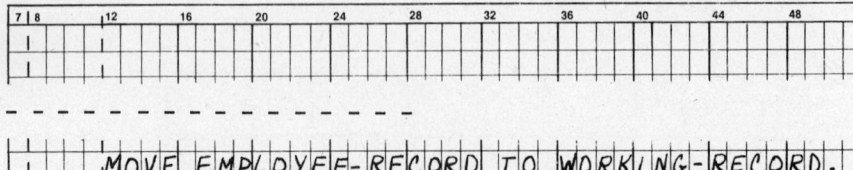

MOVE EMPLOYEE-RECORD TO WORKING-RECORD.

(Every character would be moved—usually not desirable as spacing and arrangements differ. In this case, characters from EMPLOYEE-NAME would be placed at least partly in FILLER.)

53. Suppose you wish to move all the contents of EMPLOYEE-RECORD to WORKING-RECORD, then move WORKING-RECORD to OUTPUT-RECORD and print it. What statement(s) would you add to the statement of the preceding frame?

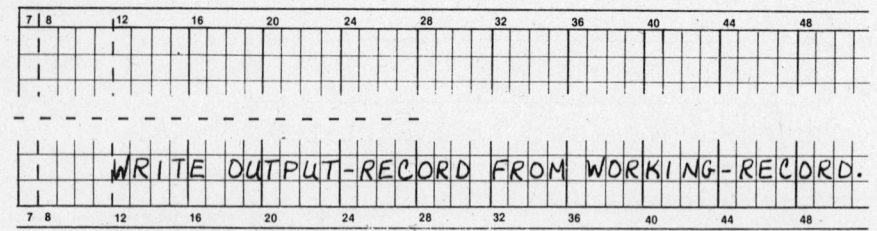

WRITE OUTPUT-RECORD FROM WORKING-RECORD.

REVIEW

54. All the information needed to write the program PRINT-A-REPORT is contained in the group of diagrams on the next pages. This program will read an input card file and prepare and print a report containing some of the data from the cards. In this program you may use most of the items you studied in this chapter. Write your program on the coding sheet provided, following the diagrams.

PRINT FILES

CARD-RECORD							
C-CODE	PERSONAL-DATA			CREDIT-DATA			
	C-NAME	C-ADDRESS	C-PHONE	YR-OPENED	MAX-CREDIT	PRESENT-DUE	PAYCODE
9 digits	21 char	25 char	10 char	2 digits	6 digits, 2 rt. of dec.	6 digits, 2 rt. of dec.	1 digit

PRINT-LINE
133 character positions

	HEADING-LINE							
	FILLER	H1	FILLER	H2	FILLER	H3	FILLER
1	10 spaces	"CUSTOMER CODE"	10 spaces	"PAYMENT HISTORY"	10 spaces	"CURRENT BALANCE"	to fill line

	INFO-LINE							
	FILLER	C-CODE	FILLER	PAYCODE	FILLER	PRESENT-DUE	FILLER
1	12 spaces	9 digits	19 spaces	1 char	21 spaces	print 6 digits, use $ and dec.	to fill line

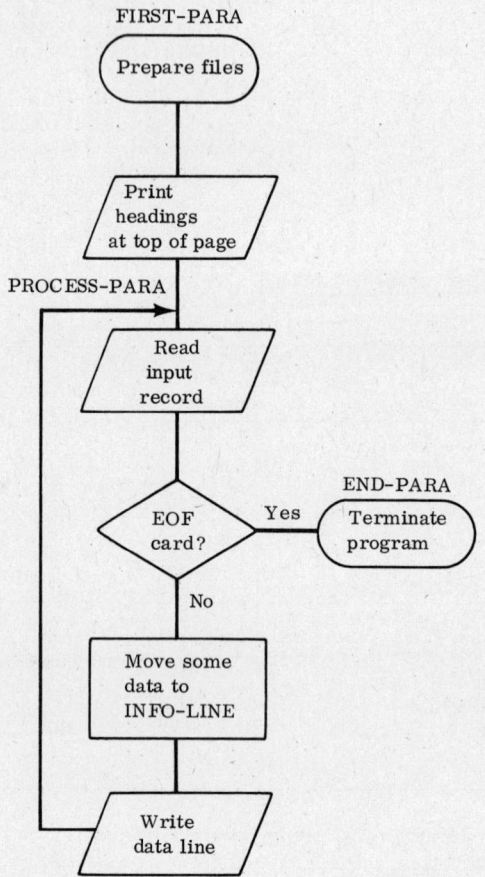

PRINT FILES 129

```
        IDENTIFICATION DIVISION.
        PROGRAM-ID. PRINT-A-REPORT.
        ENVIRONMENT DIVISION.
        INPUT-OUTPUT SECTION.
        FILE-CONTROL.
            SELECT CARD-FILE ASSIGN READ01.
            SELECT PRINT-FILE ASSIGN PRINT001.
        DATA DIVISION.
        FILE SECTION.
        FD  CARD-FILE
            LABEL RECORDS ARE OMITTED
            DATA RECORD IS CARD-RECORD.
        01  CARD-RECORD.
            02 C-CODE PIC 9(9).
            02 PERSONAL-DATA.
                03 C-NAME PIC X(21).
                03 C-ADDRESS PIC X(25).
                03 C-PHONE PIC X(10).
            02 CREDIT-DATA.
                03 YR-OPENED PIC 99.
                03 MAX-CREDIT PIC 9999V99.
                03 PRESENT-DUE PIC 9999V99.
                03 PAYCODE PIC 9.
        FD  PRINT-FILE
            LABEL RECORDS ARE OMITTED.
        01  PRINT-LINE PIC X(133).
        WORKING-STORAGE SECTION.
        01  HEADING-LINE.
            02 CCTL PIC X.
            02 FILLER PIC X(10) VALUE IS SPACES.
            02 H1 PIC X(13) VALUE IS
                "CUSTOMER CODE".
            02 FILLER PIC X(10) VALUE IS SPACES.
            02 H2 PIC X(15) VALUE IS
                "PAYMENT HISTORY".
            02 FILLER PIC X(10) VALUE IS SPACES.
```

```
        02 H3 PIC X(15) VALUE IS
           "CURRENT BALANCE".
        02 FILLER PIC X(59) VALUE IS SPACES.
01  INFO-LINE.
        02 CCTL2 PIC X.
        02 FILLER PIC X(12) VALUE IS SPACES.
        02 C-CODE PIC X(9).
        02 FILLER PIC X(19) VALUE IS SPACES.
        02 PAYCODE PIC X.
        02 FILLER PIC X(21) VALUE IS SPACES.
        02 PRESENT-DUE PIC $9999.99.
        02 FILLER PIC X(62) VALUE IS SPACES.
PROCEDURE DIVISION.
FIRST-PARA.
    OPEN INPUT CARD-FILE OUTPUT PRINT-FILE.
    MOVE 1 TO CCTL.
    WRITE PRINT-LINE FROM HEADING-LINE.
    MOVE 0 TO CCTL2.
PROCESS-PARA.
    READ CARD-FILE AT END GO TO END-PARA.
    MOVE CORRESPONDING CARD-RECORD TO
        INFO-LINE.
    WRITE PRINT-LINE FROM INFO-LINE.
    GO TO PROCESS-PARA.
END-PARA.
    CLOSE CARD-FILE PRINT-FILE.
    STOP RUN.
```

In checking your program, be sure you began entries in the appropriate areas. Check to be certain that you specified the file-name in OPEN, CLOSE, and READ statements, and the record-name in the WRITE statement. You could have used three simple MOVE statements to replace the MOVE CORRESPONDING. In that case, the data-names would have to be qualified as shown below.

```
        MOVE C-CODE OF CARD-RECORD TO C-CODE
            OF INFO-LINE.
        MOVE PAYCODE OF CREDIT-DATA TO
            PAYCODE OF INFO-LINE.
        MOVE PRESENT-DUE OF CREDIT-DATA TO
            PRESENT-DUE OF INFO-LINE.
```

CHAPTER SIX
Tape Files, Condition Types

In the preceding chapters you learned to write programs involving unit record files—both card and printer. In this chapter you will write programs involving files stored on magnetic tape. These files are not located on unit record devices, but are considered to be utility files, as they are very widely used. After learning some specifics of tape processing, you will learn some useful programming features and techniques that become essential when you write more complex programs. Specific ANS COBOL features you will study in this chapter include:

- Environment Division entries
    ASSIGN clause for magnetic tape files

- Data Division entries
    STANDARD option of LABEL RECORDS clause
    BLOCK CONTAINS clause
    Picture character S
    Level 88 condition-name

- Procedure Division techniques
    card-to-tape procedure
    record matching
    types of comparisons

Magnetic tape files use many of the same required entries you learned for card and printer files. SELECT and ASSIGN clauses are required, as is an FD entry with an associated record description entry. Tape files may be opened for input or output, and must be closed after use. READ and WRITE statements can refer to input or output tape files as well as to files on unit record devices.

ENVIRONMENT DIVISION ENTRIES

1. The magnetic tape is considered a utility device (class UT), rather than a unit record (UR) device. Which of the following could be used as a system-name for an IBM system?

    (a) UR-S-TAPE1
    (b) TAPE1
    (c) UT-S-TAPE1

    _____

    - - - - - - - - - - - - - - - - - - -

    c

2. SELECT and ASSIGN clauses must be specified for every file in a program. Assume a program uses three tape files, one card file, and one printer file.

    (a) How many SELECT clauses would you write? _____

    (b) How many ASSIGN clauses? _____

    - - - - - - - - - - - - - - - - - -

    (a) five; (b) five

3. Write SELECT and ASSIGN clauses for MASTER-TAPE, system-name TAPE7, to be used in an ANS COBOL program.

    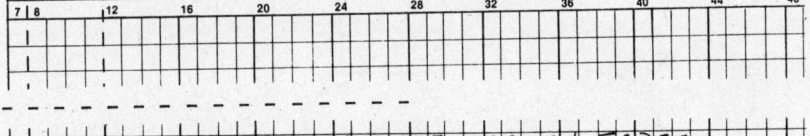

    (As with all ASSIGN clauses, the only consistency among systems is that the clause must be included, and some system-name must be specified. The system-name may include further specifications, or the specifications may be found in the job control cards.)

DATA DIVISION ENTRIES

4. Label records may be included in magnetic tape files. When these are the standard form for the system, you specify LABEL RECORDS ARE STANDARD in the FD entry. When labels for a tape file are omitted for

are of some nonstandard form, the OMITTED option is used. Write STANDARD or OMITTED after each of the following verbal descriptions.

(a) a printer file _____

(b) a magnetic tape file with nonstandard labels _____

(c) a magnetic tape on which you would like to have standard labels created _____

- - - - - - - - - - - - - - - - - - -

(a) OMITTED; (b) OMITTED; (c) STANDARD

5. The header label and trailer label records are processed automatically when standard labels are specified. This means that:

(a) label records would be created for an _____ file.
     (input/output)

(b) label records would be bypassed for an _____ file.
     (input/output)

- - - - - - - - - - - - - - - - - -

(a) output; (b) input

6. Whenever LABEL RECORDS ARE STANDARD is specified for a file, the computer system takes care of bypassing the labels if they are present, or creating them if an output file is used. Examine the system flowchart below.

(a) For which file will standard labels be created? _____

(b) For which file will the labels be bypassed? _____

- - - - - - - - - - - - - - - - - - -

(a) OUTTAPE; (b) INTAPE

7. The LABEL RECORDS clause is required for all files, including tape files. The DATA RECORD clause is:

(a) required for all files. (c) required only for card files.
(b) optional for all files. (d) required only for printer files.

---

b

---

8. Write an FD entry for MASTER-TAPE, specifying that label records are to be created by the system, and the associated record is MAS-REC.

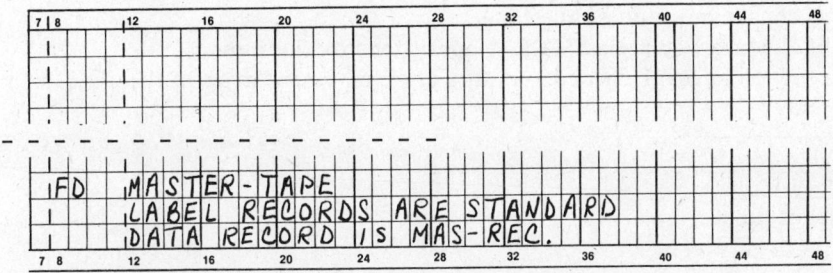

```
FD  MASTER-TAPE
    LABEL RECORDS ARE STANDARD
    DATA RECORD IS MAS-REC.
```

(Remember the period is used only after the last clause.)

Records in a card file or a printer file are distinct. That is, on cards each card is a separate record; and in a printer file, each line is a separate record. On a magnetic tape, however, records are separated only by a physical gap, a distance of tape left between the records.

Over the length of a tape, these gaps add up to a sizeable amount of wasted space. Space can be somewhat conserved by blocking of the records. When records are blocked, the inter-block gap is still present, but the inter-record gaps are much smaller, resulting in saving much space on your tape. Blocking also saves time, and it may increase the efficiency of your program. The records on the tape are read a block at a time and placed in a special part of the computer, the input area. Even though the records are still available to you one at a time, the physical work of turning the tape past the reading heads is performed much less frequently. In general, the blocking factor is given to you along with the specifications for a program.

9. When records on an input tape file are blocked, a block is read as a unit into an input area. The records are still accessed by the programmer at a rate of one per each READ statement executed. If records are in blocks of eight, the first READ statement would place one block of eight records in the input area, and the first would be available to the programmer. On execution of a second READ statement:

   (a) another block of records would be placed in the input area.
   (b) eight records would be available to the programmer.

(c) record number two would be available to the programmer.
(d) no records would be placed in the input area.

- - - - - - - - - - - - - - - - - -

c, d   (After all the records in the block have been accessed, the next READ places the next block in the input area.)

10. When an output tape file is being created, blocking could be used to:

    (a) conserve space on the tape.
    (b) cause fewer actual WRITE operations on the tape.
    (c) place several records on tape after an output area is filled.

- - - - - - - - - - - - - - - - - -

all of these

11. `BLOCK CONTAINS 12 RECORDS`

This clause for an input file specifies that twelve actual records are placed into the input area at a time.

`BLOCK CONTAINS 3 RECORDS`

This clause describes an output file. How many records will the programmer place in an output area at a time? _____

- - - - - - - - - - - - - - - - - -

one   (This is always true, no matter what the blocking factor. Here, three records from the output area would be placed on the tape every three WRITE statements. You are only concerned with one at a time, however.)

12. Consider a tape file in which records are not blocked. Seven unblocked records might be diagrammed as:

If BLOCK CONTAINS 3 RECORDS is specified, the seven records could be diagrammed as:

Write a BLOCK CONTAINS clause for a file that has records arranged like this:

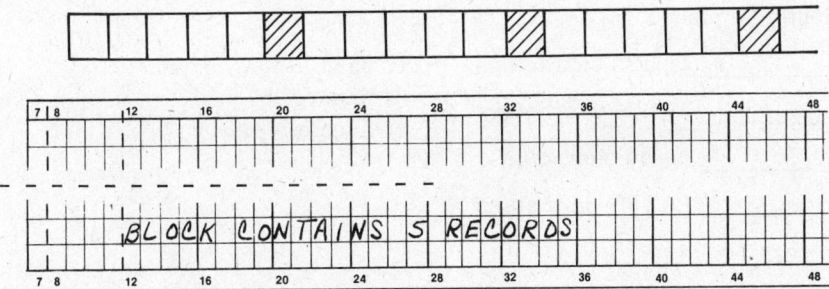

13. Write an FD entry for a magnetic tape file MAG-FILE with standard labels and associated with a record called UPDATE-DATA which is blocked in groups of eight.

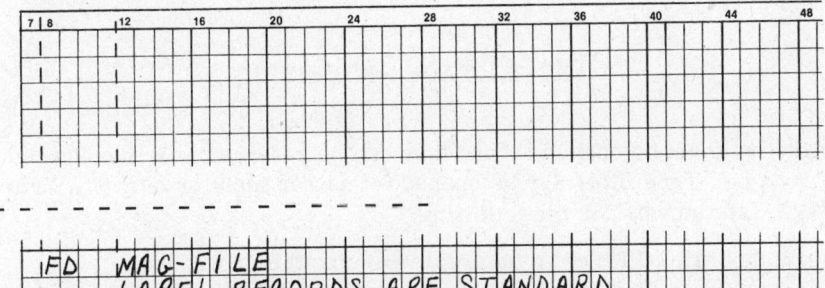

(The order of these entries is unimportant, except that FD must be first, and a period must follow the last one. The DATA RECORDS clause might have been omitted.)

Summary of FD Clauses

	LABEL RECORDS	DATA RECORD	BLOCK CONTAINS
card	OMITTED	optional	no
printer	OMITTED	optional	no
tape	OMITTED or STANDARD	optional	optional

An expansion of this chart, which includes disk files, is included in Appendix D. Refer to the chart whenever you wish. Which of these entries are used will be determined by the installation at which you run your programs.

138 ANS COBOL

14. Records in a tape file are not limited to any specific size. They could, for example, be 15 characters long or 1500 characters long. Match the following record lengths with the device on which it could most conveniently be placed.

　　　　　　 (a) 132 characters　　　1. card reader or punch
　　　　　　 (b) 156 characters　　　2. printer
　　　　　　　　　　　　　　　　　　　3. magnetic tape
　　　　　　 (c) 80 characters
　　　　　　 (d) 600 characters

- - - - - - - - - - - - - - - - - - - -

(a) 2 (a record of 132 plus the carriage-control position)
(b) 3
(c) 1
(d) 3
(Actually, any of these records could be placed on magnetic tape.)

CARD-TO-TAPE PROCEDURE

15. All files must be opened before they can be referred to in the Procedure Division. Tape files may be opened for either input or output. Write OPEN statements for the following:

    (a) a tape file (TFILE) to be created during the procedure

    (b) an existing tape file (EFILE) from which a listing will be made

- - - - - - - - - - - - - - - - - - - -

(a)　　　OPEN OUTPUT TFILE.
(b)　　　OPEN INPUT EFILE.

16. The input and output statements for tape files are basically the same as for input and output unit record files. Write an input statement to access MASTER-REC from MASTER-FILE transferring control to CLOSE-UP at the end of the file.

TAPE FILES, CONDITION TYPES 139

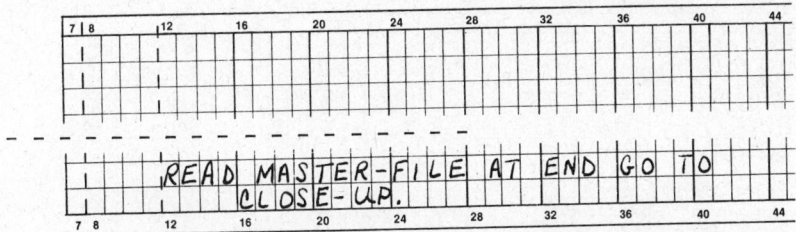

17. An output statement to place the data in PRINT-RECORD into PRINT-FILE would be written:

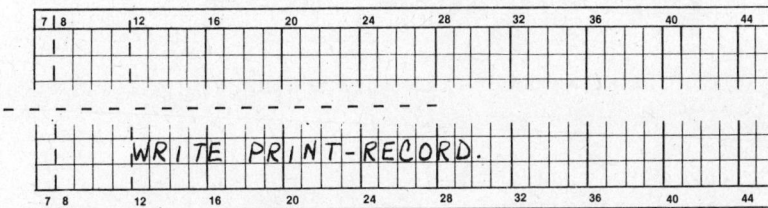

18. On the form below, complete the Environment Division and FD entries for the files shown in the system flowchart. This system flowchart represents a program to transfer the data on cards to a tape file.

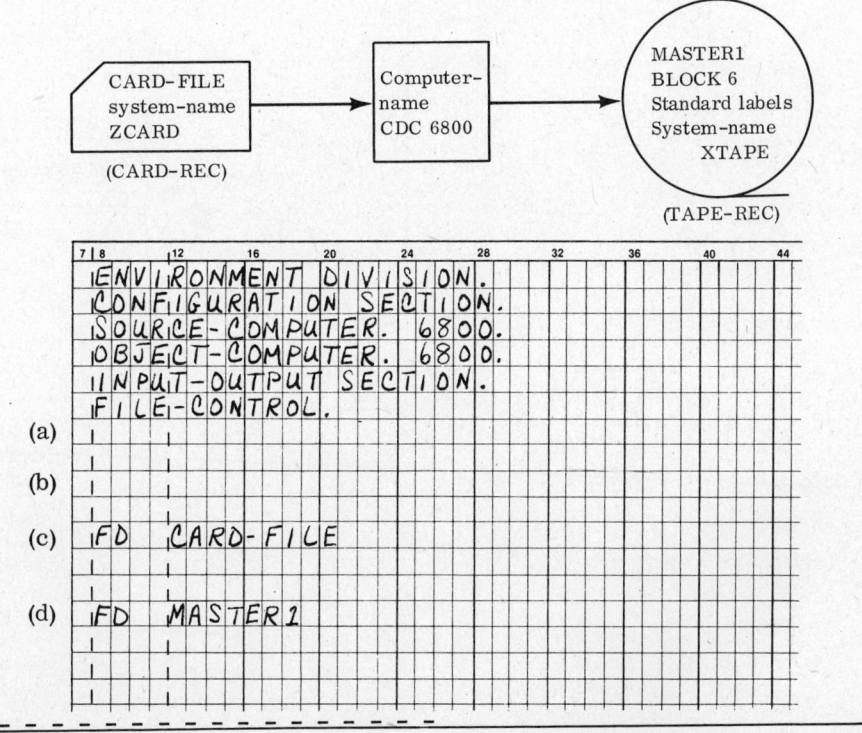

140 ANS COBOL

```
         7|8    12    16    20    24    28    32    36    40    44
        ENVIRONMENT DIVISION.
        CONFIGURATION SECTION.
        SOURCE-COMPUTER.  6800.
        OBJECT-COMPUTER.  6800.
        INPUT-OUTPUT SECTION.
        FILE-CONTROL.
(a)         SELECT CARD-FILE ASSIGN ZCARD.
(b)         SELECT MASTER1 ASSIGN XTAPE.

(c)     FD  CARD-FILE
            LABEL RECORDS ARE OMITTED.

(d)     FD  MASTER1
            LABEL RECORDS ARE STANDARD
            BLOCK CONTAINS 6 RECORDS.
```

(DATA RECORD clauses could be included in c and d.)

19. The flowchart on the right should guide you as you write an ANS COBOL Procedure Division to transfer data from cards to magnetic tape. Refer back to the preceding frame for file and record names.

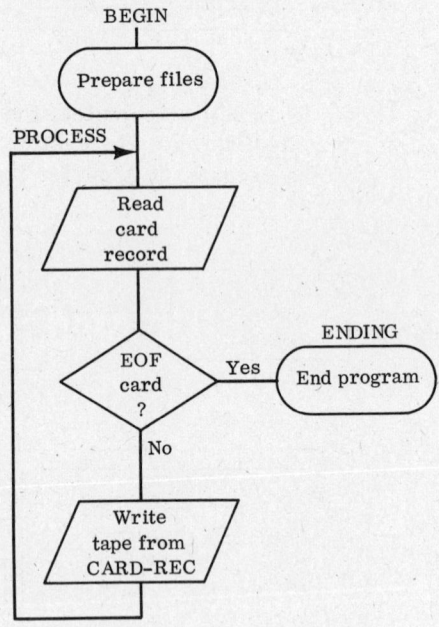

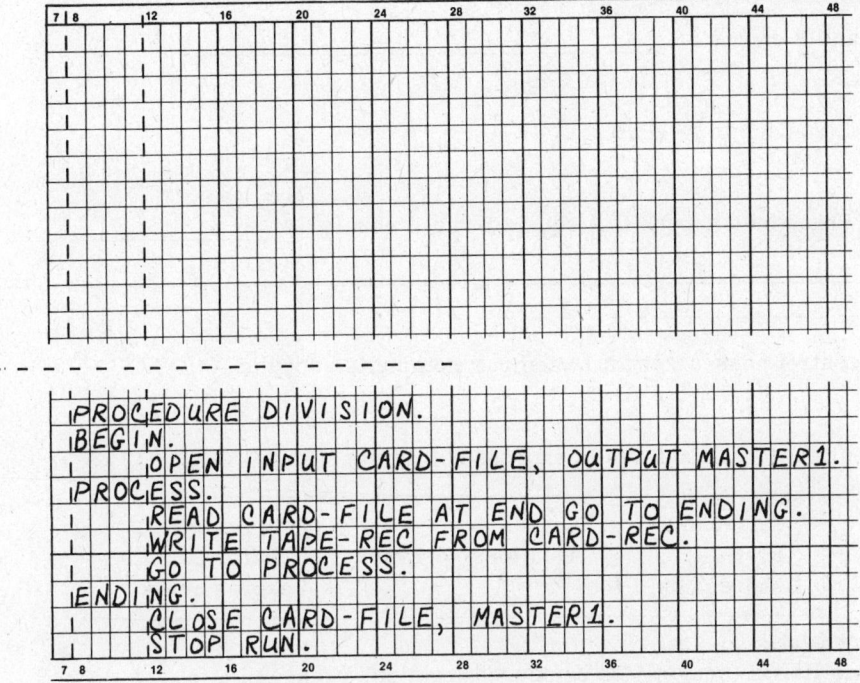

(Have you checked your spacing and periods? Commas are optional, but most periods are not.)

RELATIONAL CONDITIONS

In Chapter 3 you used an IF statement, in which you specified a condition with an action to be taken if the condition were true. In this section we will discuss conditions in more detail and learn a way to describe conditions in the Data Division using level 88.

20. IF   A GREATER THAN B   ADD 1 TO A-LARGE.

    IF   condition   action-statement

(a) In the example above, the condition is _____.

(b) The action specified will be executed if the condition is _____.
                                                                                                  (true/false)

- - - - - - - - - - - - - - - - - -

(a) A GREATER THAN B
(b) true   (otherwise, control passes directly to the next statement in the program)

142 ANS COBOL

21. In the example of the preceding frame, what would happen if A equals 7 and B equals 5? _____

- - - - - - - - - - - - - - - - - -

    1 is added to A-LARGE

22. What would happen if A equals 5 and B equals 5? _____

_____

- - - - - - - - - - - - - - - - - -

    control passes to next statement; nothing is added to A-LARGE

A relational condition is expressed this way:

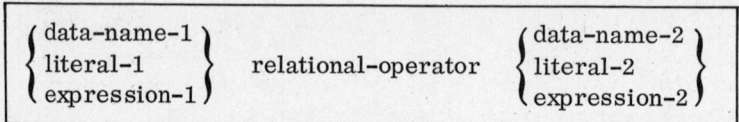

Restrictions:
1. Two literals may not be compared (related) at once.
2. Both elements must be numeric or both must be non-numeric.
3. The relational operator may be GREATER THAN, LESS THAN, or EQUAL TO; any of these may be preceded by NOT.

23. The format above explains the most commonly used condition, the relational condition. Two elements are related to each other in the specified way. If the relation is true, then the action-statement is executed. If false, control passes to the item following the ELSE clause, or the next period (this is usually the next statement). In the example below, what would be the next statement executed if NR = 7 and CODX = 6?

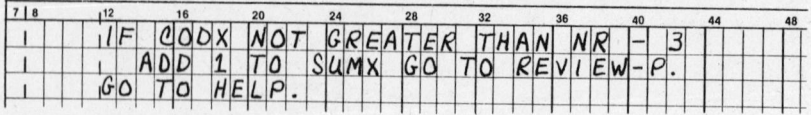

- - - - - - - - - - - - - - - - - -

    GO TO HELP   (Note that more than one statement can be included in an IF. The location of the period marks the end of IF. IF statements can also be included as action-statements, creating nested IF's. In this example, data-name CODX is compared to an expression.)

TAPE FILES, CONDITION TYPES 143

24. When two items with numeric values are related, the computer compares them algebraically. Which of the following would be compared algebraically, if all data-names are numeric?

   (a) PEN * INK EQUAL TO 0
   (b) SUMX GREATER THAN SYMBOL
   (c) 0 LESS THAN BALANCE
   (d) "17.98" EQUAL TO PRICE
   (e) FINAL-B LESS THAN 1896.30

   a, b, c, e   (d includes a non-numeric literal)

25. An algebraic comparison considers the sign (positive or negative) of the value represented. Give the truth value (true or false) of each of the following if A = -7, B = +4, and C = -1.

   (a) C GREATER THAN A + B _____

   (b) A EQUAL TO 2 * B - C _____

   (c) B NOT LESS THAN 7 * C _____

   (a) true   (-1 is larger than -3)
   (b) false (-7 does not equal 8 + 1)
   (c) true   (+4 is greater than 7 * -1)

26. In order for a sign to be used, we will introduce another Picture character. Data items in a file have a sign only if the picture for each data item includes an S as the leftmost character. The S, like the V, does not represent a character position; the sign is stored as part of the first digit in the value. Like 9 and V, S can be included in any numeric item. Write a PICTURE clause specifying an eight-digit number with four places to the right of the implied decimal point. Specify that a sign will be stored also. _____

   S9999V9999, or S9(4)V9(4)

27. If no S is included in a picture, the value is treated as positive (absolute value) in all arithmetic operations and comparisons. This is true even if the data item is named something like CREDIT-BALANCE. Which of the following pictures represent data items that would be compared algebraically? (Which ones are numeric?)

(a) S999V9
(b) $99.99
(c) XXX99
(d) 9V999
(e) 9,999,999

----

a, d (Only S, 9, and V may be included in numeric items. Only numeric items are compared algebraically. If the literal +376.98 were moved to a above, we would represent it as 376̬98. Notice that neither S nor V represents a character position.)

28. Non-numeric items can also be specified in a relational condition. Two names can be compared to find out if they are identical, or which is "greater." They are not, however, compared algebraically. Non-numeric items are compared according to the official collating sequence of ANS COBOL, as shown in Appendix B. In the alphabetic part of this sequence, you will see that Z has a higher value; it is GREATER THAN A. When two names are compared, the name that appears earlier in an alphabetic listing would be considered:

   (a) greater than the other.
   (b) less than the other.
   (c) equal to the other.
   (d) algebraically.

----

b

29. Refer to the collating sequence in Appendix B. A data item beginning 0 through 9 would be considered:

   (a) greater than one beginning with a letter.
   (b) less than one beginning with a letter.
   (c) greater than one beginning with a blank.
   (d) less than one beginning with a blank.

----

a, c (The blank is the lowest item in the collating sequence.)

Sample Values

variables	values
01 PURCHASE-RECORD.	
02 CUS-NO PIC X(5).	54570
02 ITEM-ID PIC A(5).	XXXQP
02 PRICE-EA PIC 999V99.	00763
02 TOTAL-NR PIC 999.	342
02 ITEM-EXP PIC X(62).	
01 DEALINGS.	
02 CUST-ID PIC X(5).	42381
02 PART-ID PIC A(5).	PRSTU
02 COST-EA PIC S999V99.	07500
02 ORDERED PIC 999.	047
02 PART-DESC PIC X(62).	

30. For each comparison below, specify the type of comparison (algebraic or collating sequence) and truth value (true or false) of the condition.

	Comparison	Truth Value
(a) ORDERED LESS THAN TOTAL-NR	_____	_____
(b) PRICE-EA GREATER THAN COST-EA	_____	_____
(c) CUS-NO NOT GREATER THAN CUST-ID	_____	_____
(d) CUST-ID LESS THAN PART-ID	_____	_____

(a) algebraic; true
(b) algebraic; false
(c) collating sequence; false
(d) collating sequence; false

31. A non-numeric comparison is carried out character by character, beginning at the left. The shorter item is padded on the right with blanks. Refer to the collating sequence to determine which of each pair below is greater. (The comparison stops as soon as one character is greater.)

(a) 123XYZ
    XYZ123 _____

(b) FARR
    FARWELL _____

(c) CAN-GO
    CANADA _____

(a) 123XYZ
(b) FARWELL (W is greater than R)
(c) CANADA (A is greater than -)

CONDITION-NAME CONDITIONS

32. Another type of condition is the condition-name condition, which is set up in the Data Division.

```
02  PAYSCALE PIC 9.
    88  OFFICE-TECH VALUE IS 1.
    88  PROF-ADMIN VALUE IS 2.
    88  ACADEMIC VALUE IS 3.
```

In this example, the conditional variable PAYSCALE is an elementary data item, and thus has a PICTURE clause. Level 88 specifies not a subdivision but different values that may be assigned to the conditional variable. A statement could be IF OFFICE-TECH GO TO HOURLY-PARA. Control would then be transferred to HOURLY-PARA if the value of PAYSCALE were _____.

1

33. Write a statement that would transfer control to YEARLY-PARA if the value of PAYSCALE were 3.

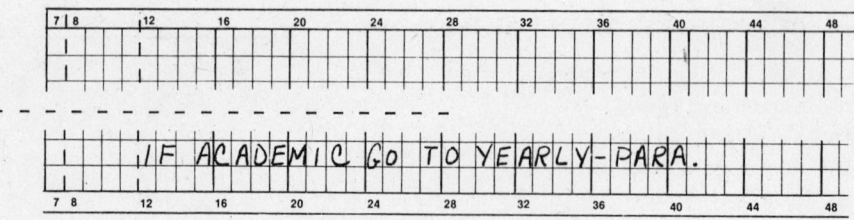

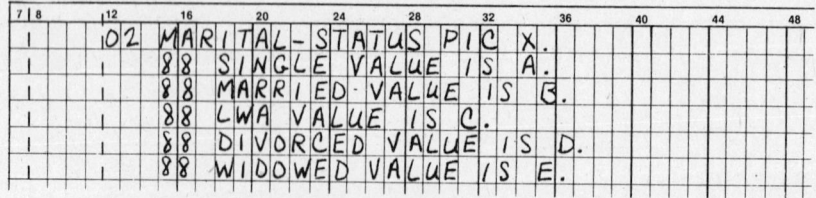

34. Refer to the condition description below.

```
02  MARITAL-STATUS PIC X.
    88  SINGLE VALUE IS A.
    88  MARRIED VALUE IS B.
    88  LWA VALUE IS C.
    88  DIVORCED VALUE IS D.
    88  WIDOWED VALUE IS E.
```

(a) The elementary data item here is _____.

(b) The conditional variable is _____.

(c) Condition-names have level number _____.

(a) MARITAL-STATUS; (b) MARITAL-STATUS; (c) 88

35. Write a statement to cause 1 to be added to SUM-S if the record indicates the person is single.

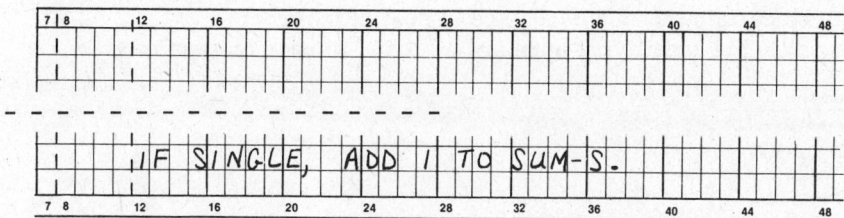

```
        IF SINGLE, ADD 1 TO SUM-S.
```

Every condition-name (level 88 item) must contain a VALUE clause. This is the only VALUE clause that may be specified in the File Section, however. VALUE clauses may be used as needed in the Working-Storage Section.

36. CLASS-LIST is a level 03 elementary data item that will contain a three-digit number. For the program under consideration it will contain 102 (FRESHMAN), 202 (SOPHOMORE), 302 (JUNIOR), or 402 (SENIOR). Write the entries to set CLASS-LIST up as a conditional variable.

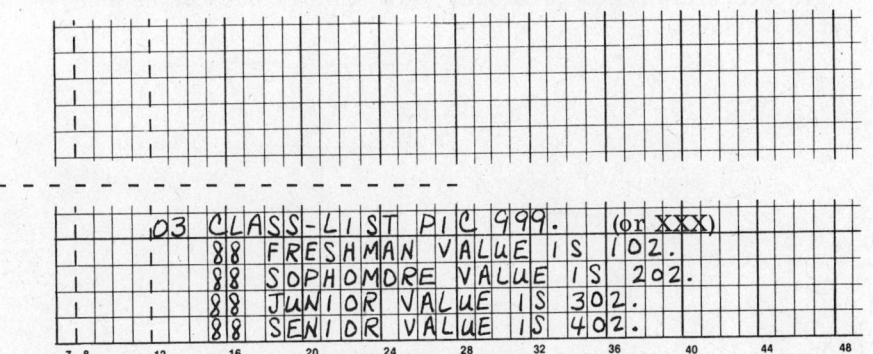

```
    03 CLASS-LIST PIC 999.    (or XXX)
       88 FRESHMAN VALUE IS 102.
       88 SOPHOMORE VALUE IS 202.
       88 JUNIOR VALUE IS 302.
       88 SENIOR VALUE IS 402.
```

You have learned to handle two types of conditions for use in IF statements. Other condition types, and amplifications of both the relational and condition-name conditions exist. As you become experienced in programming you will want to refer to the reference manual for your system to learn new ways of conditional branching within an ANS COBOL program.

37. As a programmer for a manufacturing plant, you might be asked to have a list made of certain records on a master tape file. You have a deck of cards containing stock numbers whose master records must be printed. Since each tape record (they are in sequential order) includes 120 characters, it can be moved to a printer record. Blanks will be placed at

the right. The only problem here is matching a card record with a tape record (using stock numbers) to ensure that the appropriate records are printed. In programming this problem, you would have to:

(a) read all card records first, then the tape records.
(b) be certain that the cards are in sequential order.
(c) compare identifying numbers on cards to ones on tape records.

---

b, c

38. Assume you have two separate card files. You wish to combine them into a single tape file, without duplication. For example, the first records in each file may be:

Card file 1	Card file 2
1010	1020
1030	1025
1040	1026
1060	1031
⋮	⋮

This is a record merging problem. Here is a flowchart of the merging part of the solution.

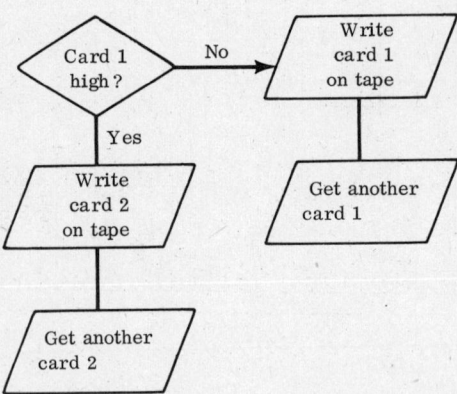

The major problem arises when you reach the end of one of the card files. Examine the flowchart segment.

(a) What must the program do if you run out of cards in Card file 1 first?

(b) What must it do if you run out of cards in Card file 2 first?

(a) Put the rest of the cards in file 2 on tape.
(b) Put the rest of the cards in file 1 on tape.

39. In general, a program must make sure that both files have reached the end. A master tape file and a transaction card deck that includes only some of them are often used to create a new master tape. This allows three possibilities for EOF:

> You run out of cards before you finish the records on input tape.
> You finish the input tape when you still have some cards left.
> The last record in each file match, so you finish both together.

Assuming that tape and card files are in ascending sequential order by an identifying number, decide how each condition might be handled.

(a) Finish transaction cards first. _____

_____

(b) Finish master tape first. _____

_____

(c) Finish both at once. _____

- - - - - - - - - - - - - - - - - -

(a) Put the rest of the input tape records on the output tape.
(b) Treat the rest of the card records as errors.
(c) Normal end of program.

REVIEW

40. The first three divisions of a program are given in Figure 6-1 on the next page. The files used include a master tape file, a card file containing customer numbers (CUST-NO) for very active customers, and a printer file for listing specific records from the tape. Both the master tape and the card file are in ascending sequence. Your problem is to find the master record for each active customer, and print certain information only if the variable PAYCODE has the value 6. In the partial program which is printed following the flowchart, you will notice in the Data Division that PAYCODE is a conditional variable. Use the flowchart as you write the Procedure Division for this record-matching problem to produce a report. Notice that we are not creating a new tape here. When the card file ends, the program can be ended. If the tape file happens to end first, display an error message and end the program. Space for writing your program begins on page 152.

150 ANS COBOL

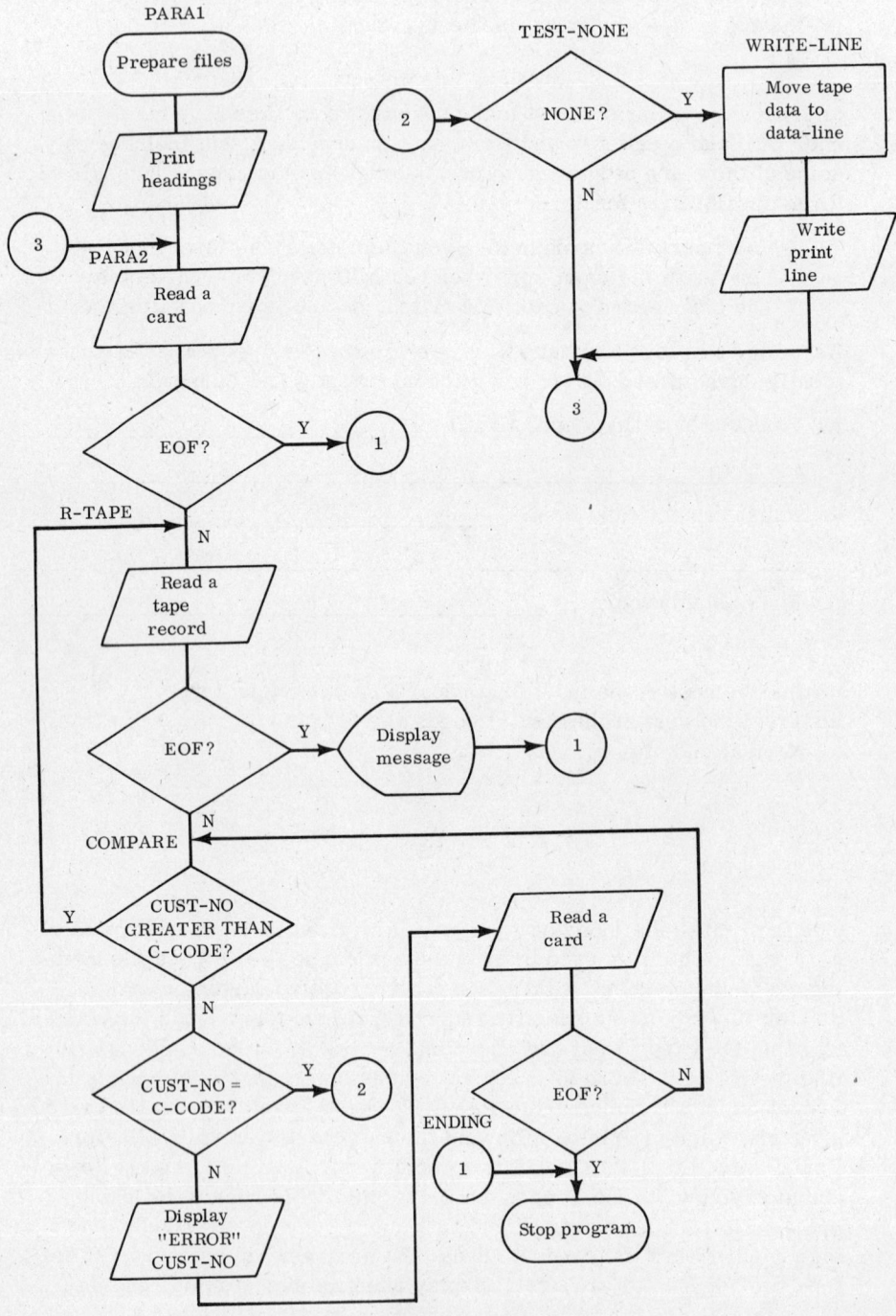

Figure 6-1

```cobol
       IDENTIFICATION DIVISION.
       PROGRAM-ID. PRINT-A-REPORT.
       ENVIRONMENT DIVISION.
       CONFIGURATION SECTION.
       SOURCE-COMPUTER. IBM-370.
       OBJECT-COMPUTER. IBM-370.
       INPUT-OUTPUT SECTION.
       FILE-CONTROL.
           SELECT TAPE-FILE ASSIGN UT-S-TAP01.
           SELECT CARD-FILE ASSIGN UR-S-CARD01.
           SELECT PRINT-FILE ASSIGN UR-S-PRINT01.

       DATA DIVISION.
       FILE SECTION.
       FD  TAPE-FILE
           LABEL RECORDS ARE STANDARD
           BLOCK CONTAINS 10 RECORDS.
       01  TAPE-RECORD.
           02  C-CODE PIC 9(9).
           02  PERSONAL-DATA.
               03  C-NAME PIC X(21).
               03  C-ADDRESS PIC X(30).
               03  C-PHONE PIC X(10).

           02  CREDIT-DATA.
               03  YR-OPENED PIC 99.
               03  MAX-CREDIT PIC 9999V99.
               03  PRESENT-DUE PIC S9999V99.
               03  PAYCODE PIC 9.
                   88  BAD VALUE IS 1.
                   88  POOR VALUE IS 2.
                   88  AVERAGE VALUE IS 3.
                   88  GOOD VALUE IS 4.
                   88  EXCELLENT VALUE IS 5.
                   88  NONE VALUE IS 6.
       FD  CARD-FILE
           LABEL RECORDS ARE OMITTED.
       01  CUSTOMER-ACTIVE.
           02  CUST-NO PIC 9(9).
           02  FILLER PIC X(71).
       FD  PRINT-FILE
           LABEL RECORDS ARE OMITTED.
       01  ONE-LINE PIC X(133).

       WORKING-STORAGE SECTION.
       01  HEAD-LINE.
           02  FILLER PIC X(59) VALUE SPACES.
           02  HEADING PIC X(16) VALUE IS
               "MISSING PAYCODES".
           02  FILLER PIC X(58) VALUE SPACES.
       01  DATA-LINE.
           02  FILLER PIC XX VALUE SPACES.
           02  C-CODE PIC 9(9).
           02  FILLER PIC X(10) VALUE SPACES.
           02  C-NAME PIC X(21).
           02  FILLER PIC X(10) VALUE SPACES.
           02  C-ADDRESS PIC X(30).
           02  FILLER PIC X(51) VALUE SPACES.
```

152 ANS COBOL

Write the Procedure Division for this program.

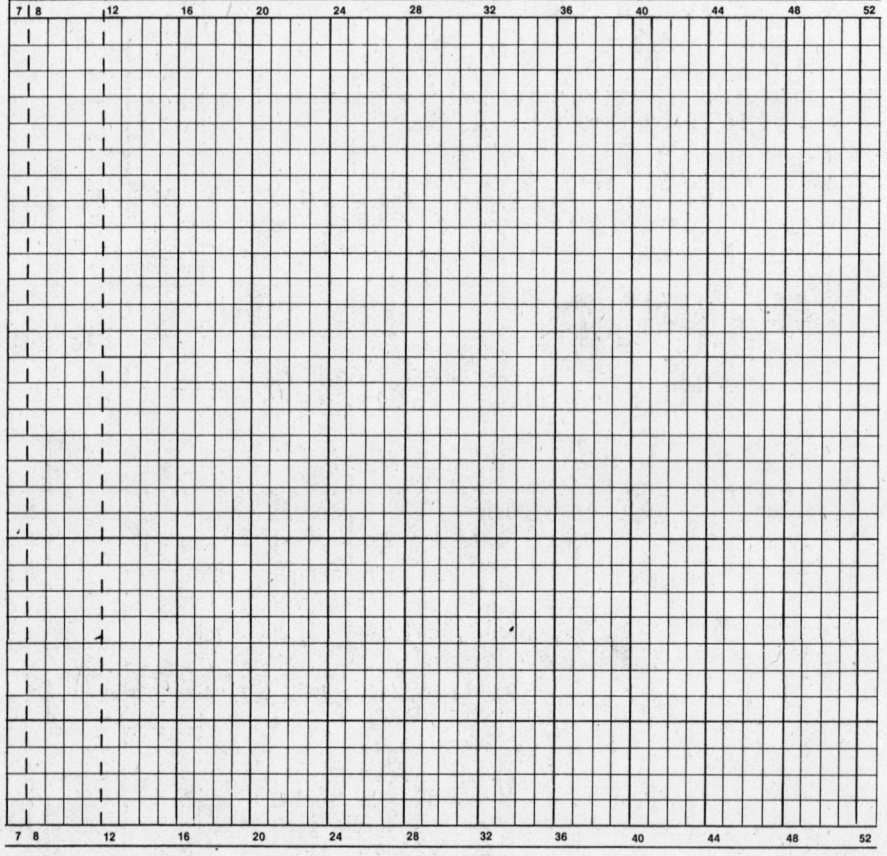

```
PROCEDURE DIVISION.
PARA1.
    OPEN INPUT TAPE-FILE CARD-FILE,
        OUTPUT PRINT-FILE.
    WRITE ONE-LINE FROM HEAD-LINE.
PARA2.
    READ CARD-FILE AT END GO TO ENDING.
R-TAPE.
    READ TAPE-FILE AT END DISPLAY "ERROR"
        GO TO ENDING.
COMPARE.
    IF CUST-NO GREATER THAN C-CODE GO TO
        R-TAPE.
    IF CUST-NO EQUAL TO C-CODE GO TO
        TEST-NONE.
    DISPLAY "ERROR" CUST-NO.
    READ CARD-FILE AT END GO TO ENDING.
    GO TO COMPARE.

TEST-NONE.
    IF NONE GO TO WRITE-LINE.
    GO TO PARA2.
WRITE-LINE.
    MOVE CORRESPONDING TAPE-RECORD TO
        DATA-LINE.
    WRITE ONE-LINE FROM DATA-LINE.
    GO TO PARA2.
ENDING.
    CLOSE TAPE-FILE CARD-FILE PRINT-FILE.
    STOP RUN.
```

CHAPTER SEVEN
Printed Reports

In this chapter you will expand your knowledge of printer files by learning many additional ways to edit data for appearance in reports. You will learn to arrange for vertical spacing in reports, so that the reports and the report items printed by the computer will be easy to read.

Specific COBOL features you will learn to use this chapter are:

- Simple insertion editing characters: 0 B + - DB CR
- Floating insertion editing characters: * + -
- BEFORE ADVANCING option of the WRITE statement
- AFTER ADVANCING option of the WRITE statement
- SPECIAL-NAMES paragraph of Configuration Section

In an earlier chapter you learned to use some simple insertion characters for editing numeric data items for use in printed reports. You have already used the editing symbols . $ Z and , in these report items. You will now learn some editing symbols which may be used in alphanumeric items, as well as more to use in numeric items.

EDITING ALPHANUMERIC AND NUMERIC DATA

Below is a table showing the result of use of two editing symbols.

Symbol	Result of Editing
0	a zero is inserted in the appropriate position
B	a blank is inserted in the appropriate position

1. The editing symbols 0 and B can be used to edit both numeric and alphanumeric data. Picture XXBXX would cause a source value of 1015 to be

printed as 10∅15. The picture XXXB99B99 would cause the value JAN1340 to be printed as: (Use ∅ to signify a blank.) _____

- - - - - - - - - - - - - - - - -

JAN∅13∅40

2. Here are several examples of edited data items.

Picture	Source Value	Report Items
XX0XX	AB3L	AB03L
99099	1234	12034
XBBX	-1	-∅∅1
90BX	1+	10∅+

   Refer to these examples as necessary to complete the table below.

Picture	Source Value	Report Items
XXXB	DAY	(a) _____
X0XBX	DAY	(b) _____
99B00	57	(c) _____
900B9	57	(d) _____

- - - - - - - - - - - - - - - - -

(a) DAY∅; (b) D0A∅Y; (c) 57∅00; (d) 500∅7

3. Specify whether each of the following pictures represents an alphanumeric or numeric data item.

   (a) 9(5)V99 _____ (c) 99XX999 _____

   (b) X(7)99 _____   (d) S99V9 _____

- - - - - - - - - - - - - - - - -

(a) numeric; (b) alphanumeric; (c) alphanumeric; (d) numeric

4. Which of the four choices in the preceding frame could be edited with the character:

   (a) $ _____

   (b) 0 _____

   (c) B _____

- - - - - - - - - - - - - - - - -

(a) a, d; (b) all; (c) all

5. The editing symbols B and 0 can be used to edit which types of data items for reports? _____

- - - - - - - - - - - - - - - - -

   numeric and alphanumeric

6. The editing symbols $, and . can be used to edit which types of items for use in reports? _____

- - - - - - - - - - - - - - - - -

   numeric only

7. The source value 39YZ is a code number. For inclusion in a printed report, it is to appear as 3ø90øYZ. Which of the pictures below describes this report item?

   (a) 9B99BXX
   (b) 9B90B99
   (c) XBX0BXX

   _____

- - - - - - - - - - - - - - - - -

   c   (a uses a 9 in the zero position; b uses 9's in alphabetic positions.)

8. The source value of ZYX is to be printed as Z0øY0X. Write its picture.

   _____

- - - - - - - - - - - - - - - - -

   X0BX0X   (Actually, A0BA0A would also be correct, but most programmers would use the X character even for alphabetic fields.)

9. Write pictures to describe the report items derived from the source values below.

Source Value	Report Item	Picture of Report Item
N37	Nøø300ø7	(a) _____
193̭2	$00193.20	(b) _____
57 (PIC XX)	5700	(c) _____

- - - - - - - - - - - - - - - - -

   (a) XBBX00BX, or XBB900B9
   (b) $00999.90, or $99999.99
   (c) XX00

EDITING OF SIGNED VALUES

10. Simple insertion editing can also be used to indicate the sign (positive or negative) of a numeric source value in a printed report. This can be done, of course, only if the source value was originally described with an S, which gives it an operational sign. Which of the values represented by their pictures below could be printed with a plus or minus sign?

    (a) 99V99
    (b) S99
    (c) S9(8)
    (d) SV9
    (e) SXX

---

b, c, d   (a is not described with an S; e is an invalid picture, since S cannot be used with alphanumeric items.)

11. Which types of data items could be edited with a plus or minus sign?

---

numeric only

Numeric Edit Symbol	Location in Picture	Effect on Report Item
+	rightmost or leftmost	+ inserted if value positive - inserted if value negative
-	rightmost or leftmost	- inserted if value negative; otherwise blank inserted
DB	rightmost	DB inserted if value negative; otherwise two blanks
CR	rightmost	CR inserted if value negative; otherwise two blanks

12. Examine the editing chart above. Which editing symbol would result in the printing of a minus sign if the value were negative? _____

+ or -

158 ANS COBOL

13. Which character would result in the printing of a plus sign if the value were positive? _____

+

14. Which of the pictures below seem correct, based on the location information given in the table?

(a) 99-99   (e) 99BCR
(b) -9999   (f) XXCR
(c) -99.99   (g) -XX
(d) DB99   (h) +09

_____

----

b, c, e, h   (In a, - is neither rightmost nor leftmost; in d, DB is not rightmost; in f and g, the data item is not numeric, even though the editing symbols are correctly placed.)

15. A data item with a source value of $\overline{2}92$ (described with PIC S999; since S is not a character position the sign is indicated above the leftmost digit) could be edited in many different ways. Some of these various editing pictures are shown below. Complete the report item for each picture, based on this source value.

Picture	Report Item
999+	(a) _____
999-	(b) _____
999DB	(c) _____
999CR	(d) _____

(a) 292-; (b) 292-; (c) 292DB; (d) 292CR

16. Now assume the source value is $\overset{+}{2}92$. Refer to the editing chart on page 157 and supply the report items below.

Picture	Report Item
999BCR	(a) _____
+999	(b) _____
-999	(c) _____

(a) 292ᵦᵦᵦ   (one ᵦ for the B, and two for the CR)
(b) +292
(c) ᵦ292

17. Complete the values of report items below.

Source Value	Picture	Report Item
28̄7̂5	99.99+	(a) _____
+̂123	999DB	(b) _____
1̄2̂3	$9.99BCR	(c) _____
+̂4438	-9(4)	(d) _____

- - - - - - - - - - - - - - - - - - - -

(a) 28.75-; (b) 123ᵦᵦ; (c) $1.23ᵦCR; (d) ᵦ4438

18. Write a picture to print a five-digit number with an actual decimal point following the leftmost digit. The operational sign is to be printed at the left whether it is positive or negative. _____

- - - - - - - - - - - - - - - - - -

+9.9999, or +9.9(4)

19. Write pictures for the following report items, all using the source value 12̂98.

    (a) 12.98ᵦDB _____   (c) -12.980 _____
    (b) $0012.98 _____   (d) 12.98CR _____

- - - - - - - - - - - - - - - -

(a) 99.99BDB
(b) $0099.99, or $9(4).99
(c) -99.990, or -99.999
(d) 99.99CR

20. Social security numbers are usually considered as three groups of digits; the first group has three, the second two, and the third four digits. If the source value were described as X(9), what picture would you write to separate the groups with a single space? _____

- - - - - - - - - - - - - - - -

XXXBXXBXXXX (This picture could not be described with 9's since the source value is alphanumeric. A source value described with X's cannot be moved to a numeric edited report item.)

FLOATING INSERTION AND ZERO SUPPRESSION CHARACTERS

Certain editing characters are capable of "floating" through a report item. In these cases, as you saw with the floating $, leading zeros may be suppressed and replaced by blanks. The editing character is then printed immediately before the first non-zero digit in the value. In the following section, you will learn to use more floating editing symbols.

21. As you recall, the leftmost digit position in a string of edit Z's must contain a Z. However, an insertion character can be inserted to the left of this position. Thus a $, a plus sign, or a minus sign could appear immediately to the left of a Z in a picture. The simple insertion character follows its usual rules and is printed in the specified position whether the Z positions are suppressed or not. A picture of +ZZZ and a source value of $\overline{0}70$ would produce an edited result of -ƀ70. Examine the source values and pictures below, then write the resulting report items. Use ƀ to represent blanks.

Source Value	Picture	Report Item
02̭98	$ZZ.ZZ	(a) _____
+̭0003	+ZZ99	(b) _____
$\overline{0}$003	-Z(4)	(c) _____
+̭0000̭8	-ZZZZ.Z	(d) _____
+̭0000̭0	-ZZZZ.Z	(e) _____

(a) $ƀ2.98; (b) +ƀƀ03; (c) -ƀƀƀ3; (d) ƀƀƀƀ.8; (e) ƀƀƀƀƀƀ

22. The plus and minus signs in the preceding frame could also be specified at the rightmost end of the picture. Only one simple insertion character may appear to the left of the Z string. Write a picture to accommodate a five-digit number with three digit positions to the right of the decimal point. The edited item should include a dollar sign, a sign only if the value is negative, and appear as all blanks if the value should happen to be zero. _____

$ZZ.ZZZ+

23. You have seen that simple insertion characters may precede a string of Z's ($ + or -) or follow the string (+ or -). You know now that the actual decimal point may be included in the string, and may even be

suppressed if all digit positions are replaced by blanks. The other insertion characters may also be included within the string of Z's. B and 0, like the comma, will be suppressed if they appear to the left of the first printed digit. Thus the source value of 06413 described with a picture Z,ZZZ.9 would be printed as ƀƀ641.3. Examine the source values and pictures below, then write the related report items.

Source Value	Picture	Report Item
0357900	$ZZ,ZZZ.ZZ	(a) _____
003̄	-ZZZ.00	(b) _____
010573	ZZBZZBZZ	(c) _____

- - - - - - - - - - - - - - - - - - -

(a) $ƀ3,579.00   (The comma is not suppressed here, as it is to the right of the first digit.)
(b) -ƀƀ3.00
(c) ƀ1ƀ05ƀ73
(B 0 and , may be suppressed; + - and $ are not unless the entire item is blanks. Actually, the B represents a blank whether it is suppressed or not.)

24. Any time the value of a data item is zero and all digit positions contain Z's, no value is printed; all reserved positions contain blanks. Give the printed report item for each of the pictures below, assuming the source value is zero. Be sure to indicate the appropriate number of blanks.

(a) $ZZ,ZZZ.99 _____

(b) $Z,ZZZ,ZZZ.ZZ _____

(c) -ZZZZZ.Z _____

(d) +ZZZBZZZ0 _____

- - - - - - - - - - - - - - - - - - -

(a) $ƀƀƀƀƀƀ.00
(b) ƀƀƀƀƀƀƀƀƀƀƀƀƀ (thirteen blanks)
(c) ƀƀƀƀƀƀƀƀ (eight blanks)
(d) ƀƀƀƀƀƀƀƀƀ (nine blanks)

25. To summarize, the floating insertion character Z causes suppression of leading zeros and placement of a blank in each suppressed position. Simple insertion characters may be used but will be suppressed under certain conditions. Assume a source value to be 000498731. Write a picture for a report item that will cause it to be printed as $ƀƀƀ4,987.31.

_____

- - - - - - - - - - - - - - - - - - -

$ZZZ9,999.99 (from three to seven or nine Z's may be used)

26. Assume a source value originally described as 9(7).9 is being edited. Write a picture that would produce a plus sign if the value were positive, then two blanks, then suppress any leading zeros and insert commas in appropriate positions. If the actual source value is zero, the entire item is to be left blank. _____

- - - - - - - - - - - - - - - - - -

+BBZ,ZZZ ZZZ.Z (all digit positions must contain Z's)

27. Another floating insertion character is the asterisk. This symbol, *, is often used for check protection, as it effectively prevents alterations of checks. Most of the rules governing the use of the * are the same as those for the Z, except that suppressed positions, whether 0, comma, or other insertion characters, are replaced with *'s rather than with blanks. A source value of 0000098 with a picture of $***,***.** would be printed as $*****9.98. Now complete the examples below.

Source Value	Picture	Report Item
12750	$*,***.99	(a) _____
0049	$****.00	(b) _____
000298	**99.99	(c) _____

- - - - - - - - - - - - - - - - -

(a) $**127.50 (comma is suppressed)
(b) $**49.00
(c) **02.98

28. The rules governing use of the asterisk differ from those governing use of the Z in one important way: an actual decimal point or a dollar sign in a string of asterisks is never suppressed. A source value of zero with a picture of **.** would be printed as **.**. With a picture of $**.** it would be printed $**.**. What would be printed if the value zero were assigned to a picture $*,***.*? _____

- - - - - - - - - - - - - - - - -

$*****.* (Remember, the comma would be replaced by an asterisk, but the dollar sign and period would not.)

29. In addition to their functions as simple insertion characters, the editing symbols $ + and - can also be used for floating insertion. In these

cases, zero suppression occurs as with Z, but the floating character is inserted immediately preceding the first printed digit. Thus $$$$ might be the picture for a source value of 009. This would produce a report item of ƀƀ$9. The insertion character is suppressed and replaced with a blank in positions to the left of where it is printed. Note that in total you need one more floating insertion character than digit positions to be edited. That is, four digit positions are edited using five dollar signs. To review the floating dollar sign, what report items would be produced from the information below?

Source Value	Picture	Report Item
0300͜00	$$,$$$.$$	(a) _____
1209͜73	$$,$$$.$$	(b) _____
0000͜84	$$,$$$.$$	(c) _____

(a) ƀƀ$300.00 (The $ here actually appears in the , position.)
(b) $1,209.73
(c) ƀƀƀƀƀ$.84

30. Write the characters that would be printed as a result of each of these pictures. The rules governing the printing of floating plus and minus are the same as for fixed signs.

Source Value	Picture	Report Item
6̄78	++,+++	(a) _____
+678	--,---	(b) _____
+7763	++,+++	(c) _____

(a) ƀƀ-678
(b) ƀƀƀ678 (The - editing symbol does not cause a plus sign to be printed.)
(c) +7,763

31. Simple insertion characters B 0 and , that appear in floating strings are suppressed and replaced with the floating character if they appear to the left of the first printed digit. As you discovered in earlier frames, the decimal point acts more like a printed digit in this case. Give the printed result for each of the following.

Source Value	Picture	Report Item
$\overline{0033333}$	++++++++	(a) _____
$\overset{+}{0008}$	-----00	(b) _____
00123̭45	$$$,$$$.99	(c) _____

- - - - - - - - - - - - - - - - - -

(a) ⌽⌽-33333
(b) ⌽⌽⌽⌽800   (Notice that the floating minus sign is suppressed here in accordance with rules for -.)
(c) ⌽⌽⌽$123.45

32. The floating insertion characters $ + and - must begin one position to the left of the leftmost digit position. Like the Z, however, either all none of the positions to the right of the decimal point must contain the floating character. Assuming that the source value is zero, the decimal point will be suppressed when floating characters $ + or - are used in all digit positions. Give the printed result of each of the following.

Source Value	Picture	Report Item
$\overset{+}{00786\!\!\downarrow\!\!982}$	+++,+++,+++	(a) _____
zero	+++,+++.+++	(b) _____
zero	+++,+++.999	(c) _____
zero	***,***.***	(d) _____

- - - - - - - - - - - - - - - - - -

(a) ⌽⌽⌽+786.982
(b) ⌽⌽⌽⌽⌽⌽⌽⌽⌽⌽⌽ (eleven blanks)
(c) ⌽⌽⌽⌽⌽⌽⌽.000 (The value zero is not positive.)
(d) *******.***

33. A few general rules apply to floating insertion characters. Only one may be used in a single picture. And when $ is floated, the plus and minus signs may be used as simple insertion characters only at the right-most position. Write a picture for a source value that might be $\overline{00386}$ or zero. The picture should result in the printing of a dollar sign immediately preceding the first non-zero digit, a sign if the value is positive or negative, and an actual decimal point. The item is to contain all blanks if the value is zero. _____

- - - - - - - - - - - - - - - - - -

$$$$$.$+

By this point, you should be able to specify any valid picture depending on your desired output. In Appendix E, you will find a summary of all editing characters described here.

VERTICAL SPACING OPTIONS

34. In this section, you will learn to specify spacing in your standard output statements. The system will place the appropriate character in the carriage-control position, so you must still leave it blank. The standard output statement for a printer is _____.

WRITE

35. The format below shows the BEFORE ADVANCING option of the WRITE statement.

> WRITE file-name BEFORE ADVANCING integer LINES

When this option is used, the printer prints a record into the specified file, then advances the number of lines specified. The statement WRITE PRINTOUT BEFORE ADVANCING 2 LINES would cause the computer to:

(a) advance two lines, then print a record on PRINTOUT
(b) print two lines, then advance.
(c) print a record on PRINTOUT, then advance two lines.

_____

---

c

36. The normal use of the WRITE statement to refer to a printer file causes single spacing if the ADVANCING option is not specified. To specify single spacing using the BEFORE ADVANCING option, you could write:

```
        BEFORE ADVANCING 1 LINES
```

(You could omit the word LINES, because it is optional in this context. If you use it, however, it must be LINES, not LINE. Don't forget: Words in all capitals in formats must be written exactly as they appear.)

37. The BEFORE ADVANCING option may specify a data-name instead of an integer, but the data item must have a nonnegative integer value. Assume COUNTX has a value of 4, and write a statement that would result in printing a record in file OUTGO, then advancing the printer four lines.

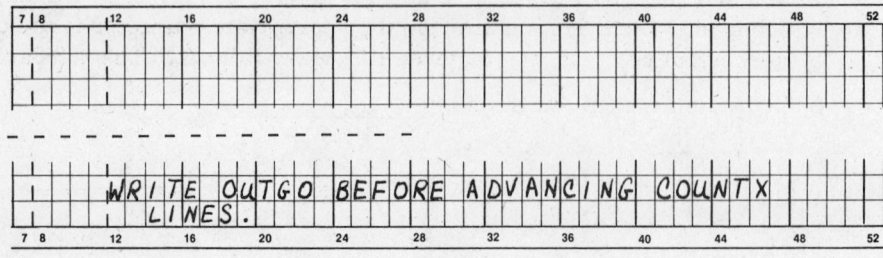

WRITE OUTGO BEFORE ADVANCING COUNTX LINES.

(Although the word LINES is optional, we will use it throughout the rest of this guide.)

38. A more complete format of the WRITE statement with two ADVANCING options is shown below.

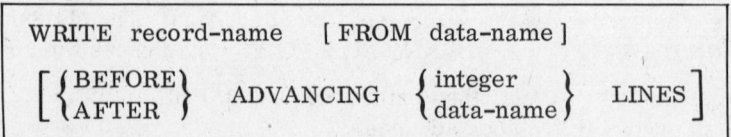

WRITE record-name [FROM data-name]
[{BEFORE / AFTER} ADVANCING {integer / data-name} LINES]

The advancing of the printer can be specified:

(a) only before the record is written.
(b) only after the record is written.
(c) both before and after the record is written.
(d) before or after the record is written, but not both.

---

d   (Recall that brackets in a format indicate an option. The FROM option and ADVANCING options are used at the programmer's discretion.)

39. Assume that one line has been printed, and the printer remains positioned at that line. What ADVANCING option would you specify to cause two blank lines to appear before the next record printed?

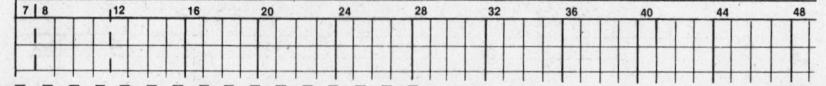

PRINTED REPORTS 167

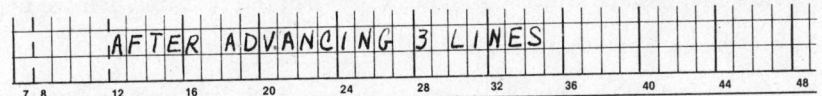

40. If an ADVANCING option is specified in one WRITE statement for a file, then each WRITE statement referring to that file must contain an ADVANCING option. Suppose that you need normal single spacing for a report, except for a blank line after the heading at the top of the page.

   (a) What ADVANCING option would you specify to print the heading?

   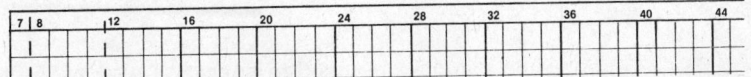

   (b) What option, if any, would you specify for the normal single spacing of the body of the report?

   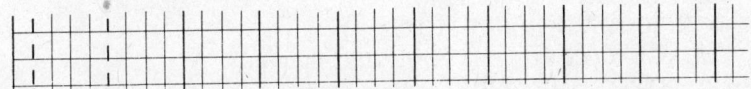

   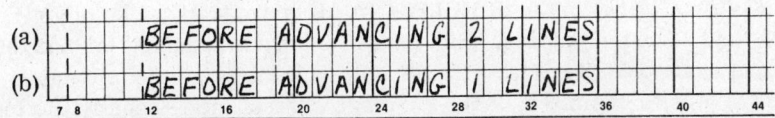

   (If you used AFTER for the b option you would have two blank lines following the heading, instead of one as desired. The body of the report would then be single spaced, however.)

41. Assume that records are being printed in accordance with the specifications below:

    ```
    H      WRITE OUT-FILE FROM HEAD2
              BEFORE ADVANCING 3 LINES.
    I      WRITE OUT-FILE FROM INFORM
              AFTER ADVANCING 3 LINES.
    S      WRITE OUT-FILE FROM SUMMARY
              AFTER ADVANCING 2 LINES.
    T      WRITE OUT-FILE FROM TOTAL
              BEFORE ADVANCING 4 LINES.
    ```

   (a) How many blank lines will appear between the line printed by statement H and the first line printed by I? _____

(b) How many blank lines will appear between the last line printed by statement I and that printed by S? _____

(c) How many blank lines will appear between the line printed by statement S and that printed by T? _____

(a) five (three caused by the statement H and two by statement I)
(b) one
(c) none (Note: Mixing BEFORE and AFTER ADVANCING options can cause problems. Except in rare programs, the use of just one option will usually be sufficient.)

42. The ADVANCING option can also be used to specify a skip to the top of the next page. To do this, we must add another paragraph to the Configuration Section of the Environment Division.

    ENVIRONMENT DIVISION.
    CONFIGURATION SECTION.
    SOURCE-COMPUTER. computer-name.
    OBJECT-COMPUTER. computer-name.
    SPECIAL-NAMES. system-literal IS mnemonic-name.

The system-literal in the SPECIAL-NAMES paragraph, like other Environment Division entries, may have a different required format for various systems. Here we will use only one fairly common format, C01, which refers to channel 1 of the carriage control tape—usually the top of the next page. A mnemonic is a memory-aiding device; the name selected is usually very descriptive of its function. Write a SPECIAL-NAMES paragraph to define the top of each page as TOP-NEXT.

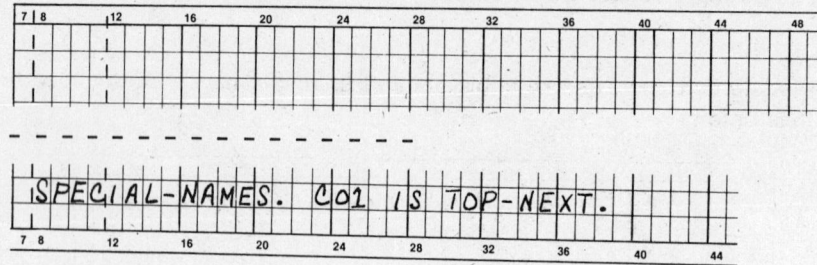

43.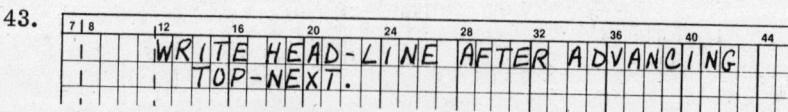

This statement would cause a line to be printed after:

(a) skipping TOP-NEXT lines.

(b) advancing to the top of the next page.
(c) C01 lines.

---

b

44. AFTER ADVANCING mnemonic-name is often used to skip to the top of the next page and print headings. Write a statement that will cause the printer to advance to the top of the next page, then write the output record PRINT-LINE from a Working-Storage record PAGE-LABEL. Use mnemonic-name TO-TOP.

```
         WRITE PRINT-LINE FROM PAGE-LABEL
            AFTER ADVANCING TO-TOP.
```

45. In the example of the preceding frame, TO-TOP must have been defined in the:

    (a) _____ Division.
    (b) _____ Section.
    (c) _____ paragraph.

(a) Environment; (b) Configuration; (c) SPECIAL-NAMES (C01 IS TO-TOP.)

46. In a multi-page report, the program must have a way of telling when to start a new page and print headings again. This is commonly done by counting lines. Counting lines involves several steps.

> A line counter must be defined in Working-Storage.
> The line counter must be increased each time a line is printed.
> The line counter must be tested before each line to see if it has reached the maximum per page.

Write statements to accomplish the following.

(a) Define LINE-COUNT as an independent variable—up to 2 positions.

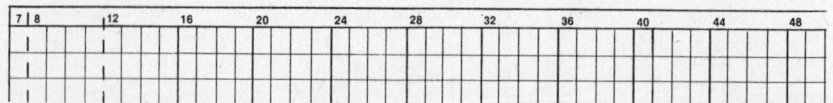

(b) Write a statement to increment the counter after a double-spaced line is printed.

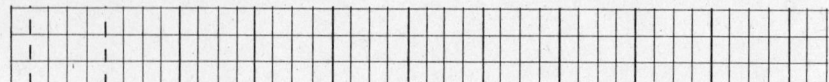

(c) Write a statement to test the counter and branch to PRINT-HEADS if it is over 60.

(d) Where would be an appropriate place to set LINE-COUNT back to zero? _____

- - - - - - - - - - - - - - - - - -

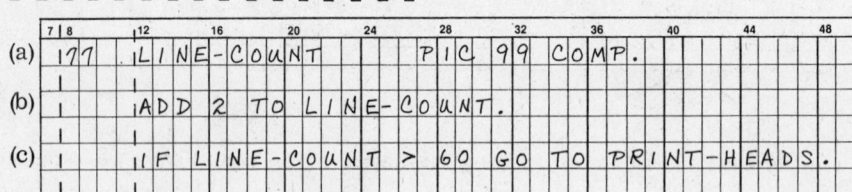

(a) 77 LINE-COUNT   PIC 99 COMP.
(b)   ADD 2 TO LINE-COUNT.
(c)   IF LINE-COUNT > 60 GO TO PRINT-HEADS.
(d) before printing the headings

REVIEW

47. Working-Storage entries describing two heading lines are shown on the program sheet on the next page. Descriptions of report items, including data-names and print columns to line up with headings are given in the table following the program sheet. Use these descriptions of edited items to write a record description for TRANS-LINE, in the blank coding form on page 172.

```
WORKING-STORAGE SECTION.
01  HEADING-1.
    02  FILLER PIC X(58) VALUE SPACES.
    02  HEAD1 PIC X(18) VALUE
        "DAILY TRANSACTIONS".
    02  FILLER PIC X(57) VALUE SPACES.
01  HEADING-2.
    02  FILLER PIC X(6) VALUE SPACES.
    02  COLA PIC X(15) VALUE
        "CUSTOMER NUMBER".
    02  FILLER PIC X(4) VALUE SPACES.
    02  COLB PIC X(4) VALUE "NAME".
    02  FILLER PIC X(25) VALUE SPACES.
    02  COLC PIC X(4) VALUE "CODE".
    02  FILLER PIC X(5) VALUE SPACES.
    02  COLD PIC X(6) VALUE "AMOUNT".
    02  FILLER PIC X(9) VALUE SPACES.
    02  COLE PIC X(11) VALUE "NEW BALANCE".
    02  FILLER PIC X(6) VALUE SPACES.
    02  COLF PIC X(7) VALUE "DUE NOW".
    02  FILLER PIC X(7) VALUE SPACES.
    02  COLG PIC X(4) VALUE "DATE".
    02  FILLER PIC X(20) VALUE SPACES.
```

Data-Name	Column	Description
C-NUMB	9	6 digits; insert 0 between sets of two.
C-NAME	26	20 characters; insert blank between 12th and 13th.
C-CODE	55	1 digit.
C-AMT	64	6 digits, 2 to right of decimal point; all digits replaced with blanks if zero.
C-NEW-BAL	79	6 digits, 2 to right of decimal point; comma in appropriate position, fixed dollar sign, sign if value negative, item all asterisks if zero.
C-DUE	96	5 digits, 2 to right of decimal point; dollar sign just before first non-zero digit. Blank if zero.
C-DATE	110	3 sets of two-digit numbers; insert blanks between sets.

```
 7 8   12    16    20    24    28    32    36    40    44    48    52
 01   TRANS-LINE.
```

```
 7 8   12    16    20    24    28    32    36    40    44    48    52
 01   TRANS-LINE.
      02  FILLER   PIC  X(8)  VALUE SPACES.
      02  C-NUMB   PIC  XX0XX0XX.
      02  FILLER   PIC  X(9)  VALUE SPACES.
      02  C-NAME   PIC  X(12) BX(8).
      02  FILLER   PIC  X(8)  VALUE SPACES.
      02  C-CODE   PIC  9.
      02  FILLER   PIC  X(8)  VALUE SPACES.
      02  C-AMT    PIC  ZZZZ.ZZ.
      02  FILLER   PIC  X(8)  VALUE SPACES.
      02  C-NEW-BAL PIC $*,***.**-.
      02  FILLER   PIC  X(7)  VALUE SPACES.
      02  C-DUE    PIC  $$$$.$$.
      02  FILLER   PIC  X(7)  VALUE SPACES.
      02  C-DATE   PIC  XXBXXBXX.
      02  FILLER   PIC  X(16) VALUE SPACES.
```

(Total 133 spaces. You could have used 9's instead of X's in the lines for C-NUMB and C-DATE.)

48. The heading and data lines described in the preceding frame are to be written on the output file OUTFILE using the output record OUTREC. The major heading is to be printed on the top line of a new page. The column headings will be printed four lines below the major heading. The information lines, edited as you have specified, will then be double-spaced. Write the statements required to cause this vertical placement of the records in the output file from the major heading through the first detail line. Use NEXT-PAGE as the mnemonic-name, and the AFTER ADVANCING option.

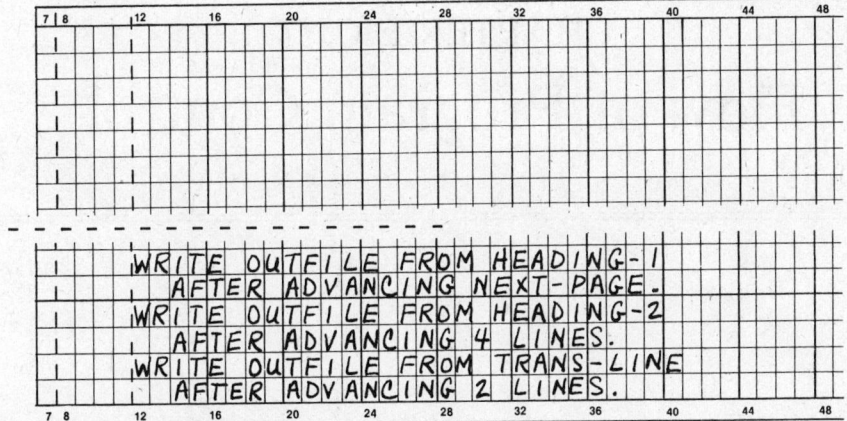

The last few frames have tested most of the material you learned in this chapter. For this reason, no complete program is included here. The chart in Appendix E, which summarizes the editing characters, will be of use to you later as you put your editing skills to work.

CHAPTER EIGHT
Flow of Program Control

Flow of control in an ANS COBOL program normally passes from one statement to the next in sequence as written by the programmer. You have already learned to alter this flow with a STOP RUN statement and with a GO TO statement; in this chapter, you will learn to use another statement. The many options of this statement make it an extremely powerful device for the programmer; they also simplify many of the coding problems he or she will face.

The specific ANS COBOL features you will learn to use in this chapter are:

- PERFORM statement
- THRU option of the PERFORM statement
- TIMES option of the PERFORM statement
- UNTIL option of the PERFORM statement
- VARYING option of the PERFORM statement
- EXIT statement
- DEPENDING ON option of the GO TO statement

PERFORM STATEMENT

1. The PERFORM statement specifies a temporary alteration in flow of control in an ANS COBOL program. The format for the PERFORM statement and an example are shown below.

   > PERFORM paragraph-name.

   example: PERFORM CALCULATIONS.

The GO TO statement, as you have already learned, causes a permanent alteration. When a PERFORM statement as above is executed, the specified paragraph is executed next, then control returns to the statement directly following PERFORM. In contrast, the GO TO statement causes, after execution of the specified paragraph:

(a) control to be returned to GO TO.
(b) control to be passed to the next paragraph.
(c) control to be returned to the statement following GO TO.
(d) a temporary transfer of control.

- - - - - - - - - - - - - - - - - -

b

2. The schematic on the right shows the order in which ANS COBOL entries might be written. List the order in which they would be executed.

    (a) PERFORM PO
    (b) WRITE
    (c) STOP
    (d) PO

START

- - - - - - - - - - - - - - - - - -

a, d, b, then c

3. Write statements to transfer control to paragraph RE-SET:

(a) temporarily.

(b) permanently.

- - - - - - - - - - - - - - - - - -

(a)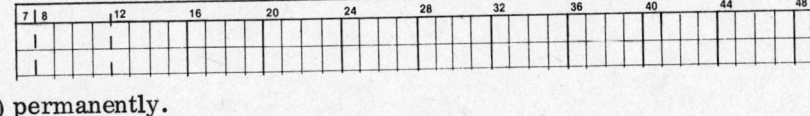
PERFORM RE-SET.

(b)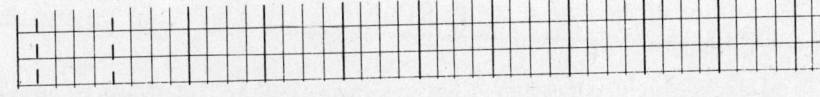
GO TO RE-SET.

4. After execution of RE-SET, control returns to the statement following one you wrote in the preceding frame. Which one? _____

- - - - - - - - - - - - - - - - - -

PERFORM RE-SET.

5. A more complete format of the PERFORM statement is shown below.

> PERFORM paragraph-name-1 [THRU paragraph-name-2]

This statement is used to specify that the next statements to be executed in your program are those found in paragraph-name-1 continuing sequentially through intervening statements until the end of paragraph-name-2. Control is then returned to the statement immediately following the PERFORM statement. Which flowchart below represents execution of the statement PERFORM PARA1 THRU PARA2. ?

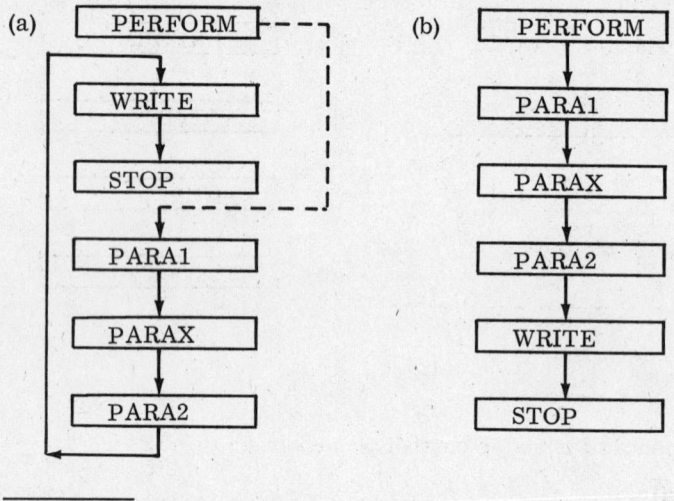

- - - - - - - - - - - - - - - - - - - -

a

6. Execution of the statement PERFORM ITEM-ANALYSIS THRU PRINTOUT. would cause:

   (a) execution of paragraphs ITEM-ANALYSIS and PRINTOUT with any intervening paragraphs.
   (b) control to return to the statement directly following PERFORM after the specified paragraphs are executed.

(c) control to be transferred to ITEM-ANALYSIS to proceed through PRINTOUT and continue as in a GO TO statement.

---

a, b

7. The THRU option of the PERFORM statement is optional. You would need to specify it only when you wish to have executed:

   (a) just one paragraph.
   (b) more than one paragraph.
   (c) at least two, but possibly more, paragraphs.

---

b, c

8. Write a statement that would cause execution of a paragraph called PRINT-HEADINGS, then return control to the statement directly following the one you write here.

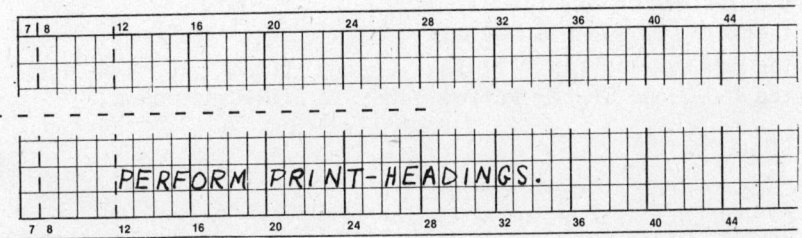

9. Write a statement to transfer control to PRINT-HEADINGS, then continue in sequence following PRINT-HEADINGS.

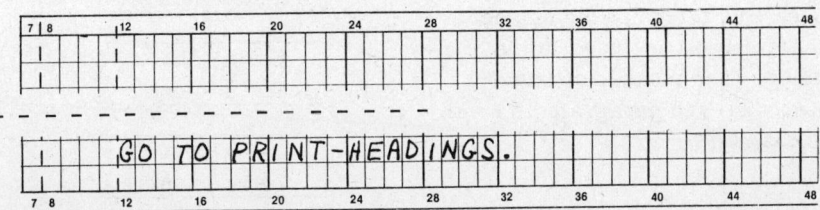

10. A sequence of paragraphs in a program are named A-PARA, B-PARA, C-PARA, and D-PARA. Write a single statement to cause execution of B-PARA, C-PARA, and D-PARA, then return control to the statement following the one you write.

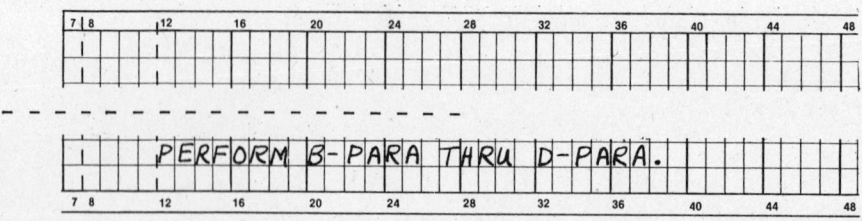

11. The range of a PERFORM statement includes all statements from the first statement in paragraph-name-1 through the last in paragraph-name-2. If paragraph-name-2 is not specified, the last statement in the range of a PERFORM would be _____.

- - - - - - - - - - - - - - - - - -

the last statement in paragraph-name-1

12. Refer back to frame 10. Which of the following statements would be in the range of PERFORM B-PARA THRU D-PARA. ?

    (a) the first statement in D-PARA
    (b) the third statement in C-PARA
    (c) the last statement in A-PARA
    (d) the statement directly following the PERFORM statement

_____

- - - - - - - - - - - - - - - - - -

a, b

13. Several PERFORM statements are given below. Give the range of each in terms of the number of statements included in the range. The number of statements in each paragraph is given on the right.

A-PARA
2 statements

B-PARA
4 statements

C-PARA
7 statements

D-PARA
5 statements

    (a) PERFORM C-PARA. Range is _____.

(b) PERFORM A-PARA THRU C-PARA. Range is _____.

(c) PERFORM B-PARA THRU C-PARA. Range is _____.

- - - - - - - - - - - - - - - - - -

(a) 7; (b) 13; (c) 11

14. In order to execute these paragraphs in the sequence C, D, A, B, a programmer would have to write two successive PERFORM statements.

        PERFORM C-PARA THRU D-PARA.
        PERFORM A-PARA THRU B-PARA.

    | A-PARA |
    | B-PARA |
    | C-PARA |
    | D-PARA |

    Write the statements that you would need to execute them in the sequence B, C, A, omitting D-PARA.

- - - - - - - - - - - - - - - - - -

```
PERFORM B-PARA THRU C-PARA.
PERFORM A-PARA.
```

15. The PERFORM and GO TO statements are both very powerful, but you must be careful when using them together. While a GO TO can be used to transfer control within the range, this should not transfer control out of the range. Refer to the solution to previous frame. Which of the statements below can safely be included in B-PARA?

    (a) GO TO C-PARA.
    (b) GO TO A-PARA.
    (c) GO TO D-PARA.

    _____

- - - - - - - - - - - - - - - - - -

a

PERFORM statements can stand alone (example 1 on the next page) or can be included in IF statements (example 2). PERFORM could also be specified in an AT END option of READ or the ON SIZE ERROR option of an arithmetic statement. The examples on the next page show two uses of PERFORM.

Notice in example 2 that PERFORMs can occur within the range of another PERFORM. GO TO statements are a different problem, as we have seen.

1.
```
        PERFORM INITIAL-ROUTINE.
           .
           .
    INITIAL-ROUTINE.
        MOVE ZEROS TO LINE-NUM, PAGE-NUM,
            TOTAL.
        MOVE SPACES TO PERSONAL-DATA.
        ACCEPT TODAYS-DATE.
```

2.
```
        IF LINE-NUM GREATER THAN 54 PERFORM
            TOP-PAGE THRU TOP-2.
           .
           .
    TOP-PAGE.
        ADD 1 TO PAGE-NUM.
        WRITE LINEX FROM D-RECORD AFTER
            ADVANCING NEXT-ONE.
    TOP-2.
        PERFORM PAGE-HEADINGS.
        MOVE 6 TO LINE-NUM.
```

TIMES OPTION OF PERFORM

16. In the PERFORM statements you have seen so far, the statements in the specified paragraph are executed once, then control is returned to the statement directly following PERFORM. If you write PERFORM A-PARA 6 TIMES, the specified paragraph is executed the given number of times before control is returned to the appropriate point in the program. If the statement PERFORM B-PARA THRU D-PARA 12 TIMES were executed, how many times would the sequence B-PARA, C-PARA, D-PARA be executed? _____

- - - - - - - - - - - - - - - - - - -

twelve times

17. Suppose you want a paragraph named QUARTER executed four times. Write a statement to cause this, then return control to the following statement.

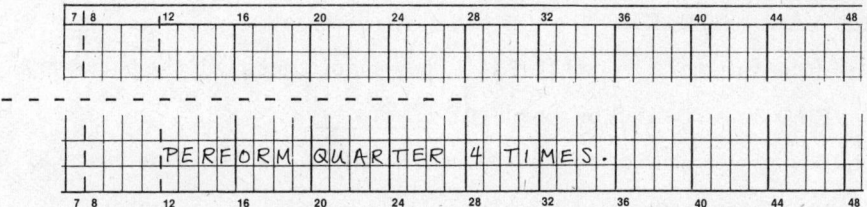

18. As the format below indicates, a data-name may be used in the TIMES option. It must, of course, have an integer value.

> PERFORM paragraph-name-1 [THRU paragraph-name-2]
> $\begin{Bmatrix} \text{integer} \\ \text{data-name} \end{Bmatrix}$ TIMES.

The data-name option is used when the number of times desired is variable for different program runs. If this value should be zero or negative, the specified paragraphs will not be executed at all. Write a statement to cause execution of paragraph P798 as often as the current value of COUNTER.

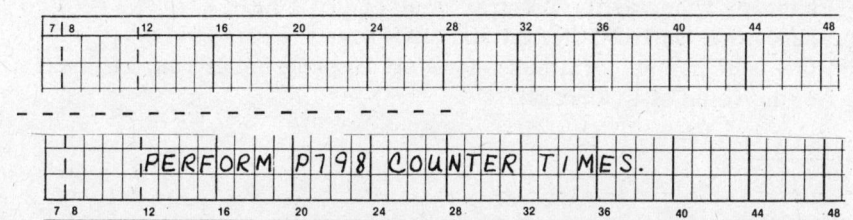

19. When the value of COUNTER is zero or negative, the statement you just wrote will not cause execution of P798. How many times would it be executed for each of the following values of COUNTER?

(a) 17 _____   (d) -0 _____

(b) -6 _____   (e) -467 _____

(c) 0 _____   (f) 688 _____

- - - - - - - - - - - - - - - - - -

(a) 17; (b) 0; (c) 0; (d) 0; (e) 0; (f) 688

20. Suppose your input cards are formatted so that the first field (NR-VALUES) contains a value equal to the number of other values on the card. Those other values are to be added by a paragraph called CHECK-AND-

182 ANS COBOL

After each input card is read, you will PERFORM CHECK-AND-ADD NR-VALUES TIMES.

(a) If the value of NR-VALUES is 7, how many times will the paragraph CHECK-AND-ADD be executed? _____

(b) Where will control be returned after CHECK-AND-ADD is executed the last time? _____

- - - - - - - - - - - - - - - - - - - -

(a) 7; (b) to the statement following PERFORM

UNTIL OPTION OF PERFORM

21. On occasion, the programmer may not be certain in advance just how many times a group of statements should be executed. In this case, he can specify a condition and the statements will be executed until the condition is satisfied. As a result of the statement PERFORM PARA-A UNTIL COUNTER EQUAL TO MAX, paragraph PARA-A would be executed:

    (a) as many times as the integral value of COUNTER.
    (b) repeatedly until COUNTER and MAX have the same value.
    (c) the same number of times whenever the program is run, regardless of the value of COUNTER.

    _____

- - - - - - - - - - - - - - - - - - - -

b

22. The condition specified in the UNTIL option is tested before the specified paragraphs are executed the first time, and again before each subsequent execution. Suppose MAX and COUNTER are both equal to 7 at the time the PERFORM statement of the preceding frame is executed. How many times would PARA-A be executed? _____

- - - - - - - - - - - - - - - - - - - -

none (The condition is true the first time it is tested.)

23. When the UNTIL option of PERFORM is specified, you must arrange for a change in the value of a variable in the condition during the execution of the specified paragraphs. Given the statement PERFORM PROCESS-P UNTIL ITEM-NR GREATER THAN 70, in paragraph PROCESS-P the programmer must:

(a) count the number of times it is executed.
(b) compare the value of ITEM-NR with 70.
(c) change the value of ITEM-NR.

_____

- - - - - - - - - - - - - - - - - -

c   (b is done automatically before each execution.)

24. Working with the statement given in the preceding frame, assume that paragraph PROCESS-P includes a statement that increments the value of ITEM-NR each time the paragraph is executed. If the value of ITEM-NR at the time control is transferred to PROCESS-P is 71, the paragraph

```
PROCESS-P.
    .
    .
    COMPUTE
      ITEM-NR =
      ITEM-NR + 3.
    .
```

will be executed _____ times.

- - - - - - - - - - - - - - - - - -

zero   (Remember that the condition is tested before execution.)

25. For each of the following original values of ITEM-NR, how many times will PROCESS-P be executed? (See preceding frame.)

(a) 69 _____   (c) 70 _____

(b) 75 _____   (d) 65 _____

- - - - - - - - - - - - - - - - -

(a) one   (then ITEM-NR = 72)
(b) none
(c) one   (then ITEM-NR = 73)
(d) two   (then ITEM-NR = 71)

26. This is the format for the UNTIL option of a PERFORM statement:

> PERFORM paragraph-name-1 [THRU paragraph-name-2]
> UNTIL condition.

Write a statement that would cause the paragraphs P1 through P6 to be executed repeatedly until the value of TOTAL is larger than the value of CREDIT.

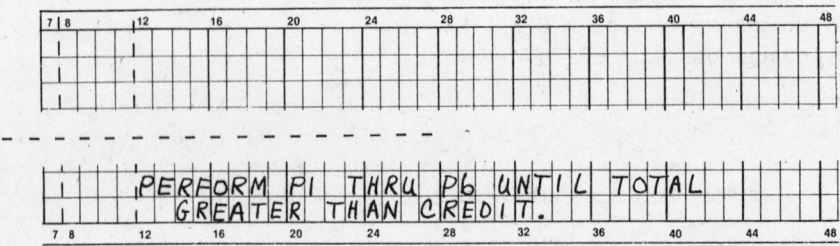

27. The statement PERFORM SUPPLY UNTIL ORDER GREATER THAN 350 will cause paragraph SUPPLY to be executed:

   (a) repeatedly until the value of ORDER is at least 351.
   (b) one time, if the original value of ORDER is 350 and ORDER is incremented in SUPPLY.
   (c) never if ORDER has a value that does not change in SUPPLY.

---

a, b

28. The paragraph shown below can be used to calculate compound interest given original values of principal (SUMX) and interest rate (PERCENT).

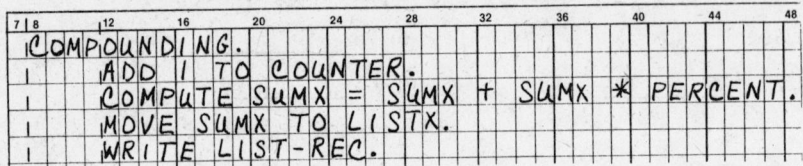

Suppose the value of SUMX is 250. You wish to know how long it will take to double that figure at the given percentage. Write a statement that will cause the appropriate number of executions.

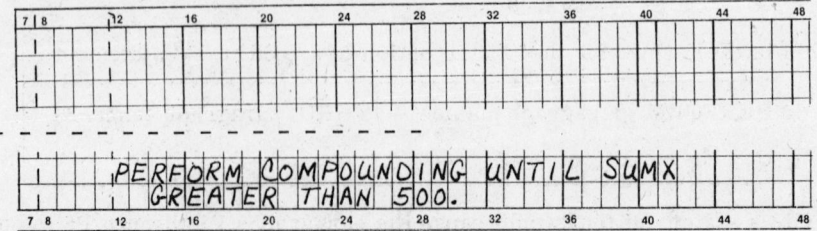

(The value of COUNTER at this point will be the number of interest periods to double your investment.)

VARYING OPTION OF PERFORM

29. A PERFORM statement with the VARYING option can be used when you do not wish to increment a variable in the procedure that is to be performed. The VARYING option specifies, in order, which variable is to change, which value it starts with, and by how much it will vary in each execution. An UNTIL segment then specifies a condition for determining when control is returned to the main sequence when the VARYING option is used.

```
        PERFORM LISTING VARYING COUNTER
            FROM A BY B UNTIL COUNTER
            GREATER THAN 60.
```

In the PERFORM statement above:

(a) The variable that is varied is _____.

(b) It is varied in increments equal to the value of _____.

(c) The original value of the variable is equal to the value of _____.

(d) Control is returned to the statement following PERFORM when

    _____.

- -

(a) COUNTER; (b) B; (c) A; (d) COUNTER GREATER THAN 60

30. When a PERFORM statement with the VARYING option is executed, events occur in a specific sequence. The format to use is shown below:

> PERFORM paragraph-name-1 [THRU paragraph-name-2]
>
> VARYING data-name-1 FROM $\begin{Bmatrix} \text{literal-2} \\ \text{data-name-2} \end{Bmatrix}$
>
> BY $\begin{Bmatrix} \text{literal-3} \\ \text{data-name-3} \end{Bmatrix}$ UNTIL condition.

First, data-name-1 is set equal to data-name-2 (or literal-2).
Second, the condition is tested; if true, control returns.
Third, specified paragraphs are executed.
Fourth, data-name-1 is incremented by data-name-3 (or literal-3).
Fifth, the program recycles through the second, third, and fourth steps.

```
        PERFORM LISTING VARYING COUNTER
            FROM BEGIN BY SPACING UNTIL
            COUNTER GREATER THAN 60.
```

For the example above complete the steps on the next page, using the actual data-names.

(a) First, COUNTER is set equal to _____.

(b) Second, _____.

(c) Third, paragraph LISTING is executed.

(d) Fourth, _____.

(e) Fifth, _____.

- - - - - - - - - - - - - - - - - - -

(a) BEGIN
(b) the condition COUNTER GREATER THAN 60 is tested
(d) COUNTER is incremented by the value of SPACING
(e) recycle b, c, and d

31. Assume that when the PERFORM example of the preceding frame is executed, COUNTER = 61, BEGIN = 1, and SPACING = 3.

    (a) When the condition is tested the first time (second step in preceding frame), the value of COUNTER is _____.

    (b) After COUNTER is incremented by SPACING the first time, its value is _____.

- - - - - - - - - - - - - - - - - - -

(a) 1 (Data-name-1 is set equal to data-name-2 before the condition is tested.)
(b) 4 (1 + 3 = 4)

32. Once execution of a PERFORM statement with the VARYING option is underway, a change in the value of data-name-2 will not affect the number of times the paragraphs are executed. Data-name-2 would occur following the word _____ in the statement.

- - - - - - - - - - - - - - - - - - -

FROM

33. The data-name which follows the word FROM in the VARYING option is used only as the very first step in varying the value of data-name-1. Therefore, changes in data-name-2 during execution would not affect the total number of times the paragraphs are executed. A change in the values of data-name-1 (which follows VARYING) or data-name-3 (which follows BY) would affect the number of executions. Consider the PERFORM statement example of the preceding frames. A change in which of the following values during execution of LISTING could affect the number of times it is executed?

(a) COUNTER
(b) BEGIN
(c) SPACING

_____

- - - - - - - - - - - - - - - - - -

a, c

34.
```
 7 8   12   16   20   24   28   32   36   40   44   48
 |           PERFORM DEPRECIATION VARYING ASSESSED
 |              FROM FINAL BY PERCENT UNTIL
 |              ASSESSED GREATER THAN COST.
```

Complete the sequence of steps below in the execution of this statement until the condition is true, as you learned in frame 30.

(a) _____ is set equal to _____.

(b) _____.

(c) Paragraph DEPRECIATION is executed.

(d) _____ is incremented by _____.

(e) _____.

(f) _____ is incremented by _____.

- - - - - - - - - - - - - - - - - -

(a) ASSESSED; FINAL
(b) The condition is tested, or ASSESSED is compared with COST.
(d) ASSESSED; PERCENT
(e) The condition is tested.
(f) ASSESSED; PERCENT (or else control returns)

35. After execution of the PERFORM statement of the preceding frame, a change in the value of which data-name will not affect the number of times DEPRECIATION is executed? _____

- - - - - - - - - - - - - - - - - -

FINAL

36. Write a statement to execute paragraph TIMELY, set NOW equal to THEN, then increment NOW by the value of NEVER until the value of NOW is less than the value of TOMORROW.

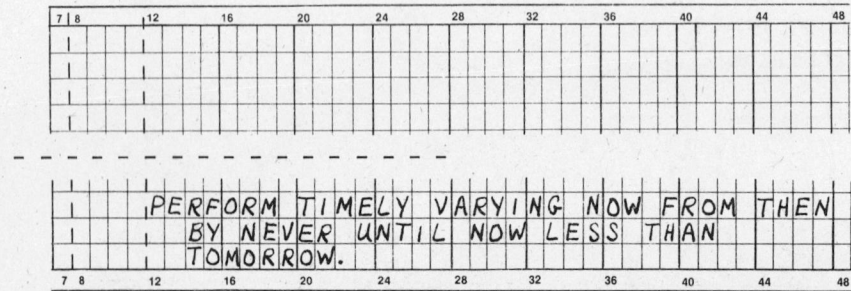

37. Whenever you specify the PERFORM statement using the VARYING option:

   (a) never change the value of the data-name following VARYING within the range of the PERFORM.
   (b) it is not necessary to change the values of the data-names specified in the option.

---

   b   (This is done by the computer.)

38. The data-names or numeric literals that are used as data-name-2 (following FROM) and data-name-3 (following BY) need not be integers, and they need not be positive. A programmer might, for example, wish to begin his value at -5 and increment it by intervals of .5. Write a statement specifying these values for varying X-RATE. The paragraph CINEMA should be executed until ATTENDANCE is more than 10,000.

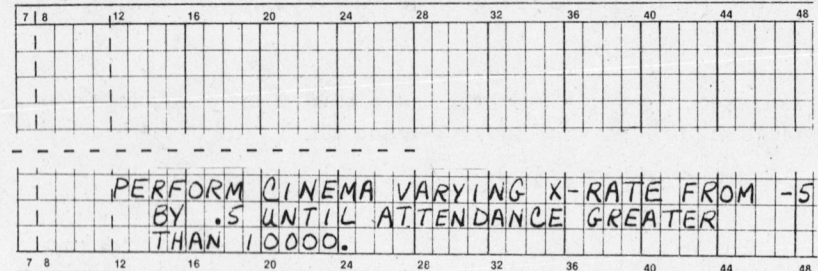

   (Commas may not be included in numeric literals.)

39. Which of the following values could be specified in the TIMES option of the PERFORM?

(a) 0
(b) .75
(c) −12

_____

- - - - - - - - - - - - - - - - - -

a, c (No executions would result, but the entries are valid.)

40. Which of the values in the preceding frame could be specified following FROM or BY when the VARYING option is used? _____

- - - - - - - - - - - - - - - - -

all of them

41. You have now written statements using all the basic variations of the PERFORM statement. Certain rules are common to all PERFORMs. A GO TO within the range of a PERFORM may not transfer control outside that range. Which of the statements below could have a GO TO within its range?

```
          7 8  12   16   20   24   28   32   36   40   44   48
(a)  1       PERFORM P1.
(b)  1       PERFORM P1 THRU P2 AGE TIMES.
(c)  1       PERFORM P3 THRU P7 UNTIL AGE = 17.
(d)  1       PERFORM P3 VARYING AGE FROM 1 BY .1
             UNTIL AGE GREATER THAN 17.
```

_____

- - - - - - - - - - - - - - - - - - - -

b, c (If the THRU option is not specified, a GO TO would always transfer control outside the range.)

42. (a) GO TO P1 could be legitimately written in which paragraph at the right? _____

(b) Which of the following could be written in P2?
1. GO TO P4.
2. GO TO P3.
3. GO TO P5.

P1.
  PERFORM P2 THRU P4.
  .
  .
  [P2]
  [P3]
  [P4]
  [P5]

_____

- - - - - - - - - - - - - - - - - - - -

(a) P5, or in P1
(b) 1, 2

43. The GO TO can be used to remove control from a PERFORM range, if it transfers control to the last statement in that range, as shown below. The EXIT statement is always the only statement in its paragraph. It is used as a termination point for a PERFORM.

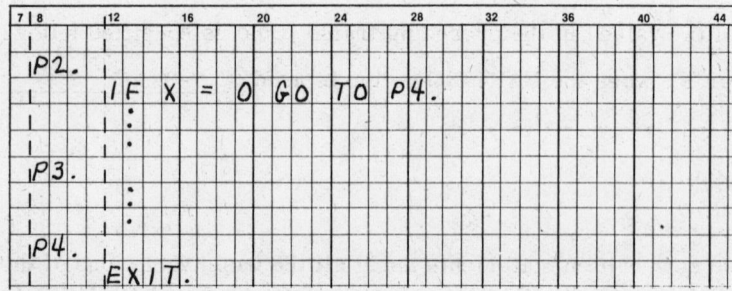

What is wrong with each of the following?

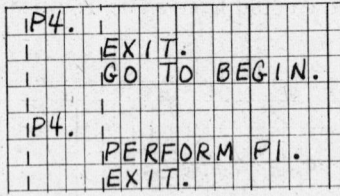

Both contain another statement in addition to EXIT.

44. A programmer will often wish to have the computer bypass all remaining statements in a PERFORM range. For this purpose the EXIT statement may be used as the last paragraph in the range. This statement, which consists of just the word EXIT followed by a period, must comprise a complete paragraph—which must be specified in the THRU option. Write a paragraph called END-POINT to be used in bypassing remaining executable statements within the range of the PERFORM.

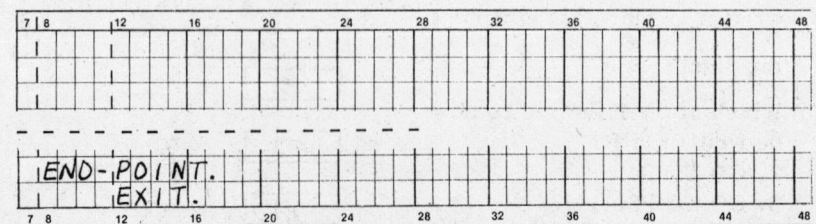

45. Suppose a program has paragraphs in this sequence: AA, BB, CC, DD, EE, FF. In AA is the statement PERFORM BB THRU EE UNTIL ALPH = Z. Paragraph EE contains the EXIT statement. Decide whether the GO TO statements below would be valid in the given paragraphs.

	Paragraph	GO TO Statement	Valid/Invalid
(a)	EE	GO TO BB.	_____
(b)	BB	GO TO AA.	_____
(c)	DD	GO TO CC.	_____
(d)	FF	GO TO AA.	_____

- - - - - - - - - - - - - - - - -

(a) invalid (EE contains only EXIT)
(b) invalid (transfers control outside the range)
(c) valid (control remains within range)
(d) valid (FF is not within the range, so there is no GO TO restriction)

46. PERFORM statements may be included within the range of other PERFORM statements. Such a statement may reference paragraphs either within or outside the range, but not both. That is, PERFORM statements may not have overlapping ranges. Which of the statements below could validly be included in PC (on the right)?

PERFORM PA THRU PD.

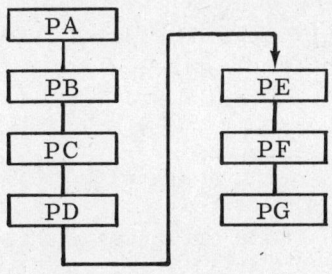

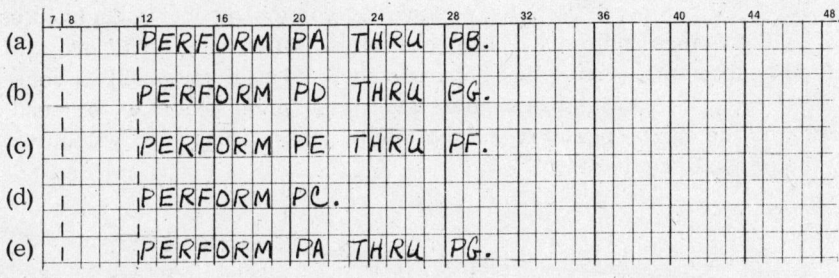

- - - - - - - - - - - - - - - - -

a, c, d (In a and d, the paragraphs are totally within; in c, totally outside; in b and e, the ranges overlap.)

192 ANS COBOL

47. In the example on the right in the preceding frame, which paragraph could contain an EXIT statement? _____

- - - - - - - - - - - - - - - - - -

    PD   (the paragraph specified in the THRU option)

48. A programmer uses an EXIT statement to:
    (a) terminate the program.
    (b) bypass the THRU option of a PERFORM statement.
    (c) return control to the statement immediately following the PERFORM.

    _____

- - - - - - - - - - - - - - - - - -

    c

49. Which of the following could validly be included in PARA-2 (on the right)?

    (a) PERFORM PARA-2 THRU PARA-3.
    (b) GO TO PARA-3.
    (c) PERFORM PARA-1.

    PERFORM PARA-2.
    ⋮
    | PARA-1 |
    | PARA-2 |
    | PARA-3 |

    _____

- - - - - - - - - - - - - - - - - -

    c   (In a, the ranges would overlap.)

As you write more complex programs, you will probably find you use PERFORMs more and more. The convenience of writing small programs (called routines) to accomplish separate parts of a larger problem contributes to this usage. A routine to calculate averages, print headings, or send a collection notice can be performed from any point in a program, without disrupting the normal sequence.

DEPENDING ON OPTION OF THE GO TO STATEMENT

The GO TO statement in its simple form transfers control unconditionally and permanently to a specified paragraph. In this section, you will learn to use the GO TO statement to specify conditional branching, depending on the value of a variable.

50.

```
     GO TO CLERICAL, SALES, MANAGE
        DEPENDING ON JOB-CODE.
```

The GO TO statement with the DEPENDING ON option above is equivalent to the IF statements below.

```
        IF JOB-CODE = 1 GO TO CLERICAL.
        IF JOB-CODE = 2 GO TO SALES.
        IF JOB-CODE = 3 GO TO MANAGE.
```

The DEPENDING ON option of the GO TO statement specifies a data-name whose value:

(a) depends on the paragraphs specified.
(b) determines to which paragraph control is transferred.
(c) is set equal to the paragraph-name.

----

b

51. This is the format for the DEPENDING ON option of the GO TO statement:

> GO TO paragraph-name-1, paragraph-name-2, . . .
> DEPENDING ON data-name

Any number (up to 2,031) of paragraph-names may be specified in a GO TO statement when the DEPENDING ON option is used. Control is transferred to the paragraph-name whose position in the list corresponds to the value of the data-name, which must represent a nonnegative integer. If the value of the data-name is zero, or greater than the number of paragraph-names listed, control continues to the statement following GO TO.

```
     GO TO MONDAY, TUESDAY, WEDNESDAY,
        THURSDAY, FRIDAY, SATURDAY,
        SUNDAY DEPENDING ON WHAT-DAY.
```

Decide to which paragraph control is transferred for each of the following values of WHAT-DAY.

(a) 4 _____   (c) 9 _____

(b) 0 _____   (d) 7 _____

(a) THURSDAY; (b) statement following GO TO; (c) statement following GO TO; (d) SUNDAY

194 ANS COBOL

52. Which of the following would cause a transfer of control to paragraph TRIDENT when the value of SCALAR is 3?

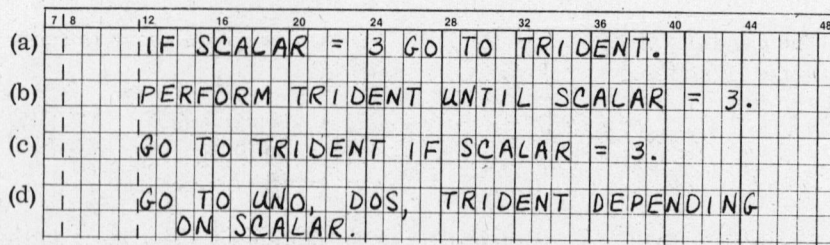

---

a, d (In b, TRIDENT would not be executed if SCALAR = 3; c is an incorrect format.)

53. The GO TO statement with the DEPENDING ON option is a conditional branching statement, as shown in the flowchart on the right. Each transfer of control occurs only under specified conditions. Which condition would cause control to be transferred to paragraph X?

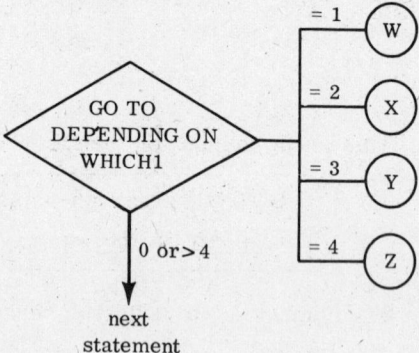

WHICH1 = 2

54. Write the conditional branching statement represented in the preceding frame.

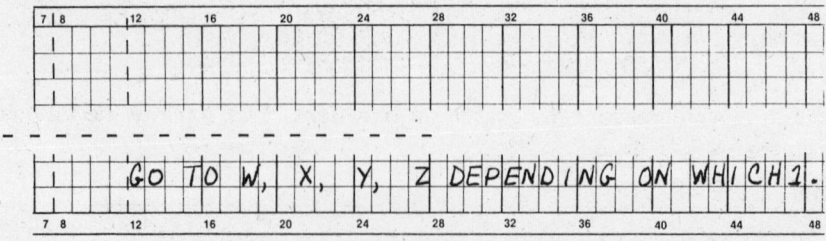

55. Write a statement that will cause transfer of control to WEEKLY if PAYDAY is 2, BIWEEKLY if PAYDAY is 4, MONTHLY if PAYDAY is 3, and BIMONTHLY if PAY is 1.

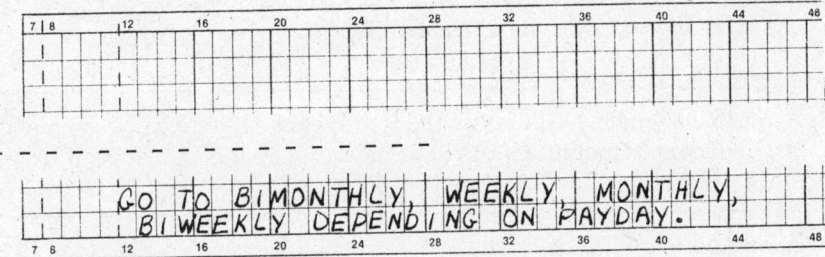

56. In execution of the statement you wrote in the preceding frame, where does the control go if the value of PAYDAY is:

   (a) 3 _____

   (b) 0 _____

   (c) 7 _____

- - - - - - - - - - - - - - - - - - -

(a) control is transferred to MONTHLY; (b) control passes to the statement following GO TO; (c) control passes to the statement following GO TO

You have learned to specify and change flow of control in a program. You can now use the PERFORM statement with the THRU, TIMES, UNTIL, and VARYING options, and the DEPENDING ON option of the GO TO statement. You can specify the effects and limitations of these controlling statements.

REVIEW

57. Instead of a complete program, the review for this chapter will consist of several brief problem descriptions. Decide which of the flow-of-control options from this chapter would be most useful in programming the solution to these problems.

   (a) Compound interest is to be calculated. Certain calculations must be done in sequence a certain number of times before the final result is achieved.

   _____

   (b) Mortgage payments are being arranged to show the amount of principal and interest included in each payment. The last one printed shows a balance of zero.

   _____

(c) Control is to be transferred to SOME-TIME, NO-TIME, or ALL-TIME based on the value of the variable CLOCK.

(d) A routine to print headings at the top of each page is to be executed at the appropriate points in a program.

(e) A routine to add the remaining transaction records to a master file after the end of the input master file is to be executed.

(f) A routine to copy remaining master record to the new master tape after the end of the transaction file is to be executed.

- - - - - - - - - - - - - - - - - -

(a) PERFORM with TIMES option; (b) PERFORM with UNTIL or VARYING option; (c) GO TO with DEPENDING ON option; (d) simple PERFORM; (e) PERFORM UNTIL; (f) PERFORM UNTIL

CHAPTER NINE
Tables

The table-handling capabilities of the ANS COBOL compiler contribute to its usefulness as a business-oriented programming language. Data items which occur repeatedly and have the same format can be described with a single data-name. Then subscripts, or identifying numbers, are used to refer to the specific occurrence of the data-name. For example, an input file may include the number of hours an employee works for each of seven days. This might be described as: 03 HOURS-WORKED OCCURS 7 TIMES PIC 99V9. The hours worked on a specific day would then be referred to with subscripts. HOURS-WORKED (2) would have as its value the number of hours the employee worked on MONDAY.

In this chapter you will learn to describe tables in either section of the Data Division. You will learn to assign values to these tables and to use them in the Procedure Division to solve problems. Specific ANS COBOL features you will learn to use are:

- Data Division entries
    OCCURS clause
    REDEFINES clause
    Double-level OCCURS

TABLE DESCRIPTION ENTRY: SINGLE OCCURS

1. A table is a collection of related data items with identical picture descriptions. For example, a table might include a list of social security numbers, a list of scores on successive exams, or a set of wholesale prices. Which of the following could be a table?

    (a) a name, an address, and a maximum credit limit
    (b) a list of state abbreviations, all described as XX
    (c) any collection of items, as long as they all have the same picture

- - - - - - - - - - - - - - - - -

    b, c   (A group of unrelated items could be a table, although it doesn't seem useful.)

2. Each item in a table can be referred to by a number that identifies its position, or subscript. For example, you may have a table of seven items that includes the names of the days of the week, where WK-DAY(1) has the value SUNDAY.

    (a) What is the value of WK-DAY (3)? _____

    (b) What term refers to the number in parentheses? _____

- - - - - - - - - - - - - - - - -

    (a) TUESDAY; (b) subscript

3. An input card may contain a variable called IN-DAY. The variable itself may be used as a subscript to access a table entry. If the IN-DAY value is 6, then the value of WK-DAY is FRIDAY. Suppose the value of IN-DAY is 4. Which of the statements below would put the corresponding value of WK-DAY on the system printer?

    (a) DISPLAY IN-DAY.
    (b) DISPLAY IN-DAY (WK-DAY).
    (c) DISPLAY WK-DAY (IN-DAY).
    (d) DISPLAY WK-DAY.

- - - - - - - - - - - - - - - - -

    c

4. A table is defined in the Data Division, using a new entry, the OCCURS clause.

```
01  WEEK-DAYS.
    02  WK-DAY  OCCURS 7 TIMES
        PIC X(9).
```

This entry sets up a table of seven items, each nine characters long. A total of 9 times 7, or 63 bytes, will be needed to store the table. You should note a few things about this definition:

        OCCURS does not appear at the 01 level.
        The PICTURE appears at the lowest level.
        The subscript is used with the OCCURS level.

Suppose you wanted to describe a table of the names of the months. Using the example as a model, write a Data Division description of MONTH-LIST.

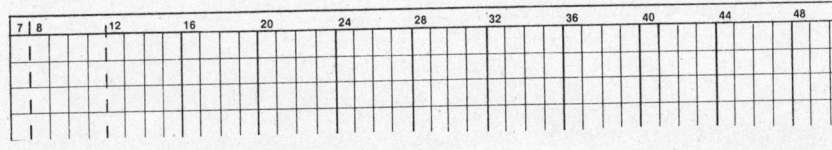

```
01  MONTH-LIST.
    02  MONTH-NAME OCCURS 12 TIMES
        PIC X(9).
```

5. Suppose an input record includes these data items:

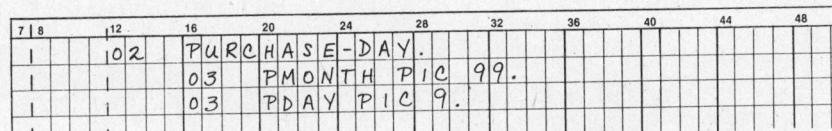

```
02  PURCHASE-DAY.
    03  PMONTH PIC 99.
    03  PDAY PIC 9.
```

What expression could you use to access the following?

(a) the name of day referred to _____

(b) the name of the month referred to _____

- - - - - - - - - - - - - - - - - - -

(a) WK-DAY (PDAY)
(b) MONTH-NAME (PMONTH)

6. Let's consider the MONTH-LIST table again. How can we set up this table, once storage is reserved for it in the Data Division? One way is by using an input file. Suppose each month-name is punched in the first nine positions of a separate card.

(a) How many cards would be in that input file? _____

(b) Write a record description for the input records.

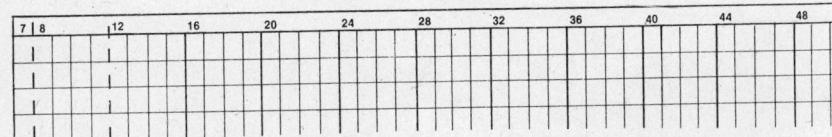

- - - - - - - - - - - - - - - - - - -

(a) 12

200 ANS COBOL

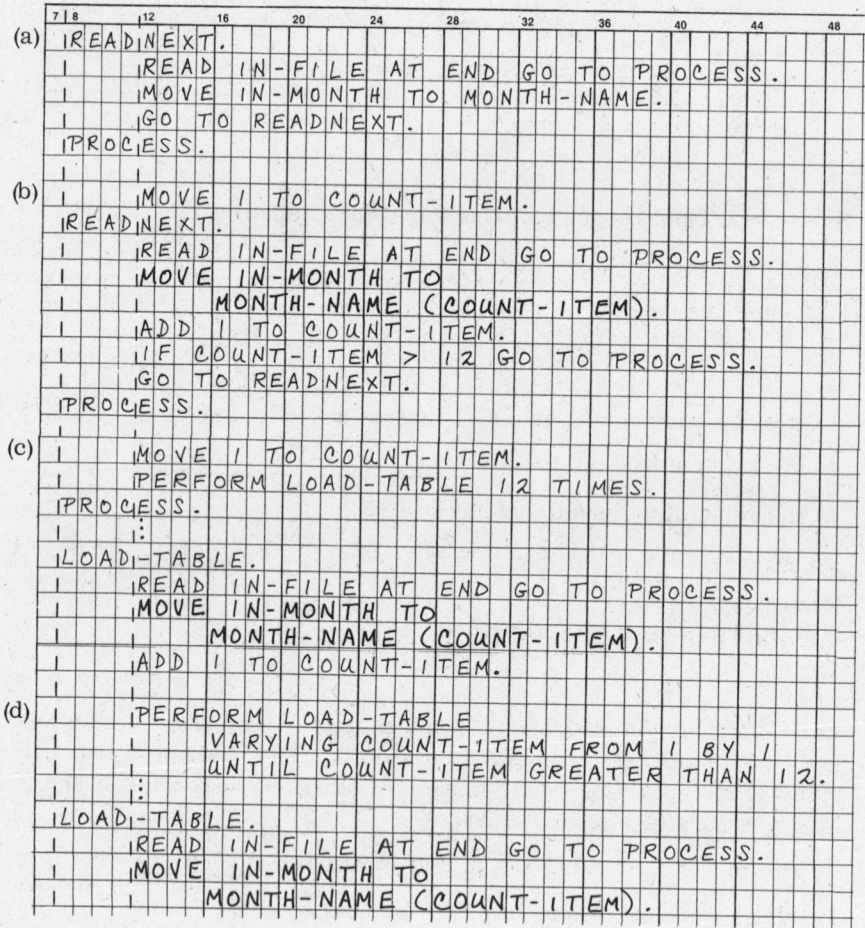

b, c, d   (All three would have the same effect.)

8. Using the VARYING option of the PERFORM verb, write the statements needed to build a table of weekdays from an input card file. Include the

PERFORM and the paragraph it performs. Use IN-FILE, IN-DAY, and COUNTER as needed.

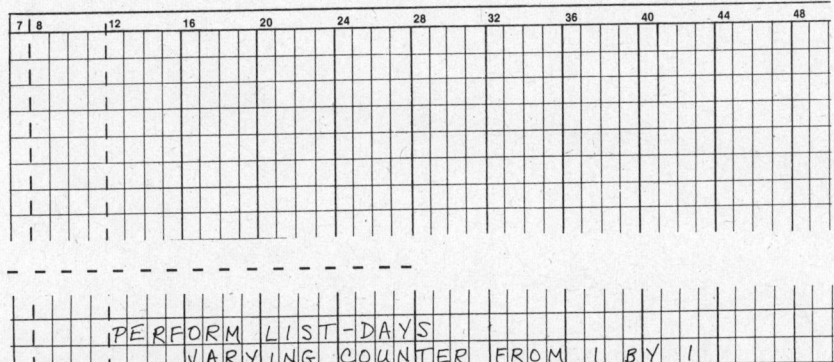

```
        PERFORM LIST-DAYS
            VARYING COUNTER FROM 1 BY 1
            UNTIL COUNTER GREATER THAN 7.
    :
LIST-DAYS.
    READ IN-FILE AT END GO TO PROCESS.
    MOVE IN-DAY TO WK-DAY (COUNTER).
```

9. Tables such as these, which aren't expected to change, can be "hard-coded" into the Working-Storage Section of a program, by using the REDEFINES clause, as shown below.

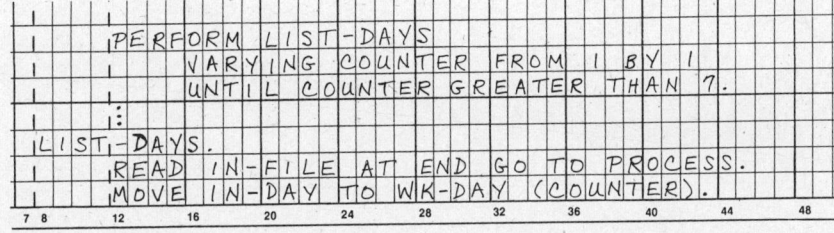

```
01  MONTHS.
    02  MONTH-1     PIC X(9) VALUE "JANUARY  ".
    02  MONTH-2     PIC X(9) VALUE "FEBRUARY ".
    :
    02  MONTH-12    PIC X(9) VALUE "DECEMBER ".
01  MONTH-LIST  REDEFINES MONTHS.
    02  MONTH-NAMES OCCURS 12 TIMES PIC X(9).
```

The REDEFINES clause allows you to use more than one name to refer to the same area of storage and must directly follow the item it redefines. The VALUE clause can be used only in Working-Storage (except in condition-names); it cannot be used in the same entry as OCCURS. A program that includes the coding above can immediately reference the table entries with a subscript, either a digit or a data-name.

Refer to the example, and code a Working-Storage record to give weekday name values to seven items. Then redefine the record as a table.

202 ANS COBOL

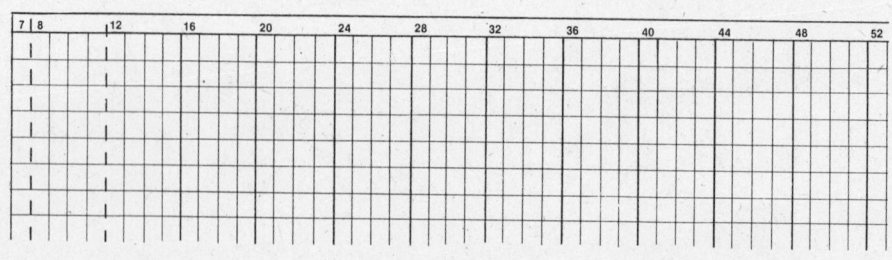

10. The entries in a table must all be the same size and format. An input record may include amounts purchased in 7 different years, from 1975 through 1981. Each entry will have 7 digits, two to the right of an implied decimal point. Use a level 02 item SUM-PURCH to refer to the entire table, and YR-SUM to refer to each item.

    (a) Write the table description.

    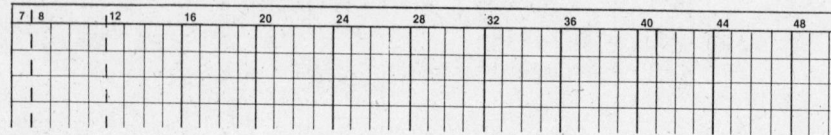

    (b) How could you refer to the purchase sum of 1978?

    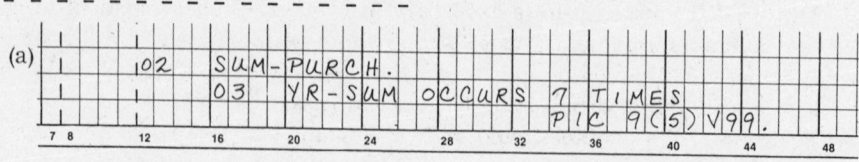

    (b) YR-SUM (4)

11. Write a statement to calculate how much a specific customer purchased in 1980 and 1981 together. Store the result in SUBTOT.

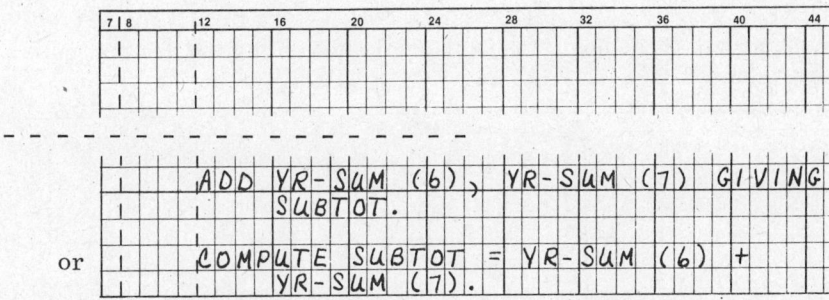

or

12. If the customer purchased more than twice as much in 1981 as he did in 1975, a new "gold-plated" credit card is to be issued. Paragraph NEW-CREDIT-CARD is to be executed, then control is to be returned to the normal sequence. Write a statement to accomplish this.

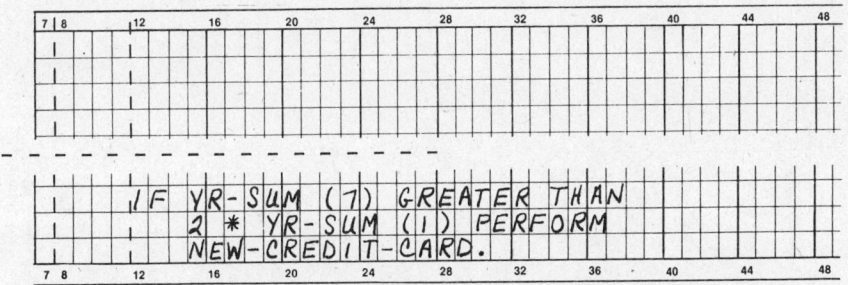

13. Write the entries necessary to describe the table SIGNALS, which contains eighteen elements of three digits each. This makes up the record TABLE-SAMPLE.

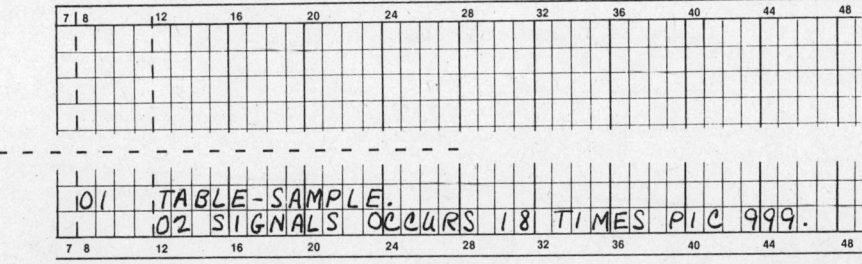

14. As indicated earlier, the REDEFINES clause in the Data Division allows the same storage area to be referred to by different names. It cannot be used at the 01 level in the File Section, and must directly follow the entry it redefines. Write Working-Storage entries to describe:

(a) a record W-REC, subdivided into seven variables, ONE, TWO, THREE, FOUR, FIVE, SIX, and SEVEN, each a signed seven-digit number with three positions to the right of the implied decimal point. Use values 4.1, 3.1, 1.2, 6.8, 7.2, 9.7, and 108.4.

(b) a table W-TABLE to occupy the same area and be referenced as W-T with subscripts.

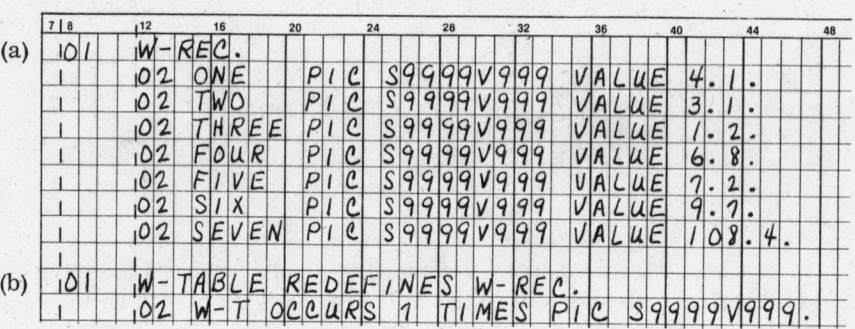

15. Based on the preceding frame, give the value of

   (a) W-T (4) _____

   (b) W-T (TM) when TM equals 2 _____

   (c) W-T (6) _____

(a) 000$\overset{+}{6}$800; (b) 000$\overset{+}{3}$100; (c) 000$\overset{+}{9}$700

16. In the record description entry below, a table is included in the input data.

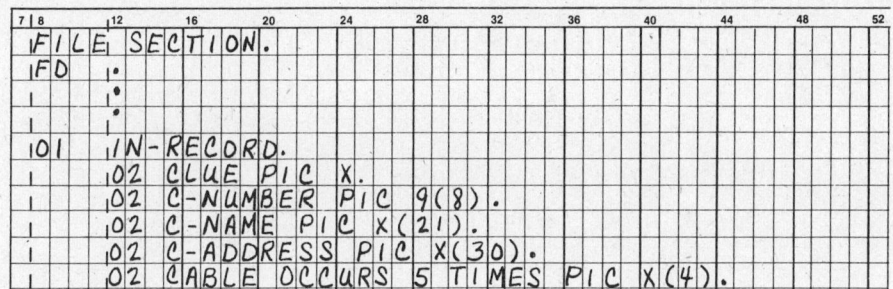

The reading of an input card will create the file, assigning values to all table elements. Assume card columns 61 through 80 contain ABCDEFG-HIJKLMNOPQRST. What is the value of:

(a) CABLE (3) _____

(b) CABLE (1) _____

(c) CABLE (5) _____

- - - - - - - - - - - - - - - - - -

(a) IJKL; (b) ABCD; (c) QRST

17. Suppose CLUE in IN-RECORD contains a number from 1 to 5. Whatever the value of CLUE, the corresponding occurrence of CABLE is to be written upon the console typewriter. Write the statement necessary to accomplish this.

```
        DISPLAY CABLE (CLUE) UPON CONSOLE.
```

18. A department store may give discounts based on the length of time a customer takes to pay his bill. The list of discounts may be described as shown below.

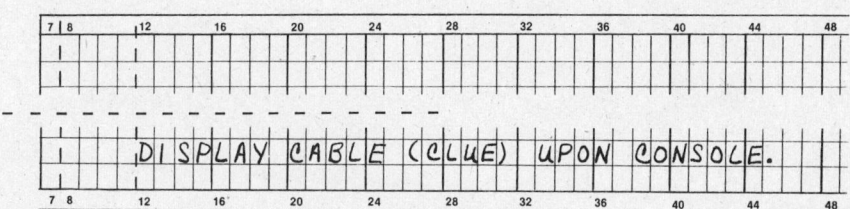

Write a description for DISCOUNT-TABLE to use the same storage area as DISCOUNT-LIST above, but be referred to as DISCOUNT with subscripts.

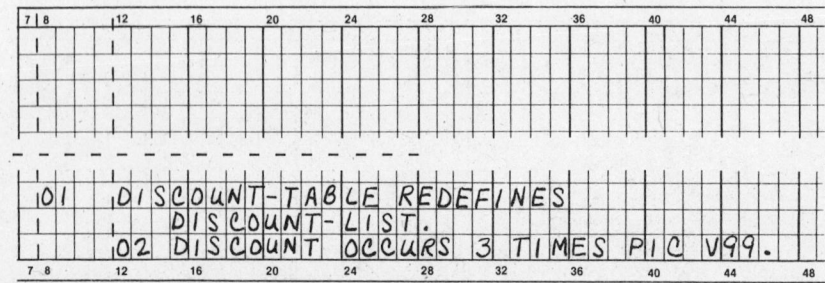

19. A spring and wire manufacturing firm has decided to give cost-of-living increases to all employees. All employees are classified according to their roles in the firm, and the percentage increase is based on position.

   1 Clerical (4%)
   2 Line Workers (5%)
   3 Foremen and Supervisors (6%)
   4 Executive (8%)

Complete the Working-Storage Section entries below to set up LIVING-TABLE, using INCREASE-RECORD to assign values of 1.04, 1.05, 1.06, and 1.08 to pictures 9V99.

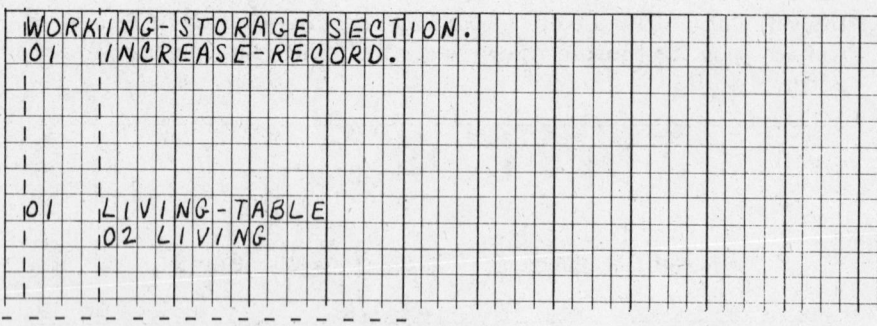

20.

PAY-REC					
NUMBERN	NAME	C	OTHER	RATE	MORE-OTHER

The payroll record, PAY-REC, shown above includes a RATE, which will be multiplied by an occurrence of LIVING from the table you created in the preceding frame. The specific occurrence of LIVING will be determined by the variable C (for classification) in PAY-REC. Before the multiplication of the increase by the current rate, RATE must be moved to HOURLY. Refer to the flowchart segment on the right as you code the statements to access a record from PAYFILE and calculate U-RATE as the updated salary. Assume all the values are valid on input. Write your statements below.

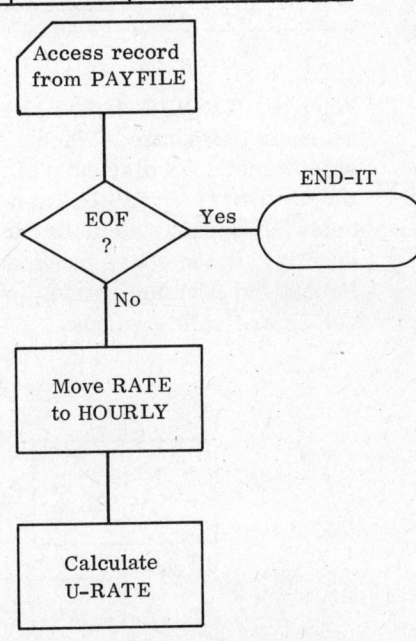

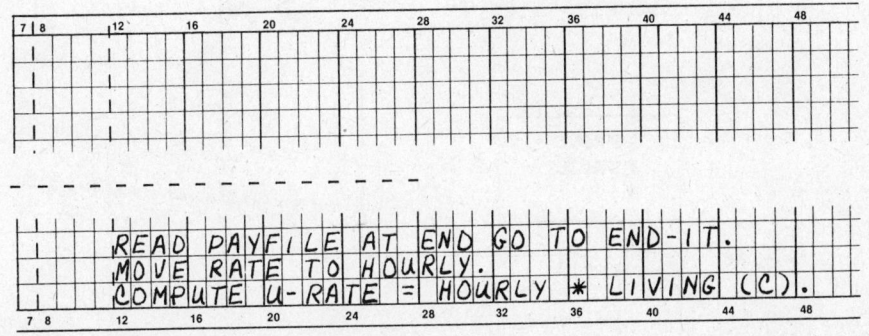

```
READ PAYFILE AT END GO TO END-IT.
MOVE RATE TO HOURLY.
COMPUTE U-RATE = HOURLY * LIVING (C).
```

(The COMPUTE statement could be replaced by MULTIPLY HOURLY BY LIVING (C) GIVING U-RATE.)

21. Write entries to describe a record SUPER-SPECIAL-TABLE, containing eight occurrences of SUPER with pictures of X(5).

208 ANS COBOL

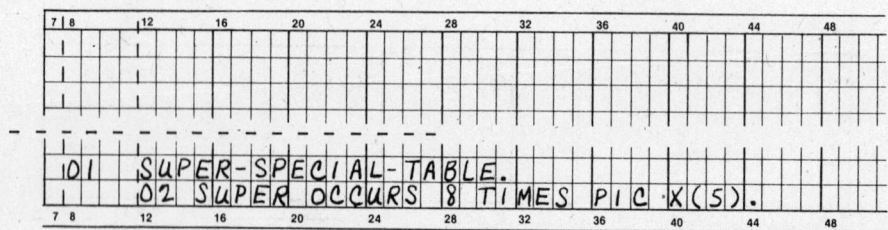

22. When SUPER-SPECIAL-TABLE is set up, the item-numbers in it are in ascending sequence. When a customer orders one of these super-special sale items, it is discounted by 20 percent. The transaction card includes the posted price (PPRICE) on which the discount is based. The flowchart below shows how the table can be searched to find if an ordered item is on sale. In the space provided following the flowchart, write ANS COBOL Procedure Division entries to program this segment. Again, assume all values are valid on input.

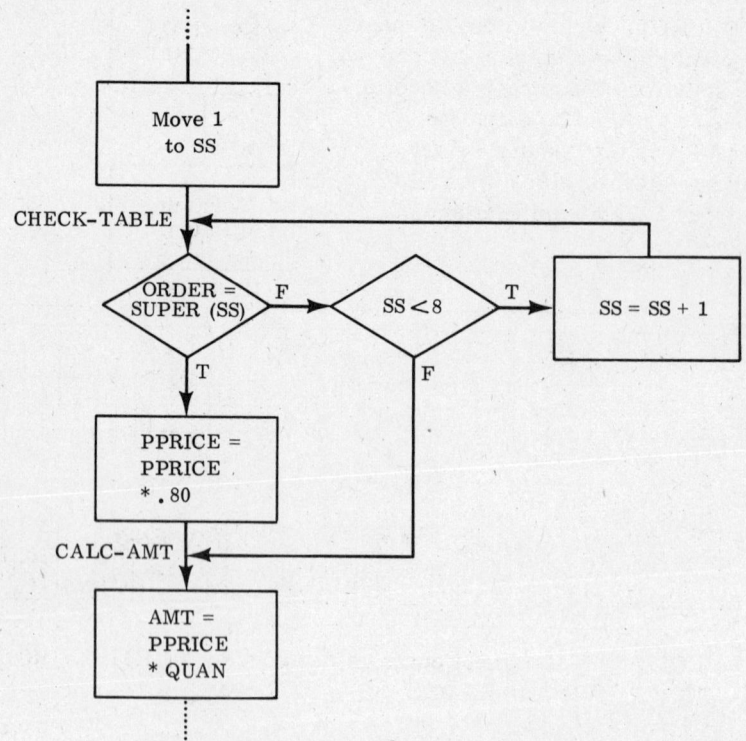

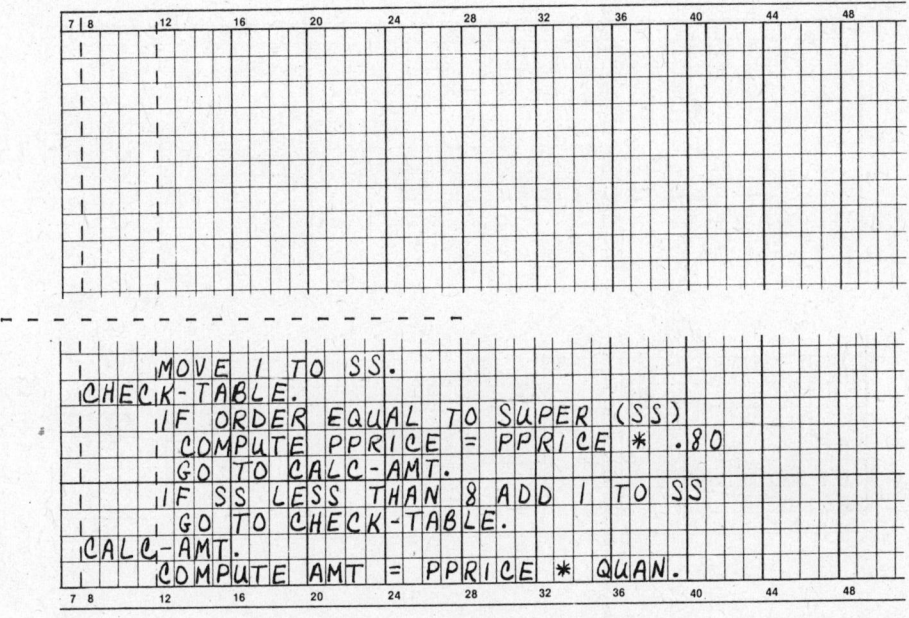

23. After execution of the statements you wrote for the preceding frame, the value of SS depends on the particular sale item that was found. A programmer may wish to keep track of the number of each item sold, and describe a table, TOTALS, to accumulate the sales. Write statements necessary to add the appropriate TOTALS.

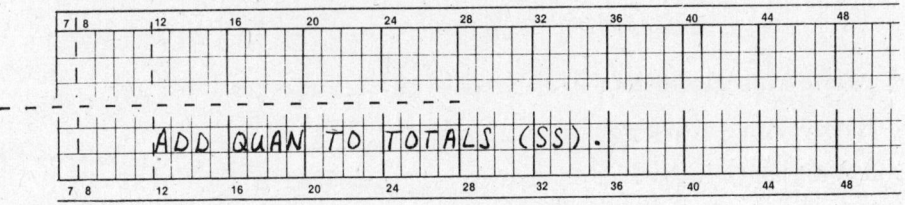

24. When you build a table during your program, as in a table to accumulate totals, you often need to initialize the table, or set it to zeros. To do this, you set each item individually to zero. Write the COBOL statements needed to set all entries in TOTALS (see last frame) to zero.

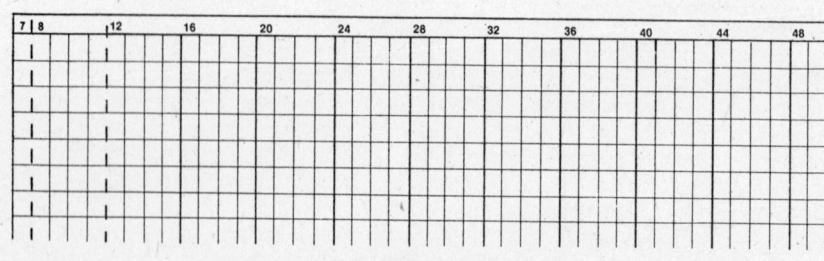

25. The Data Division segment below shows another way data items can be described. In this example, HOURS-WORKED (1) refers to both regular and overtime hours worked on Sunday. REGL (1) and OVTM (1) each refers to a single occurrence of a single data item. HOURS-WORKED (1) refers to a single occurrence of two data items.

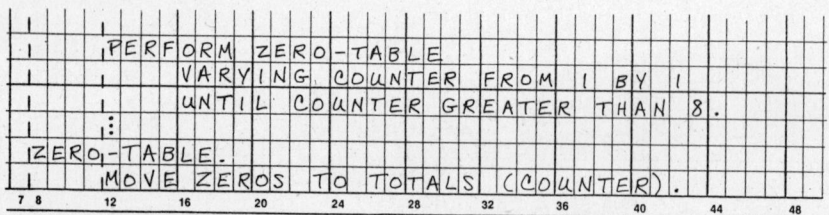

Write subscripted data-names (based on the above) to refer to:

(a) overtime hours worked on Thursday _____

(b) all hours worked on Saturday _____

(c) regular hours worked on Tuesday _____

- - - - - - - - - - - - - - - - - - -

(a) OVTM (5)
(b) HOURS-WORKED (7)
(c) REGL (3)

26. Write a statement to calculate the total number of hours worked on Saturday. Store the result in SAT.

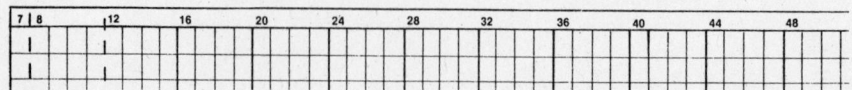

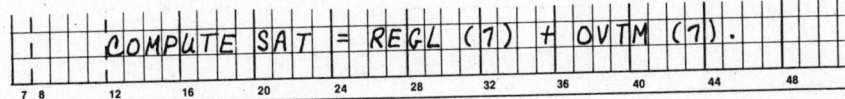

(An ADD statement is also correct.)

27. Assume that each card in an input file contains a student number and eleven scores, as shown below.

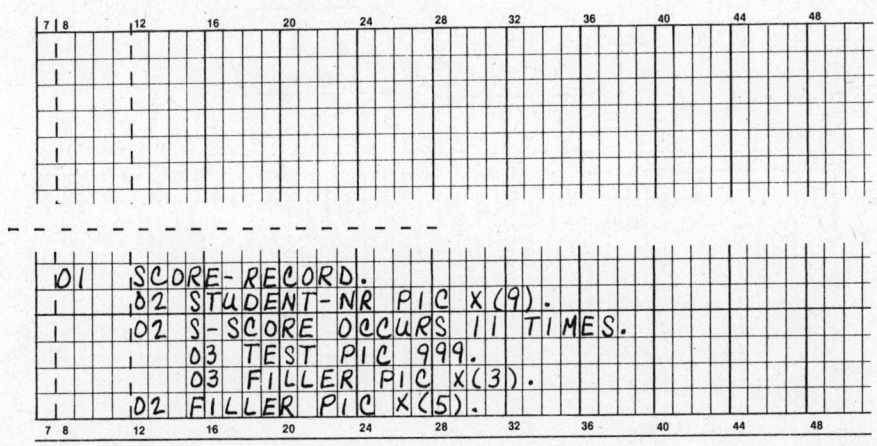

Write the record description entry.

```
01  SCORE-RECORD.
    02  STUDENT-NR PIC X(9).
    02  S-SCORE OCCURS 11 TIMES.
        03  TEST PIC 999.
        03  FILLER PIC X(3).
    02  FILLER PIC X(5).
```

28. The scores for each student are to be averaged and the result, with the student number, written on the standard typewriter console. Use K as a subscript and TEST-TOTAL as a variable to hold the sum of the scores. Refer to the flowchart on the next page as you write an ANS COBOL segment to find one student's average score. Write your program entries in the form provided below the flowchart.

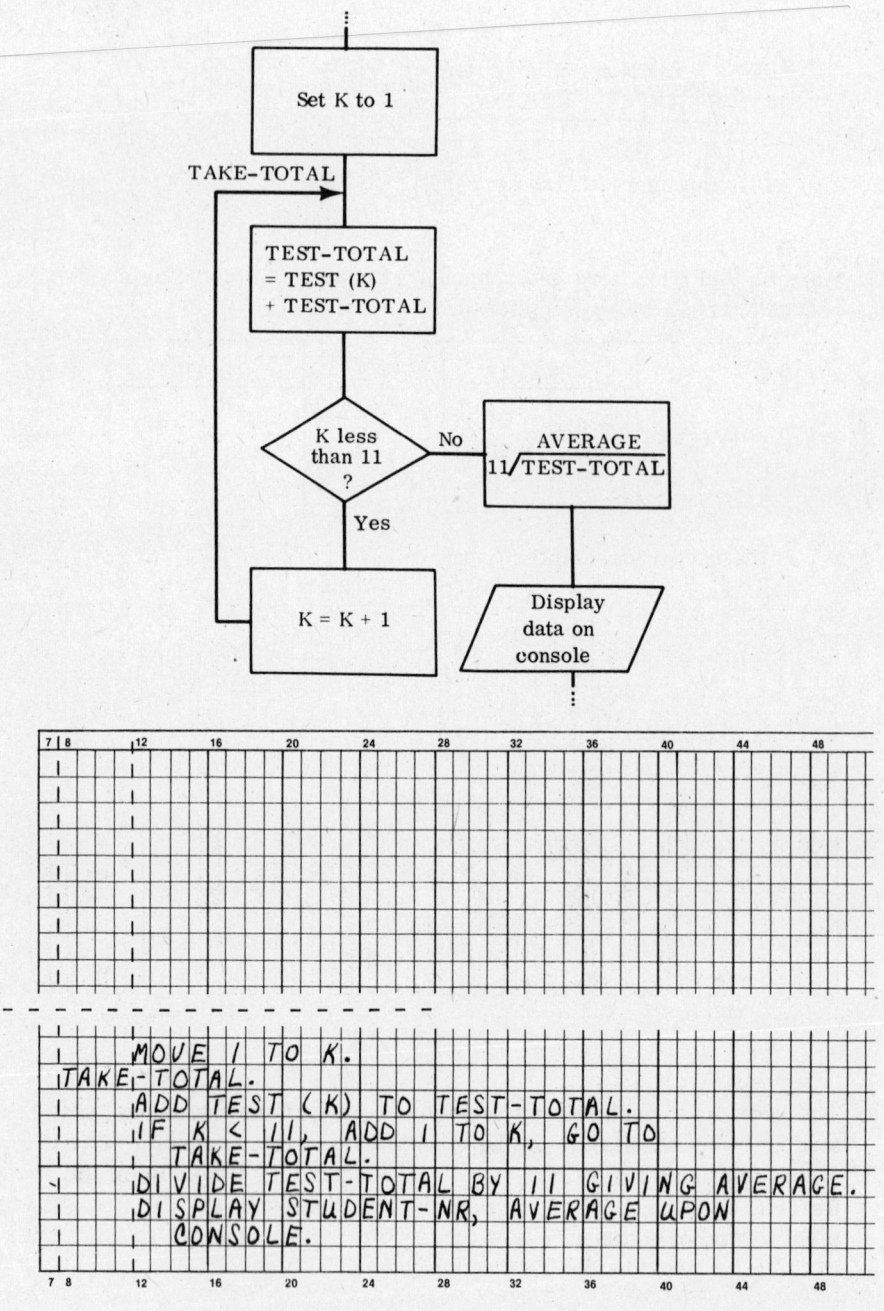

29. Input records for a sales agency include, along with identifying information for each salesman, commission sales for each of the last six months. You need a program to read these cards, select the largest of the six commission payments, and print out the salesman's name and his highest commission payment over the months. The commissions were described

as COM OCCURS 6 TIMES PIC 9(4)V99. Use the flowchart in Figure 9-1 below as you write the program on the coding form which follows.

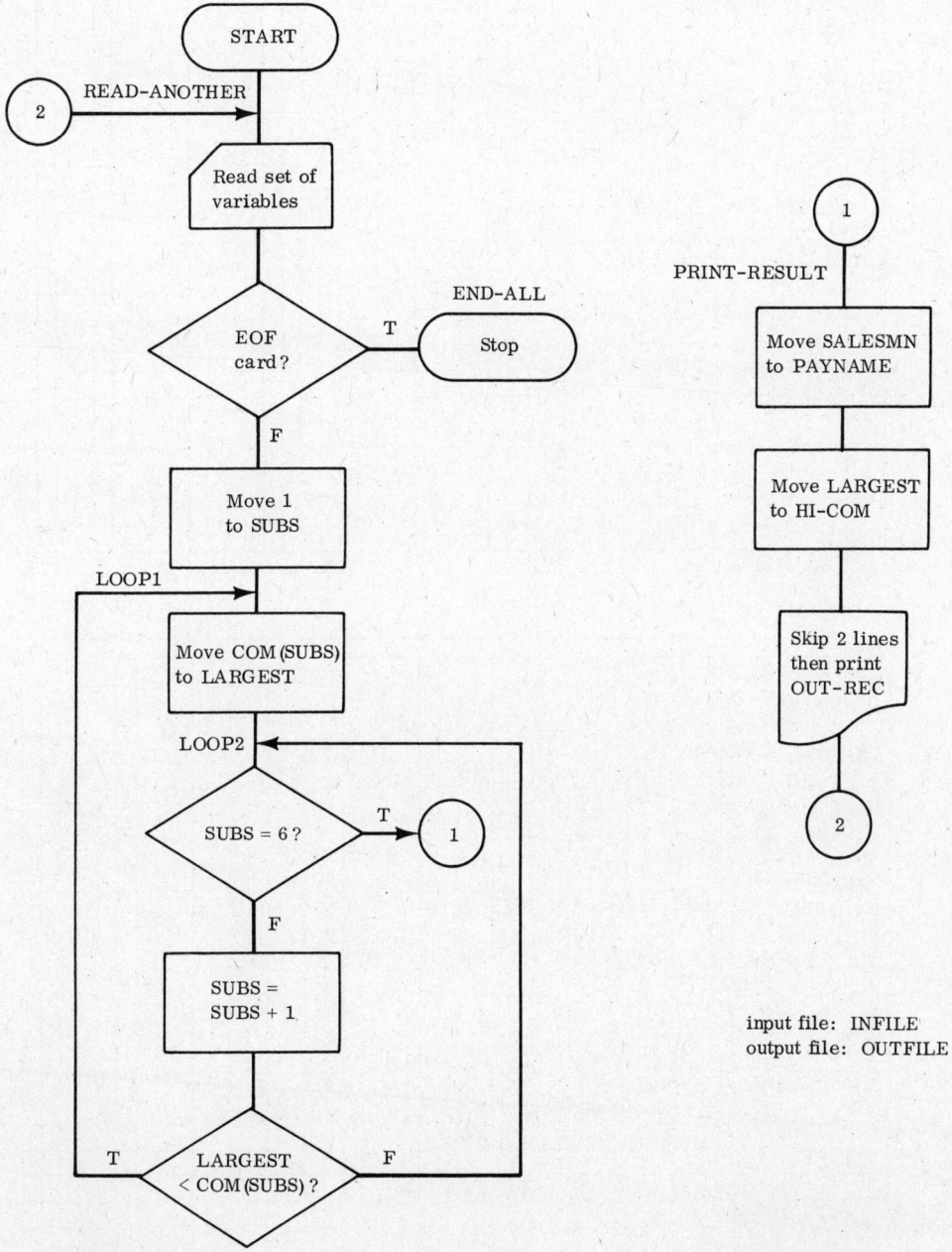

Figure 9-1

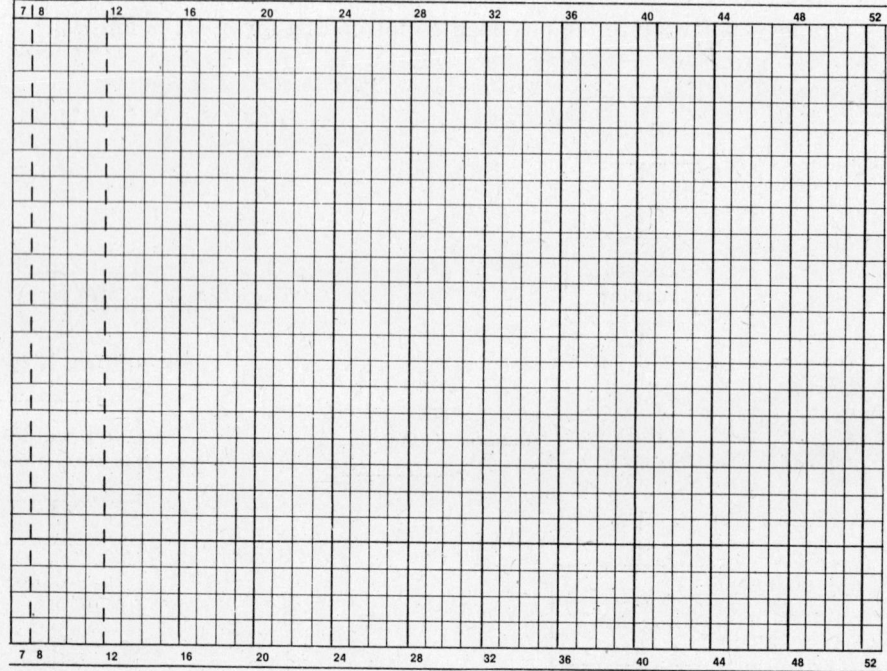

```
PROCEDURE DIVISION.
BEGINNING.
    OPEN INPUT INFILE, OUTPUT OUTFILE.
READ-ANOTHER.
    READ INFILE AT END GO END-ALL.
    MOVE 1 TO SUBS.
LOOP-1.
    MOVE COM (SUBS) TO LARGEST.
LOOP-2.
    IF SUBS EQUAL TO 6 GO TO PRINT-RESULT.
    ADD 1 TO SUBS.
    IF LARGEST LESS THAN COM (SUBS)
        GO TO LOOP-1.
    GO TO LOOP-2.
PRINT-RESULT.
    MOVE SALESMN TO PAYNAME.
    MOVE LARGEST TO HI-COM.
    WRITE OUT-REC AFTER ADVANCING 2 LINES.
    GO TO READ-ANOTHER.
END-ALL.
    CLOSE INFILE, OUTFILE.
    STOP RUN.
```

All of the tables we have considered so far have been single level; they might be called lists as well as tables. Although the single-level tables are most commonly used, double and triple levels are also permissible. Now we will consider description, referencing, and processing double-level tables.

DOUBLE-LEVEL OCCURS

Students   Scores (Pic 999)

1. Allen
2. Burgot
3. Check
4. Hitch
5. Howard
6. Kirby
7. Loveland
8. OHanlon
9. Thurber

Figure 9-2

30. A one-dimensional table might represent either a list of student names or a set of scores for any one student. A two-dimensional table can include a set of scores for each of the students. The table in Figure 9-2 would have how many elements? _____

- - - - - - - - - - - - - - - - -

72 (students * scores, or the number of elements in one dimension times the number of elements in the other)

31. The OCCURS clause may be used to denote repeated occurrences of similar items. To define a two-dimensional table, the OCCURS clause is used twice as shown below. The PICTURE clause is used only after the last OCCURS.

```
01  SALES-TABLE.
    02  SALESMAN OCCURS 14 TIMES.
        03  SALES OCCURS 12 TIMES
            PIC 9(4)V99.
```

Write the entries necessary to describe TEST-TABLE as shown in Figure 9-2.

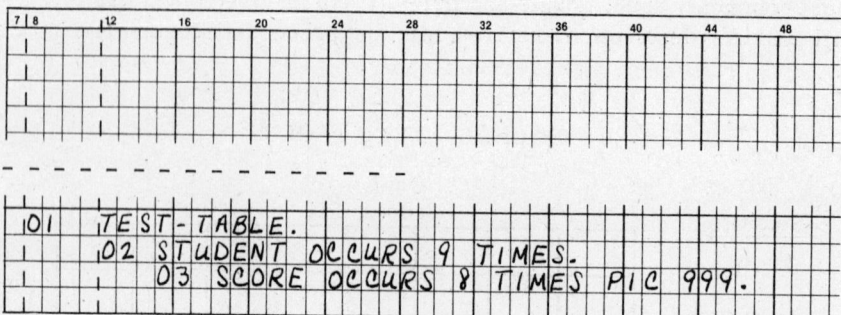

32.

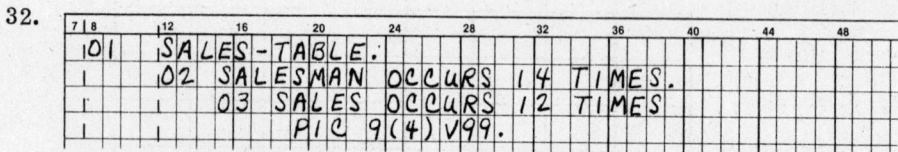

In order to refer to one entry in a two-dimensional table, you need two subscripts, written in the form (1, 2). The first subscript refers to the variable described by the first OCCURS and must be followed by a comma and a space. The second subscript refers to the variable described by the second OCCURS. Both subscripts follow the name of the last variable. Refer to the coding sheet above. Which of the following are correct?

(a) SALESMAN (2)   (c) SALES (14, 12)
(b) SALES (2)   (d) SALES (1, 17)

_____

- - - - - - - - - - - - - - - - - -

    c   (In d, the second subscript is larger than 12.)

33. Refer to Figure 9-2. SCORE (1, 8) refer to student Allen's score on the eighth test. Write the entries to refer to:

(a) OHanlon's seventh score _____

(b) Loveland's first score _____

(c) Check's fourth score _____

- - - - - - - - - - - - - - - - - -

(a) SCORE (8, 7)
(b) SCORE (7, 1)
(c) SCORE (3, 4)

34. Refer to Figure 9-2. Suppose you are interested in finding out which students, if any, received scores of 100 on a given test. The input will be a test number—the second subscript. You want to instruct the computer to find any scores of 100, and identify (DISPLAY) the first subscript, the student number. This problem works much like a one-dimensional table—you keep one subscript (the given test number) constant and vary the other to check all nine students. Use data-names from frame 31 and SUB-STU and SUB-TEST as subscripts, to write the commands you need to find and DISPLAY the value of SUB-STU when SUB-TEST is fixed, and the value of the table entry is 100.

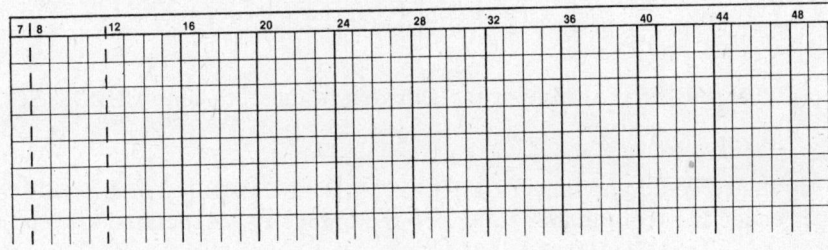

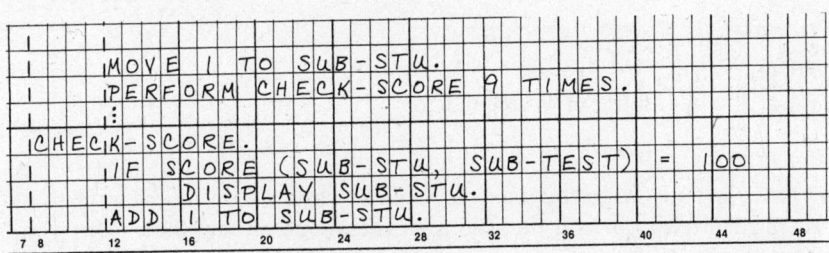

```
        MOVE 1 TO SUB-STU.
        PERFORM CHECK-SCORE 9 TIMES.
        :
CHECK-SCORE.
        IF SCORE (SUB-STU, SUB-TEST) = 100
            DISPLAY SUB-STU.
        ADD 1 TO SUB-STU.
```

35. Looking up information in a two-dimensional table often requires the use of nested IFs or nested PERFORMs. Suppose you were trying to identify any tests for which any students received a 100. We can add another level of PERFORM around the one above.

   (a) What subscript will change in the outer loop? _____

   (b) How many items will the inner loop (the coding above) be executed?

   _____

- - - - - - - - - - - - - - - - - - -

   (a) second (SUB-TEST)

   (b) 72 (9 times for each of the tests)

36. The following coding demonstrates the use of nested PERFORMs.

```
            MOVE 1 TO SUB-TEST.
            PERFORM VARY-TEST 8 TIMES.
            :
        VARY-TEST.
            MOVE 1 TO SUB-STU.
            PERFORM CHECK-SCORE 9 TIMES.
            ADD 1 TO SUB-TEST.
        CHECK-SCORE.
            IF SCORE (SUB-STU, SUB-TEST) = 100
                DISPLAY SUB-STU.
            ADD 1 TO SUB-STU.
```

(a) What will be the value of the subscripts the 19th time CHECK-SCORE is entered? _____

(b) Where could you insert DISPLAY "TEST NUMBER", SUB-TEST to cause the test number to be printed before its associated student numbers? _____

- - - - - - - - - - - - - - - - - -

(a) (3, 1)
(b) at the beginning of VARY-TEST

TEST-TABLE might be used in several ways. You might want to get a student's final average, or find the average score on any test. Or, you might be interested in the overall average for all students. In the next sequence of frames you will see how to process the data from a two-dimensional table.

37. When accessing all table elements from one row (across) or one column (down) in a two-dimensional table, you would hold constant the subscript of the variable for the specific row or column, then vary the subscript that refers to the separate elements in that specific row or column. For example, to find the average score on the fourth test, the second subscript must first be set to 4. Then the first subscript is varied from 1 through 9 as the scores of the nine students are added together. Thus the items added are SCORE (1, 4), SCORE (2, 4), SCORE (3, 4), through SCORE (9, 4). Finally, of course, the sum would be divided by nine. In averaging student Burgot's scores, the steps would be:

(a) set the _____ subscript to _____.
    (first/second)

(b) vary the _____ subscript from 1 through _____.
    (first/second)

(c) add the elements—the third element is _____.

(d) divide the sum of the elements by _____.

- - - - - - - - - - - - - - - -

(a) first; 2
(b) second; 8
(c) SCORE (2, 3)
(d) eight

38. Assume the student/score table is entered into the computer as described. Use the variable KK as the variable subscript, and write the COBOL statements to find Kirby's average. Assume the data-names you will need are SUBTOTAL and FINAL-T.

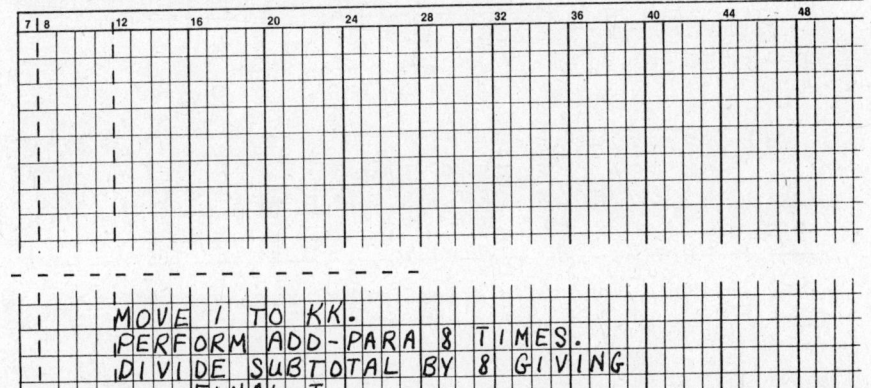

```
         MOVE 1 TO KK.
         PERFORM ADD-PARA 8 TIMES.
         DIVIDE SUBTOTAL BY 8 GIVING
             FINAL-T.
            :
 ADD-PARA.
         ADD SCORE (6, KK) TO SUBTOTAL.
         ADD 1 TO KK.
```

Other answers may also be correct. For example, you may have written:

  PERFORM ADD-PARA VARYING KK FROM 1 BY 1 UNTIL KK
    GREATER THAN 8.
  DIVIDE 8 INTO SUBTOTAL GIVING FINAL-T.
    :
    :
  ADD-PARA.
    ADD SCORE (6, KK) TO SUBTOTAL.

39. Describe TEMPERATURES as indicated in the table chart below. Each entry has a value of the form S999V9.

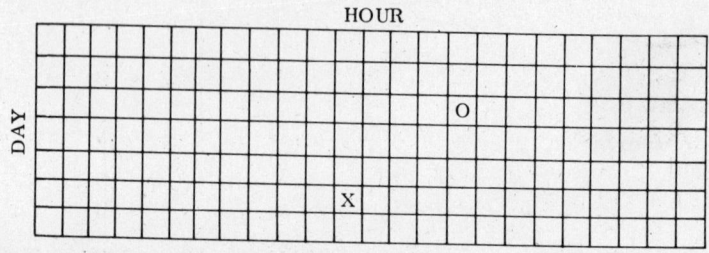

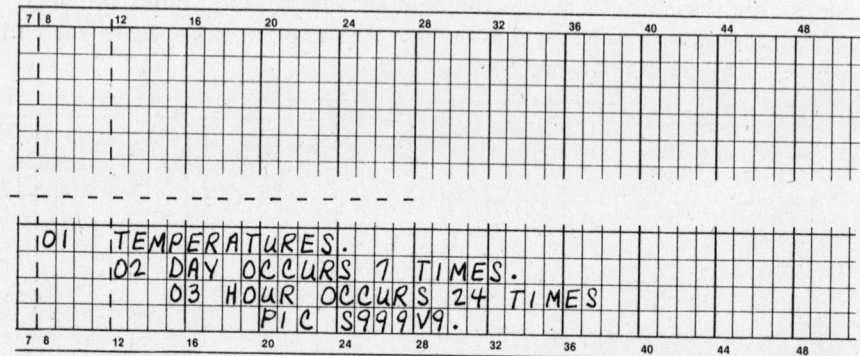

(DAY and HOUR could be reversed; the picture always follows the lowest level.)

40. Write the subscripted table element that refers to the X in the previous frame. _____

- - - - - - - - - - - - - - - - - - -

HOUR (6, 12)

Tables can be created in more than two dimensions. These are not commonly needed, but the techniques used are similar to processing two-dimensional tables. To define a three-dimensional table, you would need three levels of OCCURS; as before, you use a PICTURE only with the lowest level. To search or load a three-level table, you need three levels of IF or PERFORM.

Table handling is one of the more difficult, yet very useful features of any programming language. Several versions of COBOL provide additional statements and features to make it easier to use tables. A variable to correspond to a subscript, called an INDEX, can be defined with the OCCURS variable. This INDEX can be given a value in a SET statement. The SEARCH statement will increment the INDEX, test for a condition, and replace an IF level in a table-processing operation. Like IFs and PERFORMs, SEARCH statements can be nested to process multi-dimensional tables. You can learn about these COBOL features in the reference manual for the system you use.

CHAPTER TEN
Mass Storage Devices (Disk Files)

Earlier in this Self-Teaching Guide, we discussed uses of unit record and utility devices. In this chapter we will talk about the mass storage device. The most common mass storage device is the magnetic disk, which is usually used in disk packs of six or more disks. These resemble phonograph records stacked up, with regular tracks (corresponding to record grooves) on each side of each disk. Other mass storage devices are the magnetic drum and the data cell; since these are seldom used, examples in the guide will refer to magnetic disks. The concepts presented, however, are applicable to files located on any mass storage device.

Files located on mass storage devices may have the same organization, standard sequential, as a tape file. On the disk, however, there is a distinct advantage. The sequential file on disk can be updated without recreating the file. Records must be read in sequence, but, after updating, each can be rewritten into the location in the file from which it was accessed.

All files considered so far have been sequentially organized. They have been created in a specific sequence and can be used only in that sequence. Files on mass storage devices may also be used for direct or random access of records. If only 20 scattered records are needed from a file containing 300 or 3,000 records, sequential access would require reading of every record in the file. Random access, on the other hand, provides reading of only the desired records from the file. Many situations similar to this occur regularly in the business world. For example, all the records in a file of department store customers need not be changed every week, or even every month. And, only a few of the students enrolled in a college change their majors or names during a given term.

In order to access records directly, each record must have a unique identifier—some means of ensuring that the desired record has been located. In files called <u>direct</u> <u>files</u>, this identifier is the physical address of the record, the disk and track where it can be found, for example. In <u>indexed</u> <u>sequential</u> <u>files</u>, the identifier is some field within the associated record that is unique to that record—such as a social security number, an item-code, or a credit card number.

In this chapter we shall first consider the standard sequential file on a mass storage device; the processing of this file differs little from tape file processing. Then we shall briefly investigate direct files. We will study the organization and processing of indexed sequential files. At the end of the chapter, you will write a program to update randomly an indexed sequential file.

Specific ANS COBOL entries you will learn to use in this chapter include:

- Environment Division entries
    ACCESS IS RANDOM clause
    ACTUAL KEY clause
    RECORD KEY clause
    SYMBOLIC KEY clause

- Procedure Division entries
    I-O option of OPEN statement
    INVALID KEY option of WRITE statement
    INVALID KEY option of READ statement

STANDARD SEQUENTIAL FILES ON MASS STORAGE DEVICES

1. The disk, as a mass storage device, may be used to store standard sequential files. The standard sequential file may be accessed:

   (a) directly.
   (b) randomly.
   (c) sequentially.

   - - - - - - - - - - - - - - - - - -

   c   (Other files on a mass storage device might be accessed randomly—but not a standard sequential file.)

2. In the Environment Division, the programmer describes the equipment. The class of a disk may be either DA (direct access) or UT (utility). Since the sequential disk file is used much like a tape file, the ASSIGN clause used for IBM systems would probably be:

   (a) UT-S-FILE1
   (b) DA-S-FILE2
   (c) UT-S-FILE3

   - - - - - - - - - - - - - - - - - -

   c   (a describes a tape file; b specifies DA, which could be used here; c, with UT, is more common for standard sequential files.)

MASS STORAGE DEVICES (DISK FILES) 223

3. Write the Environment Division entries necessary for sequential disk file DISKF with external name XSEVEN.

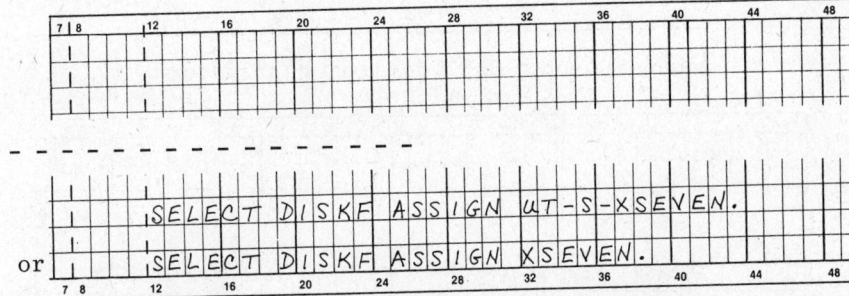

or

(The actual format and information in the ASSIGN clause again will vary with the brand and installation. The first one above is the standard IBM S/370 clause, while the second would be correct for a CDC system. When you work with a computer, be sure to check for required Environment Division entries. As you recall, many do not specify the exact device in ANS COBOL, but include such information in the job control language.)

4. The Data Division entries for sequential disk files are more standardized. All disk files must have label records; we will continue to specify standard ones. Blocking is permitted as in tape files. Write the FD entry for DISKF, with a blocking factor of 9.

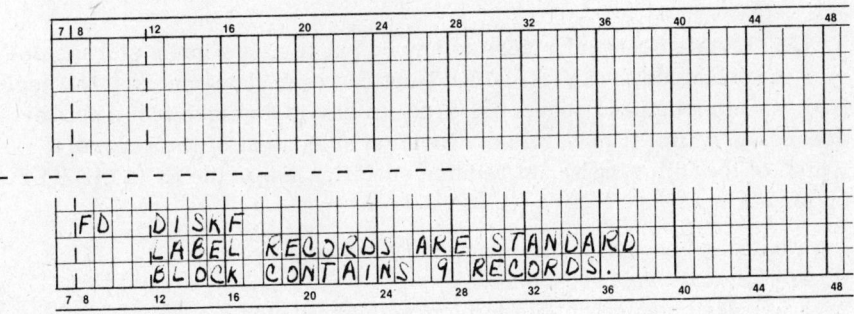

I-O OPTION OF OPEN STATEMENT

5. A standard sequential disk file can be used as input, output, or as both input and output. A file is always output when it is created. It is input when used for read only. When a file will be updated in place, we call it I-O; each record is input when it is read and output when it is put back into the file. The I-O option of the OPEN statement can be used only with files located on mass storage devices. An OPEN statement general format is shown on the next page:

```
       ┌─────────────────────────────────────┐
       │           ⎧ INPUT  ⎫                │
       │   OPEN   ⎨ OUTPUT ⎬  paragraph-name.│
       │           ⎩ I-O    ⎭                │
       └─────────────────────────────────────┘
```

Write a statement to open DISKF for updating in place.

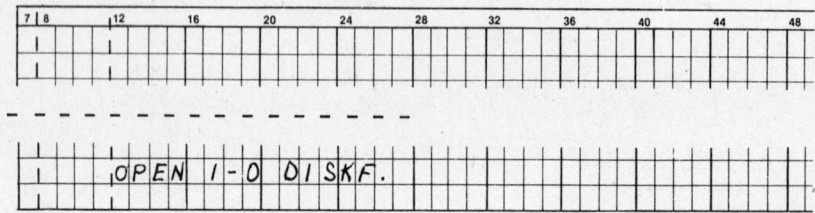

6. The I-O option is used only when the file already exists on the device. Write the appropriate OPEN statement for use when originally creating DISKF.

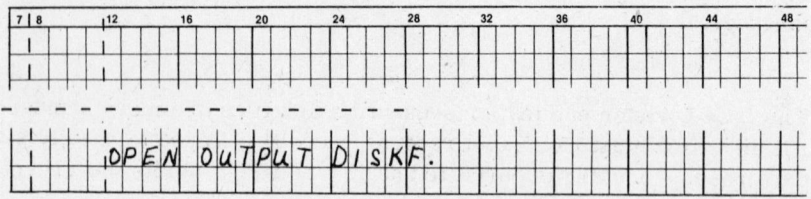

7. A WRITE statement that refers to any output file on a mass storage device must include the INVALID KEY option, even though no key is specified, as in a standard sequential file. (A key is a unique identifier for records in a file; it may refer to location or content of the record.) Which of the following would require specification of the INVALID KEY option?

   (a) a standard sequential file on magnetic tape
   (b) any file on a unit record device
   (c) a standard sequential file to be created on a disk

   ─────────────

   c

8. When applied to a standard sequential file opened as OUTPUT, the statement in the INVALID KEY option is executed only when there is no physical space in which to write the record. The format to use is given on the next page.

> WRITE   record-name   INVALID KEY   action-statement.

Refer to the format above, and write a statement to place OUT-REC in the disk output file and transfer control to START-ANEW when the allotted space is filled.

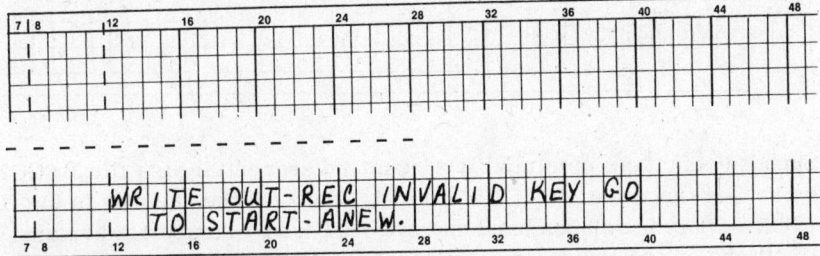

---

9. After a standard sequential file has been created, it may be opened as input or I-O. The I-O option is used for updating. Each record is read in sequence. If the record requires updating the modifications are made, then it is written back in the same place in the file. If the record is not changed, it need not be rewritten. The INVALID KEY option need not be specified for the standard sequential file opened as I-O because:

(a) the file has no key.
(b) since each record is put in the place it came from, the space will not be filled before the file is completed.
(c) no sequential files require the INVALID KEY option.

---

b   (It is needed, however, when the file is opened as OUTPUT.)

---

10. Reading a record does not remove it from a file; the process merely copies the data to another location in an input area. Therefore only records that are changed or updated must be written back into the file. When a sequential file is opened I-O, the record written is placed in the location of the last record that was read. Suppose, for example, execution of a program causes three records to be read, then the third written unchanged. How will the I-O file differ after the WRITE statement is executed?

It will be the same. (The first two records were not disturbed; the third was written identically in the same location.)

11. Write a statement to place the modified record XTRA back in the I-O file DISKF.

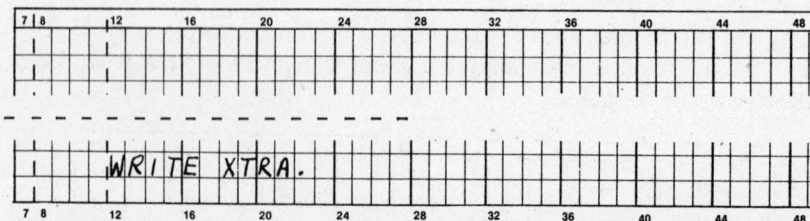

12. Suppose your task is to modify a standard sequential disk file BEGONE by setting the value of CHECKED to 1, since all the records in the file (GONE-REC) have been hand and eye verified by competent humans. Write the entire Procedure Division to update the file, using paragraph names BFIRST, BCONTINUE, and BDONE. You will have to open the file; read, update, and replace each record in the file; then close the file and end the program. Space for your program entries is given below.

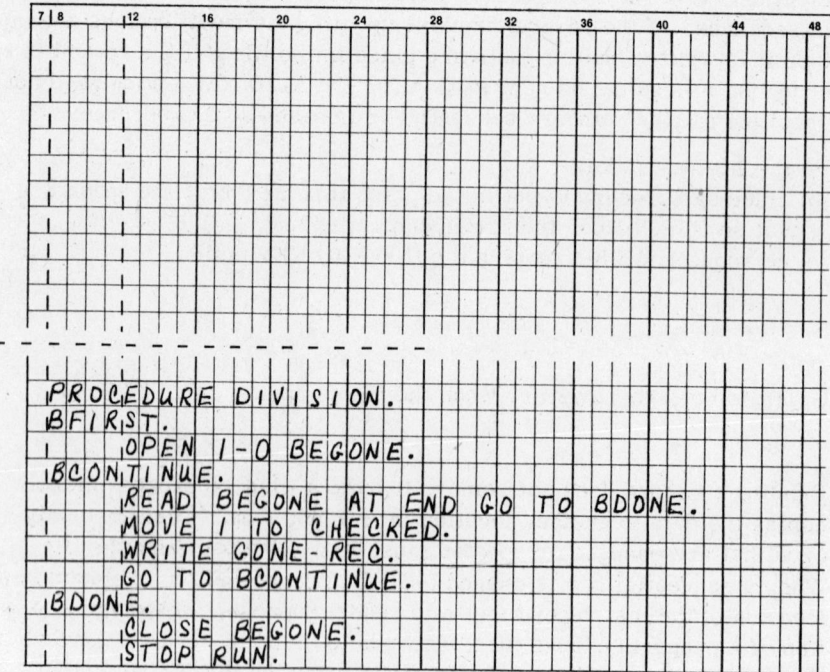

```
PROCEDURE DIVISION.
BFIRST.
    OPEN I-O BEGONE.
BCONTINUE.
    READ BEGONE AT END GO TO BDONE.
    MOVE 1 TO CHECKED.
    WRITE GONE-REC.
    GO TO BCONTINUE.
BDONE.
    CLOSE BEGONE.
    STOP RUN.
```

13. The coding in Figure 10-1 on page 228 includes most of the first three divisions of an ANS COBOL program to insert new address information into many of the records of the standard sequential disk file. You are to write the missing portion here. Describe CODEPAY-TABLE to occupy the same storage area as PAYCODE. Use SPEED as the subscripted variable.

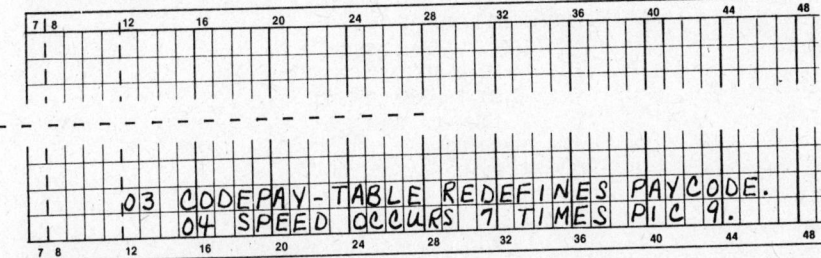

```
   03 CODEPAY-TABLE REDEFINES PAYCODE.
   04 SPEED OCCURS 7 TIMES PIC 9.
```

14. The flowchart in Figure 10-1 will guide you now as you write the Procedure Division of program TRANSIENTS. Notice that this is a record-matching program, but only the updated records need be written back into position. The correct coding appears on page 230.

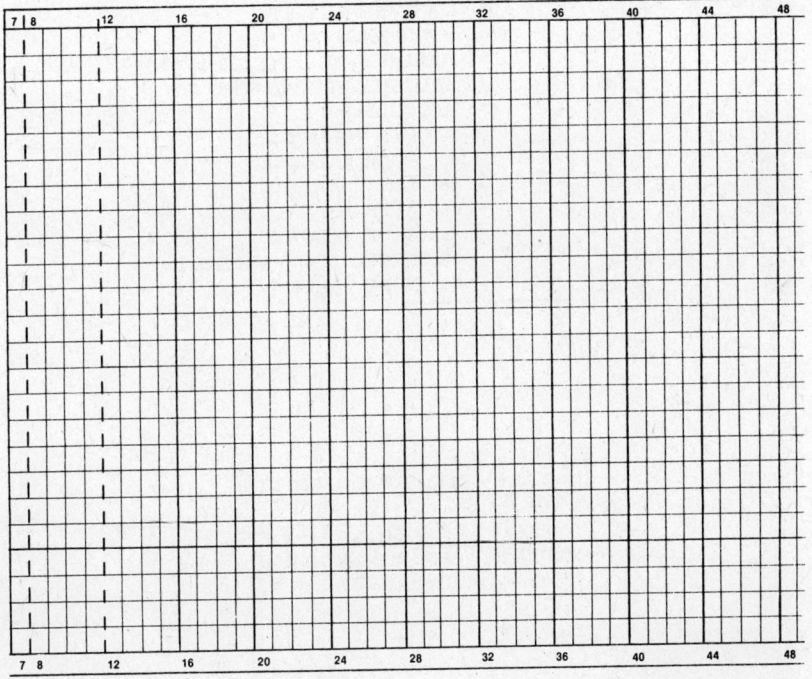

```
IDENTIFICATION DIVISION.
PROGRAM-ID. TRANSIENTS.
ENVIRONMENT DIVISION.
INPUT-OUTPUT SECTION.
FILE-CONTROL.
    SELECT UPDISK ASSIGN TO
        UT-S-PERMANT.
    SELECT TRANSACT ASSIGN TO
        UR-S-CARDIN.
DATA DIVISION.
FILE SECTION.
FD UPDISK
    LABEL RECORDS ARE STANDARD
    BLOCK CONTAINS 8 RECORDS.
01  MASTER-REC.
    02  PERSONAL.
        03  NAME PIC X(21).
        03  CUSTOMER-NUMBER PIC X(6).
        03  ADDRESS-HOME.
            04  STREET PIC X(15).
            04  CITYSTATE PIC X(15).
    02  PAYRECORD.
        03  YEAR-OPENED PIC 99.
        03  MAXIMUM-CREDIT
                PIC S9999V99.
        03  MAXIMUM-BILL PIC S9999V99.
        03  BALANCE-DUE PIC S9999V99.
        03  PAYCODE PIC 9.
            88  BAD VALUE 1.
            88  POOR VALUE 2.
            88  SLOW VALUE 3.
            88  AVERAGE VALUE 4.
            88  GOOD VALUE 5.
            88  EXCELLENT VALUE 6.
            88  NONE VALUE 7.




FD TRANSACT
    LABEL RECORDS ARE OMITTED.
01  CHANGES.
    02  C-NR PIC X(6).
    02  NEW-ADDRESS PIC X(15).
    02  FILLER PIC X(59).
```

Figure 10-1

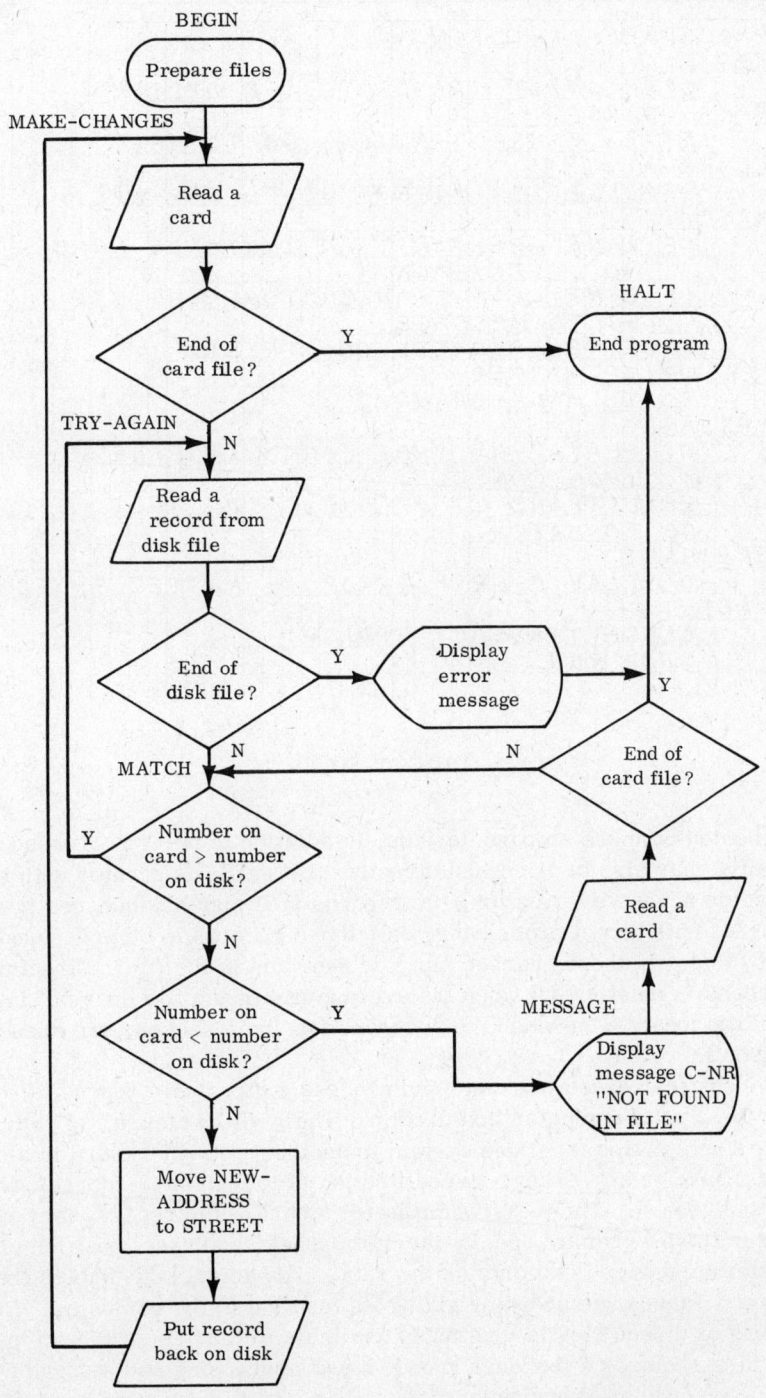

Figure 10-1 (continued)

```
PROCEDURE DIVISION.
BEGIN.
    OPEN INPUT TRANSACT, I-O UPDISK.
MAKE-CHANGES.
    READ TRANSACT AT END GO TO HALT.
TRY-AGAIN.
    READ UPDISK AT END GO TO ERR-HALT.
MATCH.
    IF C-NR GREATER THAN CUSTOMER-NUMBER
        GO TO TRY-AGAIN.
    IF C-NR LESS THAN CUSTOMER-NUMBER
        GO TO MESSAGE.
    MOVE NEW-ADDRESS TO STREET.
    WRITE MASTER-REC.
    GO TO MAKE-CHANGES.
MESSAGE.
    DISPLAY C-NR "NOT FOUND IN FILE"
        UPON CONSOLE.
    READ TRANSACT AT END GO TO HALT.
    GO TO MATCH.
ERR-HALT.
    DISPLAY C-NR " ERROR -- MASTER ENDED".
HALT.
    CLOSE TRANSACT UPDISK.
    STOP RUN.
```

DIRECT FILES

Files located on mass storage devices, in addition to being processed sequentially, may also be accessed directly. If the file is created with the appropriate access information, the records in it may be accessed in any sequence. With direct processing, only those records to be processed need be read, and only those changed must be replaced in the file. Direct or random access is most useful when the average use of the file does not involve most of its records, or when the records, for some reason, are needed in a nonsequential order.

The entries needed to create and process a direct file depend to some extent on the type of computer installation. The ASSIGN clause, as you have already seen, varies from one system to another. Every record in a direct file must have an actual key, a specification of the physical address or location of the record. This key, which is not a part of the record, may be manipulated in the program to specify the disk, track, and exact position on the mass storage device that contains the data. The actual key enables the programmer to access a record by giving its location to the computer. Random accessing of direct files is thus made available to the user. Effective use of direct files requires a thorough knowledge of addressing and storage within the device. Only an overview of direct file usage is presented here. We will not consider how to create the keys.

15. Direct files must be located on mass storage devices. The computer installations that require the programmer to specify organization in the ASSIGN clause use the code DA (which replaces UR or UT), for class, and D, for direct organization (as opposed to sequential). Which of the following might be a correct ASSIGN clause for an IBM installation?

   (a) ASSIGN TO IBM-370.
   (b) ASSIGN TO DA-D-PAYFILE.
   (c) ASSIGN TO DA-PAYF-D.

   ---

   b (The ASSIGN clause for other installations may be drastically different, and may not include any reference to file access or organization. Check with your own system.)

16. The direct file requires other File-Control entries in addition to ASSIGN and SELECT. The ACCESS clause, in the form ACCESS IS RANDOM, must be specified whenever random access is to be used. Which of the following might be an appropriate entry for a direct file?

   (a) SOURCE-COMPUTER. ACCESS IS RANDOM.
   (b) SELECT INFO ASSIGN TO 6800 ACCESS IS SEQUENTIAL.
   (c) SELECT INFO ASSIGN TO 6800 ACCESS IS RANDOM.

   ---

   c

17. Records in a direct file are accessed by means of an actual key, which gives the computer the location of the desired record. The data-name that contains the key value is specified in the ACTUAL KEY clause of the File-Control paragraph. The format for the ACTUAL KEY clause of the File-Control paragraph is shown below:

   > ACTUAL KEY IS   data-name

   Write a clause specifying that the key value will be found in a variable named A-KEY.

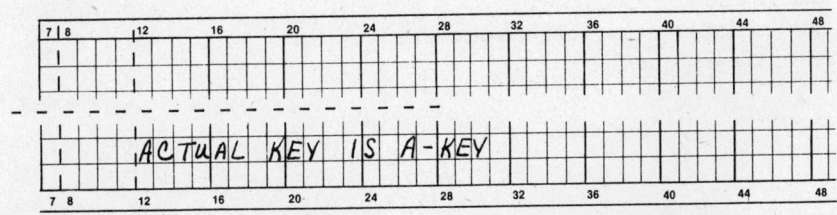

232 ANS COBOL

18. List four clauses you would use to describe a direct file in the File-Control paragraph of the Environment Division.

_____   _____

_____   _____

- - - - - - - - - - - - - - - - - -

SELECT, ASSIGN, ACCESS, ACTUAL KEY

19. file-name = UPDATO
    system-name = MASTER7
    key variable = LOCK4

Using the information above, write a complete File-Control entry for a direct file.

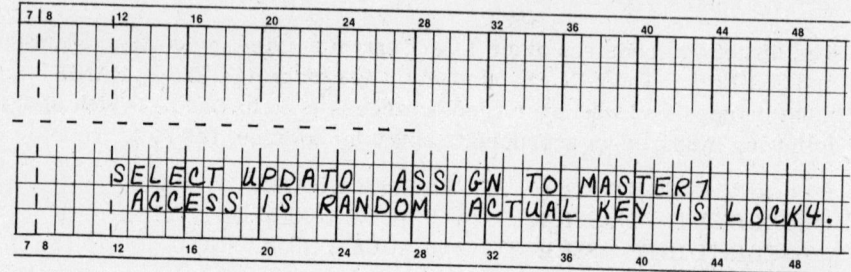

(As usual, arrangement of these entries within the B margin is flexible.)

20. The actual key that references a direct file contains information that delineates the track of the disk on which the desired record is located. It may also include information to identify the particular record on that track. The system may put restrictions on the exact format of this key content. Some IBM systems, for example, require that it have two parts. The first four bytes of the variable must be a five-integer binary item to describe location. The remainder, from 1 to 255 bytes, identifies the specific record. Whatever its internal format, however, the actual key variable must contain the required value before each READ or WRITE statement for the file is executed. In which of the following cases would you need to have a specific value assigned to the actual key variable?

(a) before accessing any record sequentially
(b) before opening a direct file
(c) before replacing a randomly accessed record
(d) after closing the file

_____

- - - - - - - - - - - - - - -

c

21. The value of the actual key variable determines:

    (a) which record is read.
    (b) where the record is written into the file.
    (c) how the file is processed.
    (d) the organization of the file.

    - - - - - - - - - - - - - - - - - - -

    a, b

22. The value of the actual key variable is associated with a record when the direct file is created. How would you open DAFILE if the records are to be associated with values of ACT-KEY?

    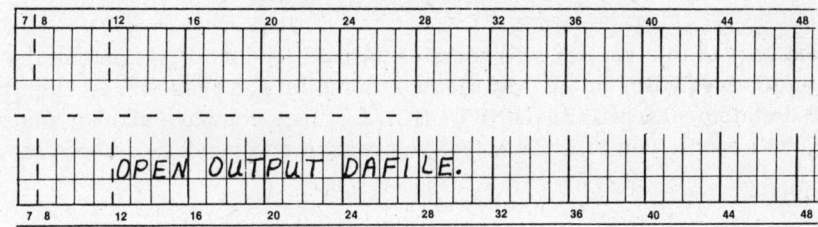

    (All files are created as OUTPUT.)

23. In the Data Division, the actual key variable must be described with a PICTURE clause, but it cannot be contained in the file it is used to access. Suppose your direct file is DAFILE. The actual key could be described:

    (a) in the Working-Storage Section.
    (b) in the Input-Output Section.
    (c) as the first entry in the record associated with DAFILE.
    (d) as part of a file called XTRA.

    - - - - - - - - - - - - - - - - - - -

    a, d   (b is not in the Data Division; the variable could not be described in c because it will be associated with that file.)

24. An actual key variable could be described in:

    (a) a record associated with a unit record device.
    (b) a level 77 item.
    (c) any file except the one it will be used to access.
    (d) none of the above.

    - - - - - - - - - - - - - - - - - - -

234 ANS COBOL

a, b, c

To use a direct file in an ANS COBOL program, you must include the appropriate Environment Division entries. These assign the file to a mass storage device, specify that records will be accessed randomly, and name an actual key whose value will let the computer know where to find the needed record. The specific format for these Environment Division entries may (and usually will) vary from one brand of computer to another, and even from one model to another within the same make. Be sure to check the programmer's guide or reference manual before you try to run a program using direct files when you have access to a system.

PROCEDURE DIVISION ENTRIES

The next part of this section will treat certain Procedure Division entries common to direct files on all ANS COBOL compilers. These three slightly modified statements, with the ANS COBOL features you have already learned to use, will enable you to write effective programs to process direct files.

25. All files must be opened before they can be used in any way. Direct files, like all files on mass storage devices, can be opened as INPUT, OUTPUT, or I-O. Match the OPEN options below with the purpose to which a file might be put.

    _____ (a) INPUT
    _____ (b) OUTPUT
    _____ (c) I-O

    1. Certain records will be changed with new credit limits imposed.
    2. The file is being created for the first time.
    3. Certain records will be accessed for faster reference. No changes will be made.
    4. Some records will be updated and others will be added.

- - - - - - - - - - - - - - - - - -

(a) 3; (b) 2; (c) 1, 4

26. Write OPEN statements for each of the following uses of a direct file, PATIENT.

    (a) A master file of data on hospital patients is to be generated.

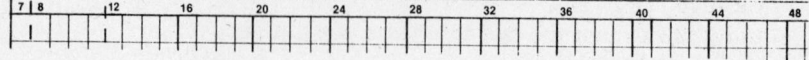

(b) The master file will be modified to reflect any new admissions and diagnoses.

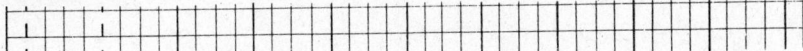

(c) The master file records that correspond to the discharges of the day will be accessed to retrieve billing information.

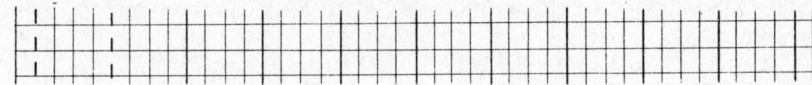

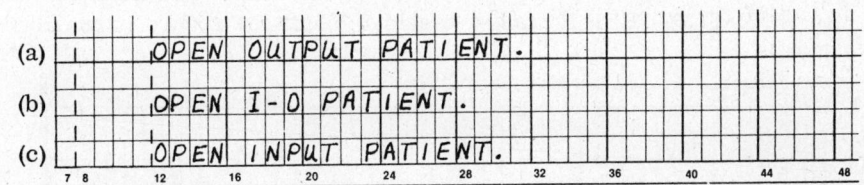

27. READ and WRITE statements that refer to direct files must include an option to check the validity of the key. The INVALID KEY option specifies an action to be taken if the key is found to be invalid. Which of the following might be an appropriate INVALID KEY option?

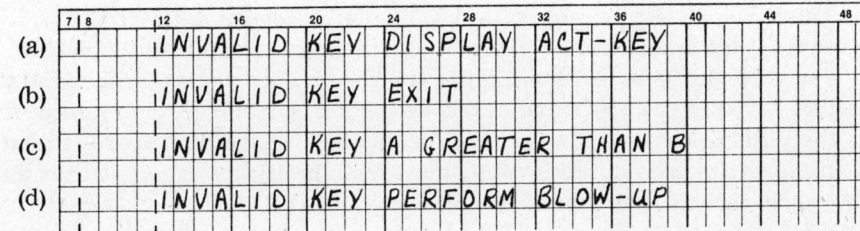

a, d (The EXIT statement must be the only statement in a paragraph; c includes a condition, not a statement.)

28. The INVALID KEY option must be specified in every READ or WRITE statement that refers to a direct file. In which of the following situations must the option be included in the appropriate statement?

(a) a standard sequential disk file opened as OUTPUT
(b) a direct file opened as I-O
(c) a direct file opened as OUTPUT
(d) an input file on magnetic tape

236 ANS COBOL

a, b, c (As you learned earlier in this chapter, standard sequential disk files opened as OUTPUT also use this option.)

29. These are the formats for the INVALID KEY options of the READ and WRITE statements:

> READ   file-name   INVALID KEY   statement.
>
> WRITE   record-name   INVALID KEY   statement.

Write a statement to place DISK-REC into DISKFILE and transfer control to SEND-FOR-HELP if the key associated with the record is considered invalid.

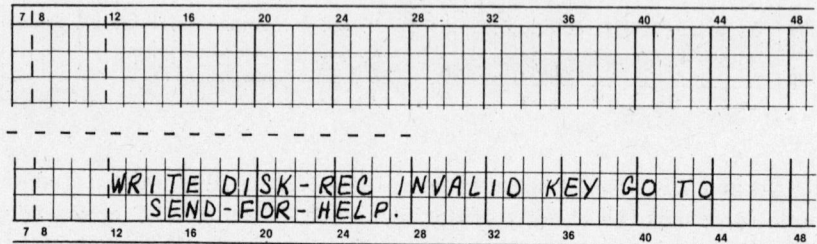

```
WRITE DISK-REC INVALID KEY GO TO
SEND-FOR-HELP.
```

30. The INVALID KEY option of a WRITE statement for a direct file is activated if the track number (as given by the current value of the actual key variable) is not within the file limits, or if no record associated with that key exists. The value of the actual key variable at the moment that the WRITE statement is executed determines where the record is written. If the key is considered invalid, however, the record is not written anywhere; instead, the statement following INVALID KEY is executed.
Which of the following would the programmer have to do before a WRITE statement could be executed for his direct file?

(a) open the file as OUTPUT or I-O
(b) ascertain that the actual key variable contained the appropriate information
(c) specify an alternative action to be taken if the variable indicates a location outside the file

---

a, b, c

The INVALID KEY option of a WRITE statement in a direct file is activated if the track specified is not in the file limits. It may also be activated if the record identifier portion of the key does not match the identification of the record in the output area. The most important fact, however, is that when the option is activated, the record is not written. The action specified should record the problem before further processing of the file obscures the fact.

31. The INVALID KEY option of a READ statement specifies an action to be taken if a record corresponding to the information in the actual key variable is not found within the file. Write a statement to access the MASRECORD in MASFILE in the locations specified in the actual key variable. If no record corresponds to that location, transfer control to ERROR-ROUTINE.

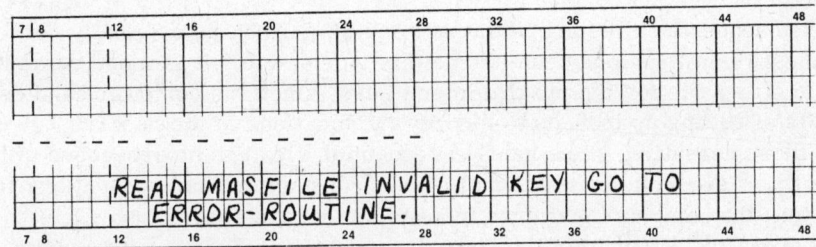

```
READ MASFILE INVALID KEY GO TO
ERROR-ROUTINE.
```

32. The AT END option of the READ statement is not specified for direct access INPUT or I-O files, since the records are accessed in random sequence. For the same reason, assigning the value of the desired actual key variable before control reaches the READ statement is essential to ensure that the required record is accessed. If the location specified is not within the file, no record is accessed and the statement following INVALID KEY is executed. Assume MASFILE is being accessed directly, as in the preceding frame. The location specified in the actual key variable is not included within the file. What happens?

_____

Control is transferred to ERROR-ROUTINE; no record is accessed.

33. When a file is opened as OUTPUT, each WRITE statement executed places the record currently in the output area into the file. When a file has been opened I-O, each WRITE statement places back into the file the record accessed by the most recently executed READ statement. When the INVALID KEY option of a READ statement is activated, the next input/output statement for that file should be _____.

_____

another READ statement (Definitely not a WRITE statement, since no record was accessed when INVALID KEY was activated. A WRITE statement would attempt to place the former record into the file. Since the key won't match, INVALID KEY would be invoked once again.)

Since we have not dealt with the construction and makeup of the actual key, we cannot realistically go into writing programs to create or access direct files. In the next section you will write a program to randomly access records in a differently organized file, the indexed sequential file.

INDEXED SEQUENTIAL FILES

Indexed sequential files are not a part of ANS COBOL as originally conceived but most compilers today can handle this type of file. It is more convenient than a direct file for the programmer to use, since the compiler handles the details of setting up indexes to identify the locations of the records. It is also more versatile, since indexed sequential files can be processed either directly or sequentially with equal ease. When an indexed sequential file is created, the computer prepares indexes so that the record identifier (something like CUST-NO within the record) is automatically associated with physical location information. Then the programmer merely refers to that identifier; the computer searches its indexes and locates the desired record. The statements used in processing indexed sequential files are very similar to those used for processing direct files. The primary difference in the ANS COBOL program lies in the names and construction of the keys.

34. In the Environment Division entries for an indexed sequential file, the SELECT and ASSIGN clauses must, of course, be included. The ACCESS clause must be specified if random processing will be used, and the default option (ACCESS IS SEQUENTIAL) may be specified if desired when using sequential processing. The RECORD KEY clause is always required. Which of the following would be a correct Environment Division entry for sequential creation of an indexed sequential file?

```
(a)     SELECT ISFILE ASSIGN DA-I-EXTNM
            ACCESS IS RANDOM
            RECORD KEY IS REC-KEY.

(b)     SELECT ISFILE ASSIGN DA-I-EXTNM
            ACCESS IS SEQUENTIAL
            RECORD KEY IS REC-KEY.

(c)     SELECT ISFILE ASSIGN DA-I-EXTNM
            ACTUAL KEY IS ACT-KEY.

(d)     SELECT ISFILE ASSIGN DA-I-EXTNM
            RECORD KEY IS REC-KEY.
```

b, d (a specifies random access; these files must be created sequentially. c specifies an actual key rather than a record key.)

35. The record key variable, in contrast to the actual key variable, must be included within the record, but it must not include the first character position. This variable may be any item that is unique in each record —a social security number, a policy number, a name, or some exotic code. In the record description below, which elementary items might be specified as a record key?

```
 7|8   |12   16   20   24   28   32   36   40   44   48
 01    EMPLOYEE-RECORD.
  1    02 LAST-NAME PIC X(12).
  1    02 FIRST-NAME PIC X(10).
  1    02 PER-HOUR PIC 99V99.
  1    02 LOCATION PIC X(35).
  1    02 TIME-CLOCK-NR PIC X(6).
  1    02 SOC-SEC-NR PIC 9(9).
```

- - - - - - - - - - - - - - - - -

TIME-CLOCK-NR and SOC-SEC-NR (LAST-NAME includes the first character of the record.)

36. Write a RECORD KEY clause for the record in the preceding frame.

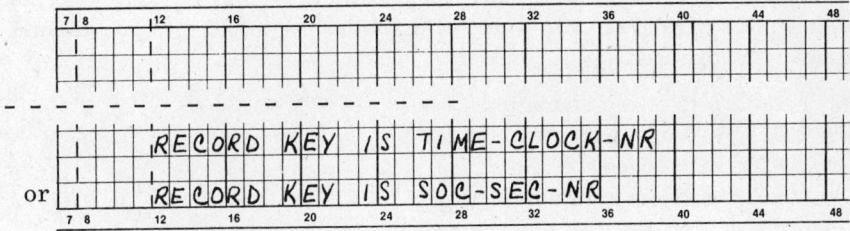

or

```
    RECORD KEY IS TIME-CLOCK-NR
    RECORD KEY IS SOC-SEC-NR
```

37. Creation of an indexed sequential file is always accomplished sequentially. Labels are used (we will continue to specify standard ones) and blocking is permitted as in standard sequential files. The output statement for indexed sequential files is identical in form to that for direct files. Write the following:

(a) an FD entry for ISFILE with blocks of four records.

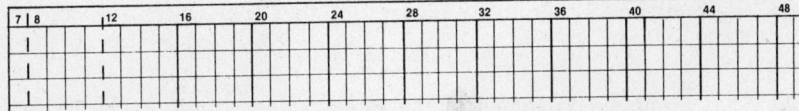

(b) an OPEN statement for creating the file.

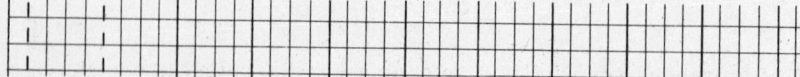

(c) a statement to place ISREC in the file and transfer control to OUT7 if an error occurs.

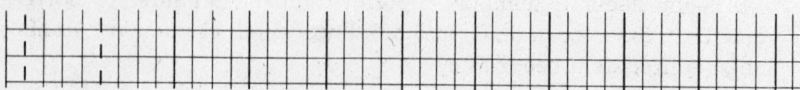

- - - - - - - - - - - - - - - - - -

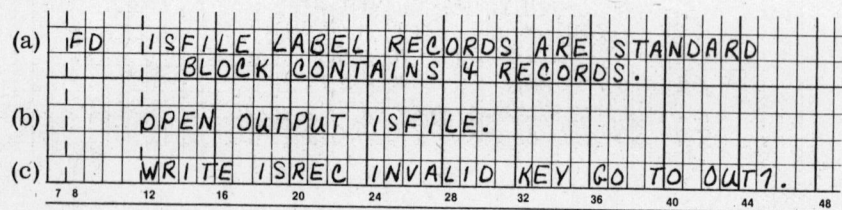

38. The INVALID KEY option of a WRITE statement referring to an indexed sequential file opened as output is activated in either of two cases. As in direct files, the clause may be activated when there is no space to write the record. In addition, however, the record key variable is considered invalid if it is not in ascending order as compared with the previous record written into the file. Suppose the latest record key variable had a value of 10678. For which of the following would the INVALID KEY clause be activated?

   (a) 10773, with space remaining
   (b) 10773, with no space remaining
   (c) 10678, with space remaining
   (d) 00693, with space remaining

- - - - - - - - - - - - - - - - -

b, c, d   (Choice b has the area already filled; c is a duplicate, not in ascending sequence; d likewise is not in ascending sequence.)

In direct file creation, as opposed to indexed sequential files, the programmer is responsible for checking the uniqueness of his record identifiers. The key in direct files merely locates, rather than identifies, the records.

39. When an indexed sequential file is processed in an I-O mode, an additional key clause must be specified in the FILE-CONTROL paragraph.

MASS STORAGE DEVICES (DISK FILES) 241

The symbolic key variable, in contrast to the record key variable, must be described as a Working-Storage item. DAFILE is an indexed sequential file to be updated. SYMBOLIC KEY IS SYM-K has been specified in the Environment Division. Which of the following is true?

(a) SYM-K must be part of the record associated with DAFILE.
(b) SYM-K may be described in the File Section if it is not associated with DAFILE.
(c) SYM-K may be a level 77 variable.
(d) SYM-K must be described in the Working-Storage Section.

----

c, d (IBM compilers use the term NOMINAL KEY rather than SYMBOLIC KEY.)

40. Write direct (D) or indexed sequential (IS) after each key type below.

(a) RECORD KEY _____

(b) ACTUAL KEY _____

(c) SYMBOLIC KEY _____

(a) IS; (b) D; (c) IS

41. An indexed sequential file opened as output must have which type of key?

----

record

42. Assume ISFILE is to be updated. ISCODE is a level 77 item and ITEM-CODE is a unique variable contained within ISREC. Write the two key clauses required if the file is to be opened I-O.

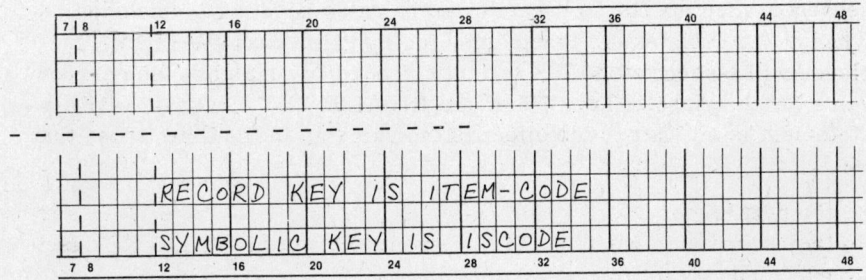

43. A value must be assigned to the symbolic key variable before every READ or WRITE statement that refers to an indexed sequential file is executed, whether the file was opened as I-O or INPUT. When the statement is executed, the compiler searches its indexes for the value contained in the symbolic key variable until it locates a record whose record key matches the symbolic key value. The index then identifies the location of that record. Refer to your response in the preceding frame. Assume you wish to read the record in ISFILE with key 10733. You would move 10733 to which variable? _____

ISCODE

44. Records can be deleted from an ISAM file when it is opened as I-O. Actually, the record isn't deleted, but "flagged," by moving HIGH-VALUES (hex FF) to the first position of the record. All ISAM files are cleaned up by utility programs periodically. Marked records are omitted at that time. Once a record is marked for deletion, it can no longer be accessed randomly. If you are sequentially accessing records, however, you will get deleted ones in sequence. Suppose your first position is described as

    02   DELETE-CODE   PIC X.

Write a statement to mark the record for deletion.

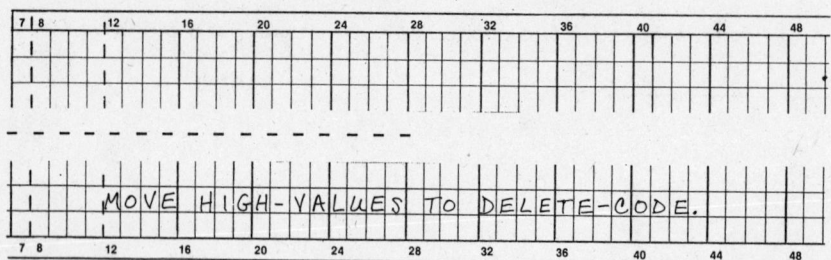

`MOVE HIGH-VALUES TO DELETE-CODE.`

45. Even though the keys in an indexed sequential file must be in ascending sequence when the file is created, every value need not be included. When a READ statement is executed for the file, the INVALID KEY clause will be activated if no record's record key matches the current value of the symbolic key. When the INVALID KEY clause of a READ statement is activated, the effect is the same as in the direct file—that is:

(a) the next higher keyed record is read.
(b) the record is read, then the statement following INVALID KEY is executed.

(c) no record is read, and the statement following INVALID KEY is executed.
(d) the result is unpredictable.

----

c

46. The WRITE statement is used to add records to an I/O ISAM file, as well as to place updated records back into it. The INVALID KEY clause is required, as it was for OUTPUT ISAM files, but the statement is executed only if the symbolic key value at the time the WRITE statement is executed is such that it would create duplicate keyed record in the file. In this case only, the record and symbolic keys are considered invalid. Write a statement to place ISREC back into the indexed sequential file, and transfer control to GOOF-UP if the key is invalid.

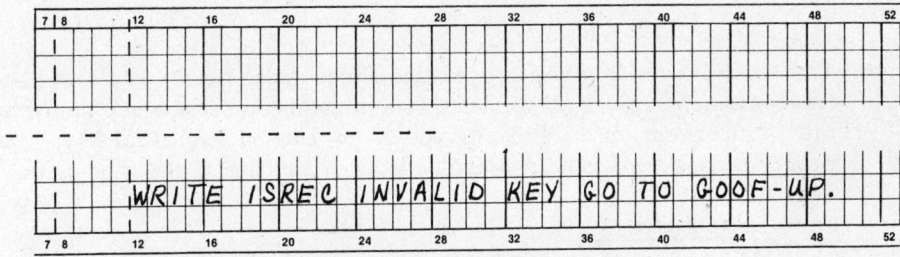

```
WRITE ISREC INVALID KEY GO TO GOOF-UP.
```

(Some IBM systems use a REWRITE statement here. Aside from the word REWRITE, it is identical to the WRITE statement.)

COMPREHENSIVE PROGRAM

Now you have all the knowledge you need to write a program to process indexed sequential files. You can specify the appropriate keys in the Environment Division and describe them in the correct sections of the Data Division. You can specify an action to be taken in the Procedure Division when the key is considered invalid. The following frames will guide you to write an extensive program to update an indexed sequential file that contains records of customers who have charge accounts at a department store. The update information will include new customer records to be added to the file, charges to be added to customers' accounts, and credits to be subtracted from others. You may consider this section a final exam in COBOL.

47. The first division of your program must identify it. Write the complete division, using at least one optional paragraph.

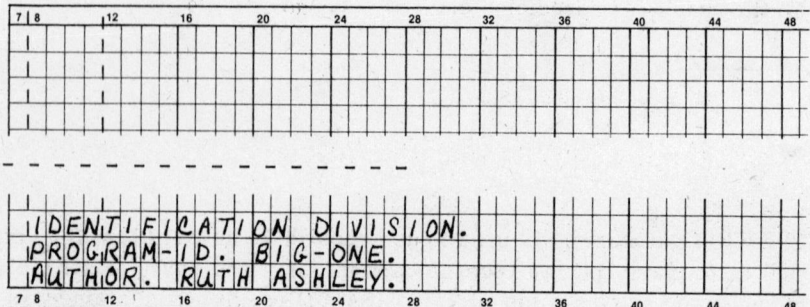

(Your optional paragraph could have been DATE-WRITTEN or REMARKS. Almost any program name could have been chosen if it began with a letter and the first eight characters were unique. Be sure to check your format; periods must have at least one space following, and hyphens must be in position.)

48. The second division gives information about the system. The system flowchart below gives all the information you need to describe the equipment for a program to randomly update an indexed sequential file. The program uses card input and print output in addition to the random access file.

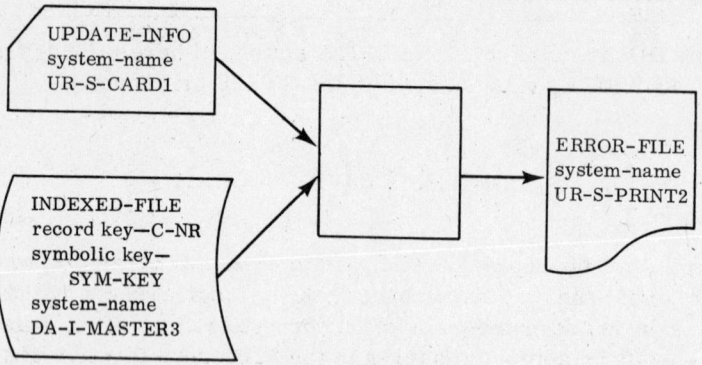

Now write the needed section of the second division for your ANS COBOL program. Space is allowed on the next page for your entries.

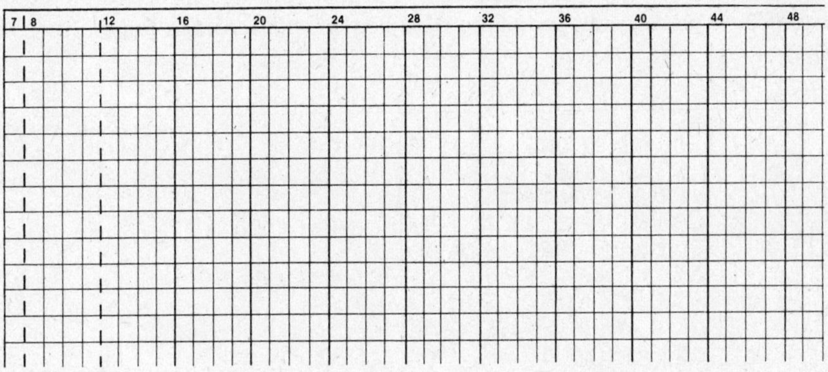

```
7 8   12    16    20    24    28    32    36    40    44    48
 ENVIRONMENT DIVISION.
 INPUT-OUTPUT SECTION.
 FILE-CONTROL.
     SELECT UPDATE-INFO ASSIGN UR-S-CARD1.
     SELECT ERROR-FILE ASSIGN UR-S-PRINT2.
     SELECT INDEXED-FILE
         ASSIGN DA-I-MASTER3
         RECORD KEY IS C-NR
         SYMBOLIC KEY IS SYM-KEY
         ACCESS IS RANDOM.
```

49. In the Data Division, the record key variable will be described in which section? _____

File Section

50. The symbolic key variable will be described in the _____ Section.

Working-Storage

The complete Data Division for your program is reproduced here. Read it carefully, noting especially the data description entries for the key variables.

```
       DATA DIVISION.
       FILE SECTION.
       FD  UPDATE-INFO
           LABEL RECORDS ARE OMITTED.
       01  UPDATE-RECORD.
           02  TRANSACTION-CODE PIC 9.
           02  CARDNO PIC X(6).
           02  NEW-NAME PIC X(21).
           02  NEW-ADDR PIC X(30).
           02  YEAR PIC XX.
           02  MAX-CREDIT PIC 9999V99.
           02  FILLER PIC X(4).
           02  ACTION PIC 9999V99.
           02  FILLER PIC X(4).
       FD  ERROR-FILE
           LABEL RECORDS ARE OMITTED.
       01  ERROR-LIST PIC X(133).

       FD  INDEXED-FILE
           LABEL RECORDS ARE STANDARD
           BLOCK CONTAINS 5 RECORDS.
       01  BAS-REC.
           02  PERSONAL.
               03  NAME PIC X(21).
               03  C-NR PIC X(6).
               03  C-ADDR PIC X(30).
           02  HISTORY.
               03  OP-YR PIC XX.
               03  MAXIM PIC 9999V99.
               03  MAX-BILL PIC 9999V99.
               03  BAL-DUE PIC 9999V99.
               03  PAYCODE PIC 9.
       WORKING-STORAGE SECTION.
       77  SYM-KEY PIC X(6).
       77  AMOUNT PIC 9999V99.
       01  LISTING.
           02  CARRIAGE PIC X.
           02  PROBLEM PIC X(80).
           02  E-MESSAGE PIC X(52).
```

51. The transaction records for this program each contain a TRANSACTION-CODE based on the type of transaction. A code of 1 indicates a new customer's record is to be added to the file. A code of 2 indicates a charge to the customer's account, and a 3 indicates a credit, either from a payment or return. The program must specify different paths for each transaction type. The flowcharts on the following pages show the flow of computer control in solving the problem, with the three different routines as separate entities. In coding your solution, you will probably find it convenient to write the three routines ADD-RECORD, ADD-CHARGE, and SUBTRACT-CREDIT first. Then write the basic program, branching to and from routines as necessary. Any time an INVALID KEY clause is activated while a record is being replaced in the file, display "INVALID KEY", C-NR, then transfer control to READ-UPDATE-INFO. As you complete this program, use the coding form provided following the flowcharts. Refer back to the Data Division and flowcharts as needed. Then compare your program with ours.

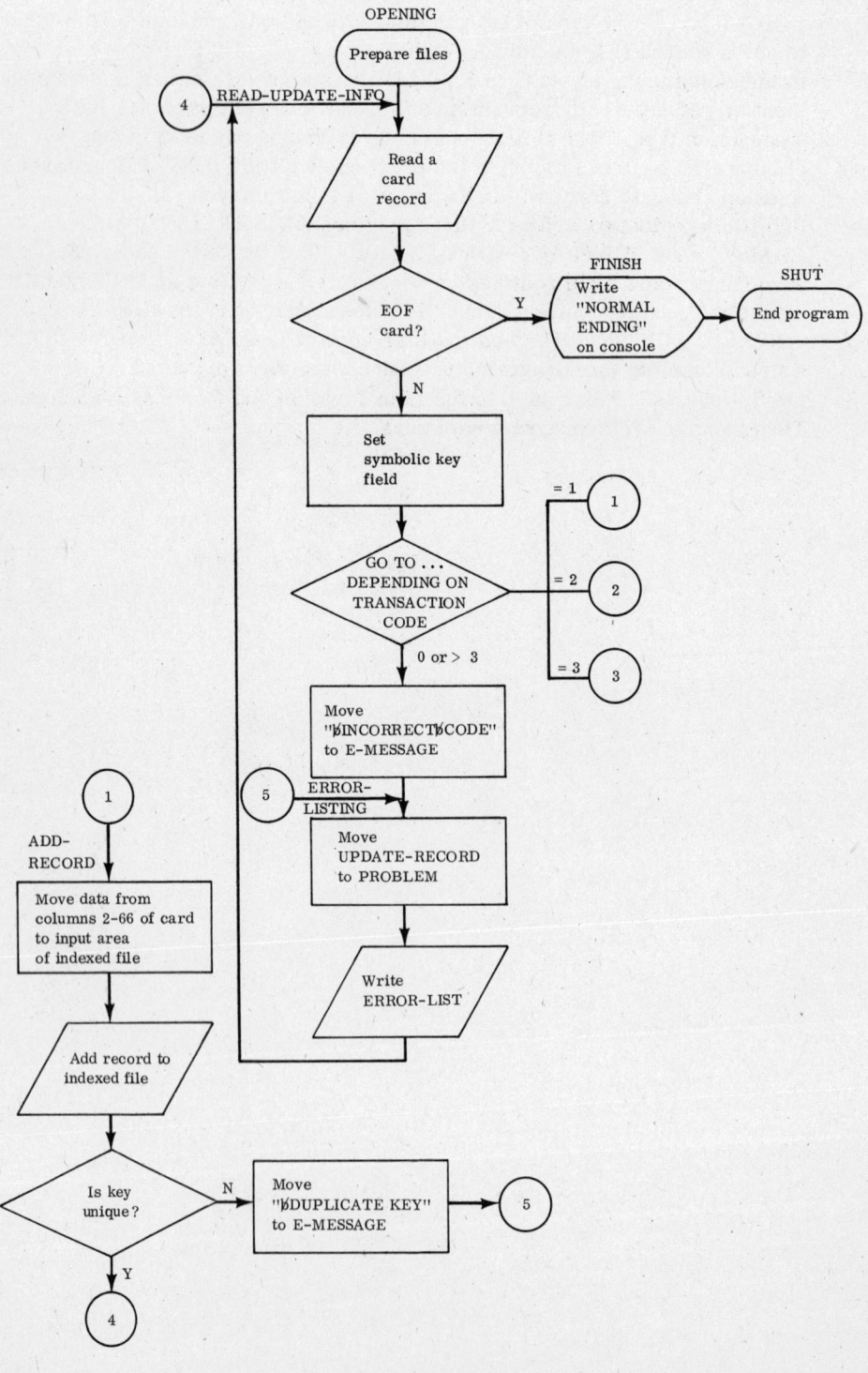

MASS STORAGE DEVICES (DISK FILES) 249

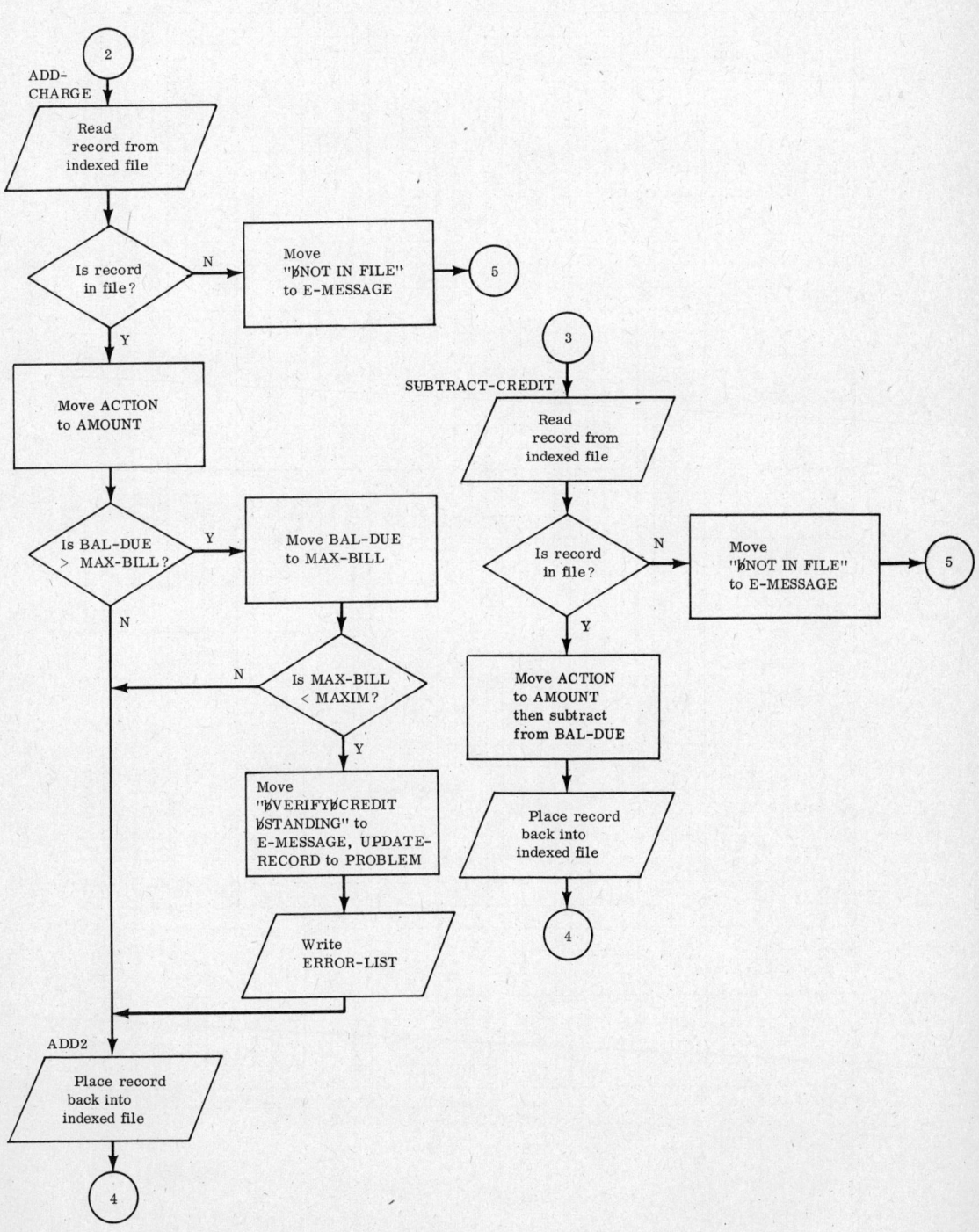

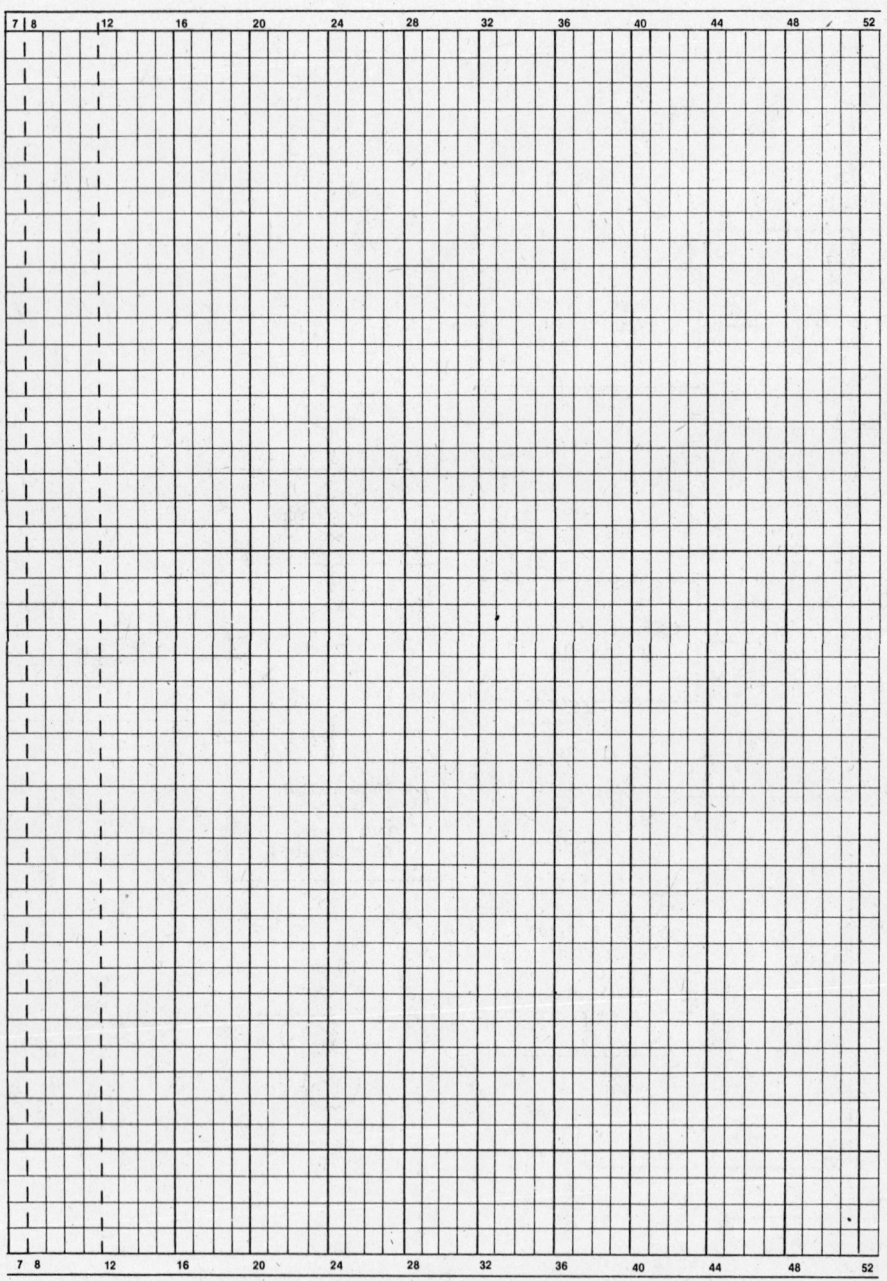

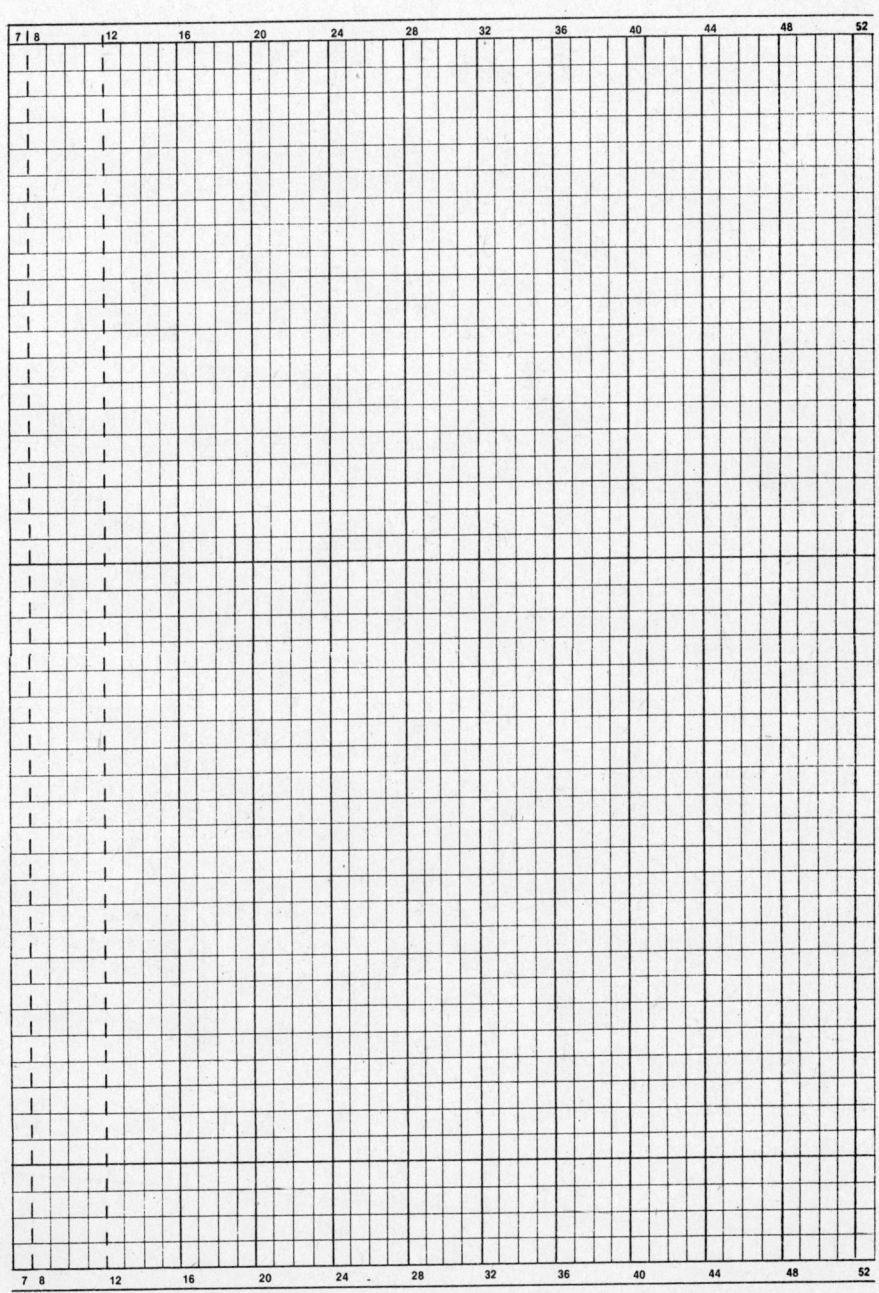

```cobol
       PROCEDURE DIVISION.
       OPENING.
           OPEN INPUT UPDATE-INFO, OUTPUT
               ERROR-FILE, I-O INDEXED-FILE.
       READ-UPDATE-INFO.
           READ UPDATE-INFO AT END GO TO FINISH.
           MOVE CARDNO TO SYM-KEY.
           GO TO ADD-RECORD ADD-CHARGE
               SUBTRACT-PAYMENT DEPENDING ON
               TRANSACTION-CODE.
           MOVE " INCORRECT CODE" TO E-MESSAGE.
       ERROR-LISTING.
           MOVE UPDATE-RECORD TO PROBLEM.
           WRITE ERROR-LIST FROM LISTING.
           GO TO READ-UPDATE-INFO.

       ADD-RECORD.
           MOVE CARDNO TO C-NR.
           MOVE NEW-NAME TO NAME.
           MOVE NEW-ADDR TO C-ADDR.
           MOVE YEAR TO OP-YR.
           MOVE MAX-CREDIT TO MAXIM.
           WRITE BAS-REC INVALID KEY MOVE
               " DUPLICATE KEY" TO E-MESSAGE GO TO
               ERROR-LISTING.
           GO TO READ-UPDATE-INFO.

       ADD-CHARGE.
           READ INDEXED-FILE INVALID KEY MOVE
               " NOT IN FILE" TO E-MESSAGE GO TO
               ERROR-LISTING.
           MOVE ACTION TO AMOUNT.
           ADD AMOUNT TO BAL-DUE.

           IF BAL-DUE GREATER THAN MAX-BILL
               MOVE BAL-DUE TO MAX-BILL.
           IF MAX-BILL LESS THAN MAXIM GO TO ADD2.
           MOVE " VERIFY CREDIT STANDING" TO
               E-MESSAGE.
           MOVE UPDATE-RECORD TO PROBLEM.
           WRITE ERROR-LIST FROM LISTING.
```

(continued on next page)

```
ADD2.
    WRITE BAS-REC INVALID KEY DISPLAY
        "INVALID KEY" C-NR GO TO
        READ-UPDATE-INFO.
    GO TO READ-UPDATE-INFO.
SUBTRACT-CREDIT.
    READ INDEXED-FILE INVALID KEY MOVE
        " NOT IN FILE" TO E-MESSAGE GO TO
        ERROR-LISTING.
    MOVE ACTION TO AMOUNT.
    SUBTRACT AMOUNT FROM BAL-DUE.
    WRITE BAS-REC INVALID KEY DISPLAY
        "INVALID KEY" C-NR.
    GO TO READ-UPDATE-INFO.
FINISH.
    DISPLAY "NORMAL ENDING" UPON CONSOLE.
WIND-UP.
    CLOSE UPDATE-INFO ERROR-FILE
        INDEXED-FILE.
    STOP RUN.
```

SUMMARY

You have learned a great deal about ANS COBOL. If you have run any of your programs, you have learned even more. You should now be able to use your local COBOL reference manual effectively in expanding your knowledge and becoming a productive COBOL programmer.

APPENDIX A
ANS COBOL Reserved Words

The words listed in this appendix are reserved words in ANS COBOL. Most of these words are reserved in all such compilers, but some may be permitted in some installations. Most installations will also have special words they have reserved. None of these reserved words may be used in a name that a programmer creates, as a program-name, a paragraph-name, or a data-name.

ABOUT
ACCEPT
ACCESS
ACTUAL
ADD
ADDRESS
ADVANCING
AFTER
ALL
ALPHABETIC
ALPHANUMERIC
ALSO
ALTER
ALTERNATE
AND
APPLY
ARE
AREA
AREAS
ASCENDING
ASSIGN
AT
AUTHOR

BEFORE
BEGINNING
BITS
BLANK

BLOCK
BOTTOM
BY

CALL
CANCEL
CD
CF
CH
CHARACTER
CHARACTERS
CLOCK-UNITS
CLOSE
COBOL
CODE
COLLATING
COLUMN
COMMA
COMMUNICATION
COMP
COMPUTATIONAL
COMPUTE
CONFIGURATION
CONSOLE
CONSTANT
CONTAINS
CONTROL
CONTROLS

COPY
CORR
CORRESPONDING
COUNT
CURRENCY

DATA
DATE
DATE-COMPILED
DATE-WRITTEN
DAY
DE
DEBUGGING
DECIMAL-POINT
DECLARATIVES
DEFINE
DELETE
DELIMITED
DELIMITER
DEPENDING
DESCENDING
DETAIL
DISPLAY
DIVIDE
DIVISION
DOWN
DUPLICATES
DYNAMIC

EGI
ELSE
EMI
ENABLE
END
END-OF-PAGE
ENTER
ENVIRONMENT
EOP
EQUAL
EQUALS
ERROR
ESI
EVERY
EXAMINE
EXCEPTION
EXIT
EXTEND

FD
FILE

FILE-CONTROL
FILE-LIMIT
FILE-LIMITS
FILLER
FINAL
FIRST
FOOTING
FOR
FROM

GENERATE
GIVING
GO
GREATER
GROUP

HEADING
HIGH-VALUE
HIGH-VALUES

I-O
I-O-CONTROL
IDENTIFICATION
IF
IN
INDEX
INDEXED
INDICATE
INITIAL
INITIATE
INPUT
INPUT-OUTPUT
INSPECT
INSTALLATION
INTO
INVALID
IS

JUST
JUSTIFIED

KEY

LABEL
LAST
LEADING
LEFT
LENGTH
LESS
LIBRARY
LIMIT

LIMITS
LINAGE
LINAGE-COUNTER
LINE
LINE-COUNTER
LINES
LINKAGE
LOCK
LOW-VALUE
LOW-VALUES

MEMORY
MERGE
MESSAGE
MINUS
MODE
MODULES
MOVE
MULTIPLE
MULTIPLY

NATIVE
NEGATIVE
NEXT
NO
NOMINAL
NOT
NOTE
NUMBER
NUMERIC

OBJECT-COMPUTER
OCCURS
OF
OFF
OH
OMITTED
ON
OPEN
OPTIONAL
OR
ORGANIZATION
OTHERWISE
OUTPUT
OVERFLOW

PAGE
PAGE-COUNTER
PERFORM
PF

PH
PIC
PICTURE
PLUS
POINT
POINTER
POSITION
POSITIVE
PRINTING
PRIORITY
PROCEDURE
PROCEED
PROCESSING
PROGRAM
PROGRAM-ID
PROTECT

QUEUE
QUOTE
QUOTES

RANDOM
RANGE
RD
READ
RECEIVE
RECORD
RECORDING
RECORDS
REDEFINES
REEL
REFERENCES
RELEASE
REMAINDER
REMARKS
REMOVAL
RENAMES
REPLACING
REPORT
REPORTING
REPORTS
RERUN
RESERVE
RESET
RETURN
REVERSED
REWIND
REWRITE
RF

ANS COBOL RESERVED WORDS

RH
RIGHT
ROUNDED
RUN

SAME
SD
SEARCH
SECTION
SECURITY
SEEK
SEGMENT
SEGMENT-LIMIT
SELECT
SEND
SENTENCE
SEPARATE
SEQUENCE
SEQUENTIAL
SET
SIGN
SIZE
SORT
SORT-MERGE
SOURCE
SOURCE-COMPUTER
SPACE
SPACES
SPECIAL-NAMES
STANDARD
START
STATUS
STOP
STRING
SUBTRACT
SUM
SUPERVISOR
SUPPRESS
SYMBOLIC
SYNC
SYNCHRONIZED

TABLE
TALLY
TALLYING
TAPE
TERMINAL
TERMINATE
TEXT
THAN
THEN
THROUGH
THRU
TIME
TIMES
TO
TOP
TRAILING
TYPE

UNEQUAL
UNIT
UNSTRING
UNTIL
UP
UPON
USAGE
USE
USING

VALUE
VALUES
VARYING

WHEN
WITH
WORDS
WORKING-STORAGE
WRITE

ZERO
ZEROES
ZEROS

APPENDIX B
Collating Sequence of COBOL Characters

The collating sequence, and even the characters considered, may vary among installations. One typical sequence (EBCDIC) is presented here. The specific sequence must be checked when you run programs in an actual installation. In this sequence, 9 has the highest value, and the blank (b̸) the lowest.

```
9 ⎫
: ⎪
: ⎬  (numeric characters)
: ⎪
0 ⎭
Z ⎫
: ⎪
: ⎬  (alphabetic characters)
: ⎪
A ⎭
"      (quotation mark)
=      (equal sign)
'      (single quote)
>      (greater than)
,      (comma)
/      (slash)
-      (minus or hyphen)
;      (semicolon)
)      (close parenthesis)
*      (asterisk)
$      (dollar sign)
+      (plus)
(      (open parenthesis)
<      (less than)
.      (decimal point or period)
       (blank, indicated often by b̸)
```

APPENDIX C
Summary of Formats

This appendix includes the formats of all Procedure Division statements discussed in this guide. In addition, a complete format for the Identification Division and for the FILE-CONTROL paragraph of the Environment Division are included. All of these formats use the following conventions.

>Words in all capitals are reserved words. Those that are underlined must be included in that format.
>Words in all small letters are to be supplied by the programmer.
>Components enclosed in brackets [ ] are optional; if used, they must be complete.
>Components enclosed in braces { } indicate that one and only one of the items in the braces must be included.
>Punctuation, where shown, is required.

Identification Division Formats

>IDENTIFICATION DIVISION.
>
>PROGRAM-ID. program-name.
>
>[AUTHOR. comment-entry.]
>
>[INSTALLATION. comment-entry.]
>
>[DATE-WRITTEN. comment-entry.]
>
>[DATE-COMPILED. comment-entry.]
>
>[SECURITY. comment-entry.]
>
>[REMARKS. comment-entry.]

Environment Division, FILE-CONTROL paragraph entries

>SELECT file-name (all files)
>
>ASSIGN TO system-name (all files)
>
>ACCESS IS $\left\{ \begin{array}{l} \underline{SEQUENTIAL} \\ \underline{RANDOM} \end{array} \right\}$ (required for random access)

ACTUAL KEY IS data-name   (direct files only)

NOMINAL KEY IS data-name   (indexed files only—IBM)

RECORD KEY IS data-name   (indexed files only)

SYMBOLIC KEY IS data-name   (indexed files only)

Procedure Division Statement Formats

ACCEPT data-name [FROM $\begin{Bmatrix} \text{CONSOLE} \\ \text{mnemonic-name} \end{Bmatrix}$].

(a) ADD $\begin{Bmatrix} \text{data-name-1} \\ \text{literal-1} \end{Bmatrix}$ TO data-name-2 [ROUNDED] [ON SIZE ERROR statement].

(b) ADD $\begin{Bmatrix} \text{data-name-1} \\ \text{literal-1} \end{Bmatrix}$ $\begin{Bmatrix} \text{data-name-2} \\ \text{literal-2} \end{Bmatrix}$ GIVING data-name-3 [ROUNDED] [ON SIZE ERROR statement].

CLOSE file-name-1 file-name-x.

COMPUTE data-name-1 [ROUNDED] = $\begin{Bmatrix} \text{data-name-2} \\ \text{literal} \\ \text{arithmetic-expression} \end{Bmatrix}$.

[ON SIZE ERROR statement]

DISPLAY $\begin{Bmatrix} \text{data-name-1} \\ \text{literal-1} \end{Bmatrix}$ $\begin{Bmatrix} \text{data-name-x} \\ \text{literal-x} \end{Bmatrix}$ [UPON $\begin{Bmatrix} \text{mnemonic-name} \\ \text{CONSOLE} \end{Bmatrix}$].

(a) DIVIDE $\begin{Bmatrix} \text{data-name-1} \\ \text{literal-1} \end{Bmatrix}$ INTO data-name-2 [ROUNDED] [ON SIZE ERROR statement].

(b) DIVIDE $\begin{Bmatrix} \text{data-name-1} \\ \text{literal-1} \end{Bmatrix}$ $\begin{Bmatrix} \text{INTO} \\ \text{BY} \end{Bmatrix}$ $\begin{Bmatrix} \text{data-name-2} \\ \text{literal-2} \end{Bmatrix}$ GIVING data-name-3 [ROUNDED] [ON SIZE ERROR statement].

EXIT.

(a) GO TO paragraph-name.

(b) GO TO paragraph-name-1 paragraph-name-2 paragraph-name-x DEPENDING ON data-name.

IF condition statement.

(a) MOVE $\begin{Bmatrix} \text{data-name-1} \\ \text{literal} \end{Bmatrix}$ TO data-name-2.

(b) MOVE $\begin{Bmatrix} \text{CORR} \\ \text{CORRESPONDING} \end{Bmatrix}$ data-name-1 TO data-name-2.

(a) <u>MULTIPLY</u> $\begin{Bmatrix} \text{data-name-1} \\ \text{literal-1} \end{Bmatrix}$ <u>BY</u> data-name-2 [<u>ROUNDED</u>]

[ON <u>SIZE</u> <u>ERROR</u> statement].

(b) <u>MULTIPLY</u> $\begin{Bmatrix} \text{data-name-1} \\ \text{literal-1} \end{Bmatrix}$ <u>BY</u> $\begin{Bmatrix} \text{data-name-2} \\ \text{literal-2} \end{Bmatrix}$ <u>GIVING</u> data-name-3

[<u>ROUNDED</u>] [ON <u>SIZE</u> <u>ERROR</u> statement].

<u>OPEN</u> $\begin{Bmatrix} \underline{\text{INPUT}} \\ \underline{\text{OUTPUT}} \\ \underline{\text{I-O}} \end{Bmatrix}$ file-name.

(a) <u>PERFORM</u> paragraph-name-1 [<u>THRU</u> paragraph-name-2].

(b) <u>PERFORM</u> paragraph-name-1 [<u>THRU</u> paragraph-name-2]

$\begin{Bmatrix} \text{data-name} \\ \text{integer} \end{Bmatrix}$ <u>TIMES</u>.

(c) <u>PERFORM</u> paragraph-name-1 [<u>THRU</u> paragraph-name-2] <u>UNTIL</u>

condition.

(d) <u>PERFORM</u> paragraph-name-1 [<u>THRU</u> paragraph-name-2] <u>VARYING</u>

data-name-1 <u>FROM</u> data-name-2 <u>BY</u> data-name-3 <u>UNTIL</u> condition.

<u>READ</u> file-name [<u>INTO</u> data-name] $\begin{Bmatrix} \underline{\text{AT END}} \\ \underline{\text{INVALID}} \text{ } \underline{\text{KEY}} \end{Bmatrix}$ statement.

<u>STOP</u> <u>RUN</u>.

(a) <u>SUBTRACT</u> $\begin{Bmatrix} \text{data-name-1} \\ \text{literal-1} \end{Bmatrix}$ <u>FROM</u> data-name-2 [<u>ROUNDED</u>]

[ON <u>SIZE</u> <u>ERROR</u> statement].

(b) <u>SUBTRACT</u> $\begin{Bmatrix} \text{data-name-1} \\ \text{literal-1} \end{Bmatrix}$ <u>FROM</u> $\begin{Bmatrix} \text{data-name-2} \\ \text{literal-2} \end{Bmatrix}$ <u>GIVING</u>

data-name-3 [<u>ROUNDED</u>] [ON <u>SIZE</u> <u>ERROR</u> statement].

(a) <u>WRITE</u> record-name [<u>FROM</u> data-name] [$\begin{Bmatrix} \underline{\text{BEFORE}} \\ \underline{\text{AFTER}} \end{Bmatrix}$ ADVANCING

$\begin{Bmatrix} \text{data-name LINES} \\ \text{integer LINES} \\ \text{special-name} \end{Bmatrix}$].

(b) <u>WRITE</u> record-name [<u>FROM</u> data-name] <u>INVALID</u> KEY statement.

APPENDIX D
Summary of FD Clauses

	LABEL RECORDS	BLOCK CONTAINS	DATA RECORD
Card	omit	not permitted	optional
Print	omit	not permitted	optional
Tape	optional	permitted	optional
Disk	required	permitted	optional

The LABEL RECORDS clause is always required; the actual labels may or may not be included.

The BLOCK CONTAINS clause is required whenever blocking is used; it may not be used for unit record files.

The DATA RECORD clause is never required, but may be used if desired.

APPENDIX E
Summary of Editing Characters

The Picture characters X A and 9 may appear where appropriate in the picture of an edited data item. The characters V and S may not appear in any edited item; in fact, V and S can appear only if no other character besides 9 appears in the item. The effects of the specific editing characters are summarized briefly below.

- **.** An actual decimal point is inserted at the position of the implied place.
- **,** A comma is inserted in the corresponding position.
- **$** single: A dollar sign is inserted in the corresponding position.
    more than one: Leading zeros are suppressed, a dollar sign is inserted to left of first printed digit or decimal point.
- **Z** Leading zeros are suppressed in Z positions.
- ***** Leading zeros in asterisk positions are printed as asterisks.
- **B** Blank inserted in position (may be used for both numeric and alphanumeric data items).
- **0** Zero is inserted (may be used for both numeric and alphanumeric data items).
- **DB** Characters DB are inserted if value of data item is negative; must be at right of item.
- **CR** Characters CR are inserted if value of data item is negative; must be at right of item.
- **+** single: Appropriate sign is inserted for positive or negative value; may be at either end.
    more than one: Leading zeros are suppressed, sign printed just left of first printed digit.
- **−** single: Minus sign is inserted if value of data item is negative; may be at either end.
    more than one: Leading zeros are suppressed; if value is negative, minus sign is printed just left of first printed digit.

Index

A, 46
ACCEPT statement, 22
ACCESS clause, 231
Actual decimal point, 111
ACTUAL KEY clause, 231
ADD statement, 54
ADVANCING options, 165
AFTER ADVANCING option, 165
Alphanumeric editing, 154
Arithmetic operators, 62
Arithmetic statements, 54
ASSIGN clause
  card files, 85
  print files, 106
  tape files, 133
  direct files, 231
  disk sequential files, 222
  indexed files, 238
Asterisk editing, 162
AT END option, 95
AUTHOR paragraph, 29

B, 154
BEFORE ADVANCING option, 165
BLOCK CONTAINS clause, 136
Blocking of records, 135

Card-to-tape procedure, 141
Carriage control character, 110
CLOSE statement, 94
Coding sheet, 6
Collating sequence, 258
Comma, 112
Comment entries, 29
Comparisons, 143
COMP option, 51

COMPUTATIONAL option, 51
COMPUTE statement, 61
Condition-name condition, 32
Configuration Section, 12, 168
CORRESPONDING option, 125
Counting, 98
CR, 157

Data Division header, 13
Data-names, 14
DATA-RECORD clause, 89
DATE-COMPILED paragraph, 30
DATE-WRITTEN paragraph, 29
DB, 157
Decimal point
  actual, 111
  implied, 48
Deleting ISAM records, 242
DEPENDING ON option, 192
Direct files, 230
DISPLAY statement, 21
DIVIDE statement, 56
Dollar sign ($), 115

Editing summary, 263
Elementary data items, 33
ELSE clause, 70
Environment Division header, 11
EXIT statement, 190

FD, 88, 137
FILE-CONTROL paragraph, 85
File description summary, 262
File Section header, 88
FILLER, 80
Floating insertion, 116, 160

Format summary, 259
FROM option, 122

GIVING option, 56
GO TO statement, 66
Group data items, 33

Heading records, 118

Identification Division header, 8
IF statement, 68
Implied decimal point, 48
Indexed sequential files, 238
INPUT option, 93
Input-Output Section, 84
INVALID KEY
  Read, 235
  Write, 224
I-O option, 223

Key clauses, 231, 239, 241

LABEL RECORDS clause, 88
Level numbers, 14, 32, 82, 146
Literals
  non-numeric, 20
  numeric, 52

Mass storage devices, 221
Mnemonic names, 168
MOVE statement, 35
MULTIPLY statement, 55

NOMINAL KEY clause, 241

OBJECT-COMPUTER paragraph, 12
OCCURS clause
  single-level, 198
  double-level, 215
OMITTED option, 88
ON SIZE ERROR option, 60
OPEN statement, 92
OUTPUT option, 93

Paragraph-names, 19
PERFORM statement, 174
PIC abbreviation, 16
Picture character summary, 240
PICTURE clause, 15
Procedure Division header, 18
PROGRAM-ID paragraph, 8
Program-names, 10

Qualified names, 123

RANDOM option, 231
Range of PERFORM, 178
READ statement, 95
RECORD KEY clause, 239
Record length
  card files, 80
  print files, 109
  tape files, 138
Record matching, 148
REDEFINES option, 201
Relational condition, 68, 141
Relational operators, 69
REMARKS paragraph, 30
Reserved word list, 254
REWRITE statement, 243
ROUNDED option, 59

S, 143
SELECT clause, 85
SEQUENTIAL option, 238
Signed values, editing of, 157
SOURCE-COMPUTER paragraph, 12
SPACES option, 119
SPECIAL-NAMES paragraph, 168
STANDARD option, 134
STOP RUN statement, 24
Subscripts, 198
SUBTRACT statement, 54
SYMBOLIC KEY, 241
System flowchart, 106

Table description entries, 197, 215
THRU option, 176
TIMES option, 180

UNTIL option, 182
USAGE clause, 51

V, 48
VALUE clause, 119
VARYING option, 185
Vertical spacing options, 165

Working-Storage Section header, 13
WRITE statement, 99, 122

X, 15

Z, 113
Zero suppression character, 113, 160